W9-AGM-809

The Cameras Weren't Always Rollin'

Larry Black

Country Road Management
Nashville, TN

Editor: Lindsey McNealy

Cover Design: Ian Black

Layout: Paula Underwood Winters

All Larry's Country Diner Photos: Phil Johnson

Printed in the United States of America

For more info on Larry Black, Larry's Country Diner, Country's Family Reunion, including DVDs and other merchandise, visit www.countryroadtv.com

ISBN: 978-0-578-59883-3

Published by: Country Road Management

CONTENTS

DEDICATION

Luann – My Wife
> We have been through thick and thin, ups and downs, richer   and
> poorer and sickness and health! You never left my side…
> > I love you.

My Sons – Ian, Adam and Jared
> I'm so proud of each of you; the husbands you are, the fathers you are,
> the men you are. Thank you for shouldering and perservering the
> continuation of my legacy. I love you, Dad.

My Grandchildren – Nathan, Nick, Devin, Brandon, Avery, Asher,
Melina, Eden, Samuel and Arial
> You make me proud! You are God's reward for my growing old.
> I will always love you, Poppa. *(Oh, remember as you read my book –
> that you do as I say and not as I've done.)*

My Daughers-in-law – Holly, Jenny, Stephanie
> You are beautiful and smart. Thank you for giving me those
> awesome grandchildren. My sons chose well. Love, Your
> Father-in-law.

This book is first and foremost for them. As you read this book it is our
hope (Luann and I) that God will touch your lives with the reality of
who God is and what He has done in our lives.

My Fans and Friends
> Thank you for sharing in my life's journey…What a ride!

Remember, the cameras are always rolling…and we don't care!

Larry Black

FOREWORD

"I've been in the business for more than 55 years, and I can honestly say that meeting Larry Black is one of the best things that has ever happened to my career. You might say that Larry Black saved my life. He sure saved my career.

My career was basically over and done with, when I got the invitation to be on Country's Family Reunion and Larry's Country Diner. Then I became a regular, any time he could use me on the Diner or on CFR. We also do their live show in Branson, and all of those appearances have led to a resurrection of my career.

And many other artists were in the same situation as I was. Most people might've thought we were retired. But we weren't. We were just looking for work! Larry has helped so many of us older artists to get back in front of people. It's been a Godsend for us.

My buddy Moe Bandy saw the exact same reaction. It just kicked our careers back into high gear, and we've been rollin' ever since.

A lot of people who enjoy the older, traditional artists are also older themselves. Many of them can't get out and drive hundreds of miles to a concert, so they are thankful that they can sit in their living room and enjoy their favorite performers on Larry's shows. Larry put me into the living rooms of millions of people.

When we sign autographs after our concerts, every night I'll have so many people come up and say that they saw me on the

Diner, or on Family Reunion. Folks will say, "Gene, when you see Larry Black, be sure to tell him 'thank you' for bringing real country music to us."

Thanks to all the exposure his TV shows gave me, my career is now hotter than it's even been. I'm working more dates than I was twenty years ago, and I owe it all to Larry.

What you see on TV is the real Larry Black. He has been an actor in the movies and TV, but there is no acting on the Diner. That's who he really is. He is one of the most straight-up people I've ever been acquainted with, and when I'm shaking his hand, I know that I'm shaking the hand of a true, personal friend. He's got my cell phone number, and I don't give that out to very many people.

I've got a special appreciation for Larry. Just saying "thanks" is not good enough for everything that he has done for me. There's no way I could say enough good things about Larry Black. He's my friend, and I wouldn't take anything for our friendship."

— Gene Watson

JUNE 18, 2015

Well Larry… you've really done it this time.

After your pretty eventful life, and after more than a few close calls with death… this is how it ends.

At the bottom of a Montana mountain. With a 1,000 pound ATV on top of you.

I wonder how many bones I broke in that fall. I'm sure everyone will be impressed when they total them up for my autopsy.

The things you think of as you're near death.

I'm pretty sure I'm bleeding internally… I hope no ants get on my face… I will probably go into shock soon, or I might already be there, and not know it... maybe they'll do a tribute to me on the Diner. I hope Gatlin doesn't host it. He'll steal all my spotlight.

If I die here, in this totally stupid way, my wife is going to kill me!

And just one more thought comes, before I close my eyes to get away from all this pain… this horrible accident would be a great way to start off my autobiography. I could kind of look back at my life as it flashes before my eyes. Too bad I won't be alive to write that book. It would have been a good one.

And then… I died.

I was okay with it. I knew where I was going.

But you know that old saying, "He lived to tell the tale"? Well, through a true miracle from God, that is exactly what happened to me. My life should have ended that day in Montana. But it didn't. I lived to tell my story.

– Larry Black

THE PROMISE

We always start each Larry's Country Diner TV show with "The Promise"… So I think it would be appropriate for me to start my autobiography with "The Promise" here as well. As I try to tell my life story, I surely know I can use all the help I can get.

"As long as he sought the Lord, God made him to prosper." – 2 Chronicles 26:5

That is a verse that I have tried to live by for my entire life. I'm sure there have been times when I've come up short in it, but I have always tried to seek the Lord in everything I did. I knew if I did, He would see me through. He always has.

LIGHTS, CAMERA, ACTION!

"Where the cameras are always rollin'... and we don't care!" Of course, that's the catchphrase of our Larry's Country Diner show that my wife Luann came up with.

But there were no cameras around yet, when I rolled into this world on November 10, 1943. They tell me the snow was more than five feet deep in Vermillion, South Dakota on the day I was born. The snow was piled up so high that cows were walking over their fences. My dad had to fight through the snow to get home from the service to see his new baby boy.

A little snow was no big deal to my parents. They had survived much greater challenges. My mother was born in Stover, Missouri, and she had the very unique name of Orpha Mae Grose. Some people mistake it for *Oprah*, but it is *Orpha*. And while my mother was born in Missouri, a short time later, her family moved up to Pierre, South Dakota.

In the 1930s, divorce was quite rare. So when my mother's parents divorced, she suddenly found herself in a "broken" home. That's what they called divorced families back then... broken. With such a label, my mom was looked down on by her classmates. Mom lived with her dad, who later remarried, and had another daughter.

Her father did day work for local farmers, but he was also a hunter. He had lots of hunting dogs, and he fed his family from his hunts. Mom's home in South Dakota was located along the edge of an Indian reservation. While the Indians lived in teepees, my mom and her family lived in a little, tar paper shack.

While mom's mother, my grandma Vivian, was a rare divorcee, she was also ahead of her time in another way. She was a female business owner. And guess what that business was… she ran a Diner!

When I was young, we would go to visit her, and I will always remember the big tip jar she had sitting on the counter. When my brother and I came in, Grandma would take the coins from that jar and give them to us. She baked bread, and always seemed to have a big loaf of bread on the table. It smelled so good. I thought that maybe I could take just a little bit from the inside of it and no one would know… but the truth was it tasted so good, I ended up taking out the entire middle part of the loaf. I hollowed it out, and then I put it back together! I often wonder what my Grandma would think about her grandson running a diner on TV now!

Mother was bullied at school, just because her mother was divorced. But she found love and compassion in the Four Square Church in Pierre. The church had a female pastor (quite rare at the time). Sister Lelasure mentored my mother, and when mom gave her heart to Jesus, she also gave the Lord a special sign of her commitment to Him. Back then, to some, wearing makeup was taboo, a sign of the world. Mom wanted to serve God as best as she could, so she decided that she would not wear lipstick. My mom lived 89 years, and never wore lipstick of any kind.

As a teenager, she worked for the Governor of South Dakota. She worked in the Governor's mansion, assisting Mrs. Lee. Mom served food and helped to put on very nice dinners. And the Governor's wife taught her many things about entertaining the wealthy and influential. That would serve her well later in life, when she became a pastor's wife.

My father, Edwin Lawrence Black, was born and raised in Meckling, South Dakota. My dad's father was a sharecropper, and dad and his four brothers and two sisters all worked with his family on the farm. In school, he enjoyed playing basketball.

One of dad's sisters, my Aunt Verle, actually met mom at a youth rally, and thought she would be a good person for her brother to meet. After a short courtship, Edwin and Orpha were married by C.T. Beam, the pastor of the Assemblies of God in Vermillion. Brother Beam mentored my father for the rest of his life, and would later recommend that he go to North Central Bible Institute.

My brother Richard was the first son of Edwin and Orpha Black. And just twenty months later, they would welcome another… me. Both my parents had wanted a baby girl, so much so that they both cried when they found out they were having another boy. Way to make a guy feel appreciated!

Mom might have been crying for another reason, though. I weighed in at 10 pounds and 1 ounce. I was a big boy. She was in the Dakota Hospital for seven and a half days, and the total bill was $45.00! They charged her $4.00 a day, with a total medication charge of $1.60! My, how times have changed. I wouldn't believe it, if my mom hadn't saved the hospital bill receipt. You can see a copy of it attached in the photo section of this very book.

When it came time to name me, my parents both knew they wanted to call me Larry. But even though my dad's middle name was Lawrence, for my official name, they opted for another one they found under the "L's" in a baby name book.

Can you believe my "real" name is Loren Lee? But you can call me Larry. Please do.

In the baby book my mother created for me, she wrote that I went to church for the first time when I was twelve days old. When I was born in 1943, my dad was getting ready to head off to World War II. Mom spent the next few months moving from place to place, trying to keep her family close to my dad, as he waited to go overseas. When he was in the service, they lived both in Amarillo, Texas and in Charleston, South Carolina.

When I was still in diapers, mom was traveling from Texas to South Carolina to join up with dad. On the way, she spent the night at the Union Station in Nashville, Tennessee. She had my brother Richard on a halter, and held me in her arms. As she tried to get a few minutes of sleep on the hard train station bench, a vagrant came over and started harassing her.

A policeman told the man to go away, and said, "Ma'am, don't worry. I'll keep watch over you and your boys tonight. You get some sleep." I know that God had his hand on us.

Ironically, many years later, in that same Union Station, my son Adam would hold his rehearsal dinner before his wedding. It would also serve as the location for another event in our lives, which I will talk about later in this book.

After serving his country, my dad returned to Vermillion and got a job at a laundry. One day, when I was two years old, he took me to work with him. And while he was out of the room, I somehow managed to pull a set of steam pipes down from the ceiling. I burned my knuckle, and had a scar on my hand for many years. I didn't get to enjoy many more "Take Your Child to Work" days after that!

My dad's days in the laundry were also numbered though, as he would soon find his true calling. Thanks to the GI Bill, he was able to enroll in the Central Bible Institute in Springfield, Missouri. As he prepared for the ministry, our family settled into our new home in Springfield.

While dad was attending college, mom tried her best to keep up with our bills. She always had to work to make money for our family.

She took in washing and ironing for people. She also made a deal with the manager of the Gospel Publishing House on Booneville Avenue, where he allowed her to set up a small concession stand in the back of the building. Each noon hour, people would come down and buy bagged sandwiches that mom had prepared earlier that morning. My brother and I also helped out, selling candy bars and gum. We found that most people couldn't say no to a pair of cute little three-and-five-year-old boys!

One of the people I met selling candy was a man by the name of Art Oman, who did all of the cartoon work for the Pentecostal

Evangel Magazine. He was a very creative artist, and he took the time to teach me how to do some different drawings. I always thought it was neat that he was an artist whose name was Art.

Years later, when I was a teenager, I went to say hello to him, and he still remembered me from our first meeting when I was only three years old!

Springfield, Missouri was the headquarters of the Assembly of God, and that allowed my father to make a lot of friends who were part of the hierarchy of the church. Some of the stalwarts of the movement visited our house. My mom could put on great dinners, and she would prepare big, fancy meals.

A few of those high-ups in the church always maintained a kind of aloofness. They knew they were the foundation of the church, and they were always on their very best behavior. But most of them lightened up when they came to visit. I found out that all of them were just human… but they were also some of the neatest people I'd ever met. They had the best stories of how God moved in their lives, and in the lives of others. They told of miracles that had happened to them. I was just a little boy, but I really savored my time with those people.

I also liked to have company come over, because I knew I would have some new victims for my practical jokes! My mom and dad both loved to laugh. I'm sure I got my sense of humor from my parents; and they were both willing to let me play a few pranks on these important religious leaders!

My favorite practical joke involved a book that had the scandalous title, "Forbidden Scenes of Hollywood". The cover had a picture of a scantily clad woman emblazoned onto it. But it wasn't a real book. The inside was hollowed out, and it had a little explosive cap, like one from a cap gun. And when someone went to open the book, that cap would explode.

Before one of the church leaders arrived, I sat the book onto a table by the chair they would soon be sitting in. It never failed that, as soon as everyone had left the room, the visitor would pick up that book, and we would all hear it that cap go off! The temptation was too much. I'd come in laughing and say, "So you wanted to see the Forbidden Scenes!"

Raymond T. Richey was my favorite practical joke "victim". I was always playing a prank on him. Brother Richey spent his whole life traveling the world, holding tent revivals. They say that more than one million people came forward to give their hearts to the Lord during Bro. Richey's services. He was born in 1893, so by the time I met him, I just saw him as a little old man.

Of course, Brother Richey had a very serious side, but he also had a sense of humor that just wouldn't quit. He was willing to let me joke with him, and then he would joke right back. As we were having dinner one night, I accidentally dropped a piece of buttered bread on my leg, and he asked, "Did it land butter side down?"

"Yep!" I said. He laughed. "That's what I prayed for! I gotcha!"

Brother Richey really got me back for all my pranks one day, while I was at school. I had an amateur ham radio set up in our utility room, which I called my "ham shack". And when I got home from school that afternoon, everything in that room was moved around. He'd hung the headphones across the room, and had plugged all my wires into the wrong place, leaving only a note behind that said, *"I gotcha!"*

Brother Richey was in his seventies, but he was still so vibrant, and still willing to play jokes with a teenager. He was a great minister, and a very loving man.

Years later, when we had moved to Alabama, many of the church leaders we'd met in Springfield would come to visit. Burt Webb was the Superintendent of the General Counsel of the Assembly of God. Dad had him come speak in our church a couple times, and then they would go fishing in Pensacola, Florida. All the guys from Springfield really loved to come to Mobile, because dad would take them deep sea fishing!

But the church leaders were not the only visitors we had in our home. I remember a young man who moved into town and wanted to get involved with the youth in our church. I heard my father whisper to my mom that the man was a communist who was looking for a home. On another occasion, there was an evangelist passing through town who was deaf, and while he stayed with us, he taught me how to perform sign language. Many decades later, when I was hospitalized with a tube down my throat, I would make use of that sign language to communicate with the nurses who were taking care of me.

It was during this time that I found out exactly how hard of a worker my father was. While he was still in college, he made a commitment to pastor an Assembly of God church in Morrisville, Missouri. Morrisville was just outside of Springfield. But before he could become the church pastor, he would first have to build the church… almost completely by himself!

Dad was a good carpenter, and my Pop did it all. He preached, went to school, and in his "free time", he would take a wheelbarrow up into the hills of the Ozarks and fill it with rocks. He'd bring those all the way back down, dump them, and go back to get another load, time after time. He used those rocks to construct his new church. Sometimes he would get a little help from a few other people in the congregation, but not very often.

It is amazing that my dad was able to complete that church on his own. But he would never have said that. My mom wouldn't either. I still have a photograph that she took of the church. On the back, she wrote, *"The church God helped us build."*

Four decades later, I took my son Jared back to that church. The Assembly of God has now grown into a big church, and most of the original building is gone… but in the basement, you can still see the wall that my dad built with his bare hands. It was very touching for Jared. He took a little piece of the rock that his grandpa had touched. My dad really did leave behind an incredible legacy of love and ministry in all the churches he pastored.

As he was building that little church, dad would occasionally let me and my brother fill up his wheelbarrow with rocks. I'm sure he welcomed a few minutes' break. But we were so little at the time that we really weren't much help. So while he worked around the clock, he let us be kids. Richard was usually outside playing some type of sport, but I could most always be found inside, lying in front of our radio.

My favorite radio shows were The Lone Ranger, Sky King, Roy Rogers, The Cisco Kid, and Bobby Benson and the B-Bar-B

Riders. During those shows, the cereal companies would run ads that offered kids a special decoding ring. They made it sound so amazing! My mom let me order one, and then, even though I was only four years old, she let me walk down to the post office by myself. Morrisville was so small that everyone in town knew everyone else. All of the roads were dirt. They weren't paved at all. And back then, a four year old could walk the streets without a worry of somebody harming them or trying to take them.

I walked to that post office each day until my decoder ring finally arrived. I was so excited! Until I opened the envelope. Even at the age of four, I knew I had been ripped off. That ring was so flimsy, and nothing like the radio ads had described. I was so disappointed.

And soon, there was another walk home that I will never forget. This also relates to my mother's vow to never wear lipstick. As I passed by the high school one day, I saw one of the young girls who went to our church. She was thirteen years old, and I really liked her. Even at four years old, I kind of had a crush on her.

Back then, in the Pentecostal church, you didn't wear makeup. They really stressed that Christian girls didn't do something that sinful. And when I saw that this thirteen year old girl, who I liked, was wearing lipstick, I just started crying. I cried all the way home, because I knew that girl was going to Hell.

Another interesting aspect of the Pentecostal church I discovered came when I watched members of the congregation speaking in tongues. I couldn't understand a word they were saying, but my father explained to me that the Holy Spirit was supernaturally directing each person's prayers. It was a little bit frightening, when I was younger. To deal with that fear, I'd make jokes, saying, "Sheila Mugundy... I'm talking in tongues... Startamyhonda." But I know that speaking in tongues is real. It's not something that people are making up.

My dad also spoke in tongues, but not very often. When I was fourteen, we had one of our yearly revivals in Dad's church and inevitably there would be a service dedicated to 'receiving' the Baptism. That meant that at the end of the sermon an invitation would be given to come to the altar to 'seek the Holy Spirit'. I wanted whatever God had for me, so I would go to the altar "seeking". I had heard so many people express their experience when they 'received' the Holy Spirit and I wanted the same kind of experience. But that didn't happen for me, at least not then.

But as I matured, I began to understand that speaking in tongues is praying in a heavenly language. I began to see that 'speaking in tongues' is actually the Holy Spirit making intercession for you. I could see why the Holy Spirit was important for my relationship with The Father. But I didn't learn that for another ten years.

I was working for WEIV, a radio station in Ithaca, NY, owned by the Christian Broadcasting Network. I had just finished my shift and was driving home. I turned on our station as Scott Ross was beginning his show by interviewing Harald Bredesen about the Holy Spirit. (A side note about Harald...he was the pastor of the First Reformed Church of Mount Vernon, New York. He was asked by a couple Notre Dame professors to meet with several divinity students, and that was the start of the Charismatic movement in the Catholic church.)

As I listened to his interview with Scott, Harald's down to earth presentation rejuvenated in me the desire to speak in tongues. That day, driving down the hill from the radio station, I told the Lord I was going to exercise the gift he'd given, and I've never regretted it. It continues to be an active part of my prayer life. The thought of allowing the Holy Spirit to pray through the spirit to the Father about something I'm unaware or aware of is incredibly comforting.

The Great Flood hit Missouri in July of 1951, and my parents took a job clearing mud out of a yard for a local family. I can't even begin to describe the total destruction that that mud had caused. Mom and dad told Richard and I that if we helped them, when we were finished, they would give us anything we wanted. And of course, we each wanted Red Ryder BB guns!

Dad constructed a ramp that he used to push wheelbarrows full of mud from the yard of that house, up over a hill, and then back into the river. He and mom worked like Trojans, and Richard and I helped them as much as we could for two weeks. And sure enough, when we were finished... we both got our BB guns.

One night, dad drove home from Springfield and parked his car in front of our house, like always. But somehow, this time he parked on top of a big bed of leaves. During the night, the heat from his car caught those leaves on fire, and they combusted, burning all four tires off of the vehicle. We're talking about major smoke!

Speaking of smoking... one of my very first memories is from when I was just four years old. We lived next door to a family that had a whole bunch of kids, and every one of those kids under that roof smoked! Even the little kids smoked. They had a baby who walked around in diapers, puffing on a cigarette! I never forgot that.

A couple years later, we left the smoking babies and moved to Slater, Missouri, where dad pastored a small church and attended Missouri Valley College. During this time, he also worked at a downtown hotel as an overnight clerk. Yes, my father was a hard worker!

My dad was a great pastor. I watched him many, many times be woken up in the middle of the night to go and be with someone who was in the hospital. He was called to be a pastor, but all during his career, my father was never a dynamic preacher.

As a little boy, I was really not all that interested in the sermon of any preacher. Instead, you could usually find me under a church pew, with my head on a hymnal, trying to take a nap. It always seemed to be hot in the church back then, and since we had no air conditioning, the coolest place was in the shade, under the pews! As I lay down there, I would also look up at all the gum that had been stuck onto the bottoms of those seats. People would chew it, and when the service started, they'd stick it up under their seat. I became fascinated with all the different colors of gum. I could tell which one was Dentyne, because it was red. But I would have to lick the others to see if they were Spearmint, Doublemint or Juicy Fruit.

As I got older, and grew too big to nap under the pews, if there was ever an occasion where my brother or I would act up during church, the only thing my dad could do from the pulpit, for the moment… was give us a look. But when he gave us one of his stern looks, we knew that we would surely be dealt with later.

One day, I did something in church, and I knew I would get it when we got home. But I had been sick. Richard knew that I was ill, and he asked dad, "Can I take his whipping for him?" And dad whipped him. Richard took the spanking for me. Not many brothers would do that. But as I watched, it also hurt me; to see my brother spanked, when I knew that I was the one who deserved it.

Our parents did spank us. The last one I got, I was fifteen years old. Mom took a wooden ruler and started spanking my rear end. She broke the ruler in half, and then started using her hand. I couldn't help it, I started laughing, and then she started laughing. My mom always said that after I was spanked, I was the sweetest kid in the world… for a few days, at least.

But mom and dad kept me in line at home, and that discipline continued at school. I was once at the water fountain, and my teacher slapped me. We had just been standing in line to get a drink when she slapped me. I still don't know why… I figure I was laughing and cutting up. I was five years old.

I always liked to talk in school. On my report cards, the teacher would always give me an "Unsatisfactory" in conduct. And when my parents asked why I was unsatisfactory, the teacher said: "He talks all the time."

When I came into the first grade, I began to take piano lessons. My teacher, Mrs. Reed, initially thought that I was too young, but she reluctantly agreed to give me a try for a month, to see if I was up to it. Her brother was a very good musician, and after a few weeks, he told her that I "had a great talent."

I began taking trombone lessons in the second grade. I couldn't reach the sixth position on the instrument, because my arms weren't long enough, but I was able to grab an extension on the trombone so that I could get to that sixth position. I was the youngest boy in that school who had ever played trombone, and a year later, I was even allowed to play in the high school band.

My brother Richard was a tremendous trumpet player, and he was also always in band. And he and I always played in church. I could read music, but in church, I also learned how to play by ear. Our church in Slater was located right across the street from the high school, and we had a bunch of young people there who were all incredibly gifted musically. In our tiny church, we had a sousaphone player, a clarinetist, a flute player, my brother playing trumpet, and me playing trombone. We had guitar players, a drummer, and even one guy who played the spoons! All of those were kids who played in the school band, but they would also make time to come over on Sunday morning, Sunday night, and then on Wednesday night, to play in church. We had a very lively band. We had so many extra players that they would cover up for any mistakes I might make, so I just had a ball. My brother and I played in every church that my Dad had, all the way through our high school years. It was a lot of fun. That's where my love for music really started.

For my second grade class picture, I stood next to Ida Jane Murray. I really fell hard for Ida Jane. I gave her a ring that I had bought at the local Ben Franklin store, and I think it embarrassed her; she put heavy duty tape all over it. She covered it with that tape and gave it back to me. I guess that meant she was undecided!

In the summer of 1953, dad left the church in Slater, and our entire family did a three-month evangelistic revival tour. We would stay a week in each new church, and then we'd move on to another location. And for each of those revivals, Richard and I would dress up like little cowboys. We wore cowboy hats, boots and western shirts, and I'd sing a song called "Christian Cowboy". Many decades later, I'd sing that song on one of the Country's Family Reunions, too. And a few years after that, my grandson, Sam Bam, did it on the Diner! It was fun to watch him, as he hammed it up a little bit and made it fun. He did his own choreography. I had been eight years old when I was singing that song, and he was around that same age when he did it on TV.

During our revivals, Richard and I did trombone and trumpet duets, and mom played the piano as we sang. We provided all the music, while dad brought the message. And it was during one of those revivals that I got saved. I will always remember where it happened: at the Assembly of God Church in Pleasant Hill, Missouri.

The best part about our evangelistic tour was probably our name. We were called "The Black Evangelistic Team"! I'm sure that created some confusion more than once, as four of the whitest people on earth rolled into town!

One of the gas stations in Slater had a guy who came out and pumped your gas. He'd check the oil and wash your windshield, as he tried to get all the gossip you knew, which he'd pass on to the next customer. When we came through, the guy told the next customer that "there's a white minister in town with two black boys!"

After one of our revival services, the church pastor's wife, who happened to be very pretty, came up to me and said, "You have beautiful lips," as she kissed me... on the lips. I didn't kiss her back. I later learned that she might have done the same (and more) with one or two of the much more grown-up men in her congregation.

On our way to a Christ Ambassador rally in Sedalia, Missouri, our car was sideswiped by another car, just as it passed us. Dad got out to talk to the other driver, and discovered that he was a teenager who had been drinking. The guy sped away, and we followed him.

When the kid got to a bridge, he lost control and turned his car over. It landed in the water, and he was killed. I went with dad to the morgue, and he let me go in with him, as he prayed over the deceased teen. It was the first time I had ever seen a dead body.

In Springfield, Missouri, I was able to start the fourth grade. Dad had gotten a job doing carpentry there, while he auditioned for different churches. Churches that needed a pastor would bring in different candidates and let them preach a sermon or two, and then they would hold a vote on them.

I was just getting settled at my new school when dad received a call from the First Assembly of God Church in Mobile, Alabama, who asked him to come down to "try out" as their new pastor. So he brought his entire family along to try and wow them! Richard and I sang, dad preached, and the church members liked the family concept. They hired dad, and on November 10, 1953, my birthday, we moved to Mobile.

Looking back, there was probably little need for dad to try so hard to get the pastor job in Mobile. They wanted him as their pastor, but they didn't have enough money to pay him a salary! Dad agreed they could pay him with a percentage of what was given in the offering plate. I don't know if you have seen some church offering plates, but that was a very risky thing to do!

Each week, our entire family would have fun guessing what the offering would be that Sunday. If it was enough, my dad would treat us all to dinner later at the Dairy Castle. If the offering had been really big, we could even add a milkshake to our meal!

But one thing that my father refused to spend money on was our hair. Dad cut my hair for the first seventeen years of my life! He even cut it when I was in college, when I would come home to visit. And of course, he also cut my brother's hair.

One day, a bunch of kids from our church were at our house as he was preparing to cut my hair, and as kids will do, they started joking. "Cut all of his hair! Take it all off." Dad asked me what I wanted, and I just said, "Go ahead."

He took the shears and shaved my head bald. I didn't care. It wasn't much different from the flat top I wore for almost two decades.

We lived in a little house in Crichton, outside of Mobile. The young lady next door to us had a TV. This was in the very early days of television, and she would let me come over to her house after school so that I could watch the westerns. It was much better seeing the cowboys and Indians on TV, rather than listening to them on the radio! I was seeing exactly what the Lone Ranger, the Cisco Kid and Sky King really looked like!

But we wouldn't get a television in our own home for a long time. The people of our church thought that TV was evil. But there was one person in our congregation who had a television, and mom and dad would let us ride our bikes over to their house to watch TV. We started going over there a couple times a week, and as we were riding our bikes back late at night, our parents would get concerned that someone might hit us in the dark. So, this got dad to buy a television and put it in our bedroom.

That Sunday, he got up in church and said, "I want to confess to something. I've already started hearing rumors that my family is hiding a TV set in our backroom. I want to tell you that we do have a television. But it is not hidden. We put it in our boys' room." He explained why he had bought it, and he assured everyone that if they came to our house to visit, they would never have to see the TV. Little did he know that his son would grow up to have his own TV show one day!

When we moved to Mobile, I found out that we were what they call "Yankees". I remember coming home from school and asking mom, "What's a carpetbagger?"

But I was very pleased when my fourth grade teacher used me as an example of how to use proper English. The other boys would say, "Can I git a glass of wadder?" But I would say, "May I have a glass of water?"

It also seemed that almost everyone in Mobile ended each sentence with "ya hear?" The teacher enjoyed my proper English, but the other kids weren't very impressed.

I attended my fourth, fifth and sixth grades there in Mobile, and one of my absolute favorite teachers was Mrs. Tinkham, who taught fifth grade. She was young and beautiful, and I remember that she had exceptional clavicle bones. I always tried to do my best for her.

Mrs. Tinkham once gave us an assignment to write about a national park that we'd visited. She mentioned that she loved Yellowstone. And since I was born in South Dakota, which was close to Montana, I figured I must have visited Yellowstone. So I wrote my essay with a very vivid description of my time at the legendary location. But there was just one problem... I had never been there!

Ironically though, many years later, we would have a home just 65 miles from Yellowstone. I think it was my way of making it up to Mrs. Tinkham.

When we weren't in school, we were entertaining at PTA meetings, talent shows, and any other event or venue that would have us. We sang at all the big events, and the Black Brothers became known all around the state of Alabama. We once even won a talent show, where the prize was getting the chance to do a benefit show at the Veteran's Home in Biloxi, Mississippi.

As we grew up, Richard and I spent many years singing and playing music together. We even sang at the funerals of our mom and dad. Our mother's funeral was the last time we ever sang together.

I would make my very first television appearance in Mobile, Alabama, as well. Richard and I were on a local station, on a show called "Martha Maitland's Playground Reporter", a half-hour show that aired each Saturday. On it, Martha would go to different school to find talented children, and we were on that a couple times.

But we missed out on a chance at bigger TV stardom, when a talent scout for the Ted Mack Amateur Hour asked our parents if Richard and I would be on their show. Kid and family acts were just starting to get popular at the time.

But my mom told them no. She didn't want us to "get out into the world" at our young age. She didn't think it would be good for us. It was just something that mom and dad wanted to protect us from. We didn't find out until many years later that she had turned them down, but I don't regret that we didn't get to do it.

One of the best things about our years in Alabama, though, were the summer youth camps! These were always a special time. The camps were at Oak Mountain State Park, just outside of Birmingham. My dad was a good cook, so he was responsible for the camp kitchen. Richard and I got to go to for free, since he worked in the kitchen. Of course, we would work there too, washing the dishes.

The camp was very rustic, and the grounds were a lot like the Ozarks. They had a huge lake, and we'd go swimming in it every day. The Assembly of God didn't allow "mixed bathing", and I could never understand that, so I said, "I don't want to bathe with the girls. I just want to swim with them!" But they didn't allow it.

At my very young age, I found out that "mixed bathing" was what I would call a "geographical sin". Let me try to explain that...

When I was eight years old, in Slater, Missouri, everyone swam together in the local pool. But a year later, when we moved to Mobile, Alabama, I was told that I couldn't go to the city pool, because the boys and girls all swam together there. And when I was fourteen years old, at youth camp, the boys swam at a certain time and the girls swam at a different time. But when we moved to Fort Lauderdale, Florida, on the first Sunday we were there, the church had a beach party. And when I saw the Sunday School teacher wearing a bikini, I was totally confused. I started questioning some of things I had always been taught in church. I think "mixed bathing" was more of a cultural thing than a true sin.

But my first taste of "real sin" would also come around that same time. Back then, our church forbid us to shoot pool, bowl, dance or roller skate. Roller skating was like dancing on wheels! I was walking in downtown Mobile when I walked past a bowling alley. I looked around to see if there was anyone who might know me, and then I stepped inside the door.

As soon as I got inside, I thought, "This is what sin feels like." I took a long look, and then stepped back outside. I thought, "The pleasures of sin are fun for a season... or a frame or two."

Another thing that was considered a sin was putting money into a jukebox. Worse yet, my parents always said, "That is just throwing money away!" Of course, I wanted to try it! I knew that there was a jukebox at the local miniature golf place, about a half block from our church. At the time, I loved the group The Cadets, and one day, I casually walked by the jukebox, glanced at the song numbers… and walked on.

Then I came back, and tried to back up toward the jukebox, so that no one saw me. I quickly dropped a quarter into the slot, and hit the selection for "Stranded in the Jungle" five times (you could pick five songs for a quarter back then). Then I ran outside! I sat down on the steps of our church, just down the road, and I listened to my song playing… five times. When we started the Larry's Country Diner TV show, one of the very first additions I made to the Diner was a huge, beautiful Crosley jukebox!

We moved so many times as I was growing up. Dad would get a different church, in a new town, and usually in a new state, and we had to pack up everything and start all over. But I loved it! I enjoyed meeting new people and making new friends. I was invigorated with each move. I always had my brother with me until I made new friends, and it wouldn't take me long to get new relationships to take the place of my old friends. I learned not to put down heavy roots… because I always knew that there would be another move coming in a year or two.

When we made those moves, as my father drove, Richard and I would play a game called "Zip", where we would look out the window and count cows and horses. When we passed one, the first one to see it would say, "Zip!"

Whoever had seen the most cows and horses by the time we reached our destination won. I'm pretty sure my dad thought it was a good way to keep our mouths zipped during a long drive!

When I was twelve, I wanted to join the Boy Scouts. To get in, you were supposed to be thirteen, but since my brother was already going, and since I was a "PK" (preacher's kid), they let me join them.

Besides being young, I also had another challenge... I didn't know diddly squat about camping! And mom and dad weren't much help, as they didn't know very much about camping either.

Before I had headed off to camp, my mom had given me a pot pie for my supper! So I went to the campfire, took the pot pie out of the box, took the cellophane off of it, and just laid the pie in the fire. Luckily, one of the other scouts came over and got it out! He traded me my pot pie for the sandwich he was going to eat.

Some of the boy scouts had a party, and they invited girls. And with no supervision, things escalated to "playing post office". I had never kissed a girl, and nobody wanted to play post office with me. I was the homely, fat postmaster! So I guess I just had to sort the letters by myself! Of course, my older, much better looking brother got a lot of post office activity.

My first case of puppy love was Sammie Dorough. Sammie lived in Jasper, Alabama. We met at camp in Birmingham. She had short, black hair. I thought she was a cutie. I really liked her, and I thought she liked me. And after the camp was over, we wrote to each other for several months... but then, we just gradually lost touch.

Losing your first love is rough, but there was one particular incident that was even more traumatic for me. In Mobile, we lived just across the street from Brookley Air Force Base. There was a very steep hill near the base, and all my pals liked to take refrigerator boxes and slide down that hill. But of course, I came up with a "better" idea, as I tried to ride my bike down the hill.

Everything went fine, until I got to the bottom. And as I came to a very sudden stop, I went over the handlebars. Did I break my arm, or a collarbone? No, that would have been less painful… and much less embarrassing. No, as I flew over the front wheel of my bicycle, my groin caught the handlebars and I ripped my testicle sack! My friends could see me bleeding through my pants. Luckily, to patch me back together, the doctor used glue instead of stiches.

I also managed to get some stiches a short time later, all because I wanted to play hooky from school. To get out of going that day, I told my mom that I had a stomachache. Much to my dismay, mom insisted on taking me to the doctor. After checking me over, to my complete horror, the doctor informed me I needed to get my appendix taken out! They took me straight to the hospital, where I had the operation. I never pretended to be sick again.

After I had healed up, I started my first job. At the age of thirteen, I worked as a soda jerk at a Green's Drug Store in Mobile, just across the street from our church and parsonage. I loved Nu-Grape soda pop and Ruffles potato chips. You could buy them both together for 15 cents. And next door to the drug store was Alexander's Television and Radio Shop. It's funny how a local radio and TV business could have such a huge influence on a thirteen year old kid.

I was already a ham. I still am… in more ways than one. I'm a licensed amateur ham radio operator. My first call letters were

W2HUT. I fell in love with amateur radio when I saw a man talking on his radio set in his car, parked outside of Green's Drug Store. I walked over to him and started asking all about it. One thing I've learned about ham radio operators is that they are always willing to help anyone else who is interested in their hobby. I still remember that man's call letters. They were W4WPS.

Once I'd learned Morse code and earned my very own ham radio novice license, I started hanging out at Alexander's TV and Radio Shop. And even though I was still barely in my teens, the owner would let me play around with radio repairs. I eventually got good enough that, when someone brought their radio in, if it had a bad AC filter or condenser, I could fix it for them. They were always surprised to watch this young kid repair their radio.

When we moved to Fort Lauderdale, I wanted to get my general amateur radio license, which was a step up from my novice license. Back then, you had to read 13 words per minute in Morse code to get the general license. My dad had to take me all the way to the FCC office in Miami to take the test.

Once I got there, I quickly found out that the test was not easy, and I failed it. I went home and studied, and tried to get my code speed up. Again, my dad drove me to Miami, and again, I flunked the test. But I didn't give up, and my father didn't give up on me, either. Three different times, he took me to Miami to take that test. I never forgot that he was willing to do something like that for his son.

I passed the test on my third try, and joined the amateur radio club in Fort Lauderdale, Florida. That same year, the Westside Optimist Club named me as their Boy of the Year.

Amateur radio has changed so much over the years. Today, a lot of it is computerized, but it was much more fun to spin that dial until I found someone to talk with. I still have my license, and I'd like to get one more radio set before I die. I'd like to have it at our place in Montana.

As a fourteen year old, I also bagged groceries at the Piggly Wiggly store. I was a good employee.

One day at school, I was sitting in class, cutting up as usual, when I suddenly began to feel both of my legs going numb. When I got home, I assured my parents that I was not joking when I told them my legs had gone "asleep". And when the sensation had not gone away by the next morning, my parents took me to a doctor of Osteopathy. They found that I had a curvature of the spine, and discovered that one side of my last vertebrae was overdeveloped, while the other side was underdeveloped. The doctor said that there was a new drug they were trying out. He said it was like liquid cement, and he injected it into my spine. Now I wouldn't usually suggest getting cement shot into your back, but it actually worked!

Most of my free time during junior high and high school was spent on music. I had continued to play the trombone during those years, and over time, I worked my way up to Student Band Conductor. I loved the trips our band took. We played in the Mardi Gras parades, and that was always a hoot. People would throw beads at us, and they'd try to throw things into our instruments. It was wild.

Our Stranahan High School Band marched in the Orange Bowl Parade for a couple years, and we even competed for the State Championship. We didn't win, but we did get runner-up. I was always "second chair first" in the band. No matter how hard I tried, I could never advance to "first chair first".

Since I had first learned how to play in churches, I almost never read the music. I played by ear, and I could tell where my harmony part needed to go. All the other trombone players had their little music stands on their trombones, right in front of them, but I didn't need one. During my junior and senior years, I was one of four students chosen to represent our school in the State Choral Festival.

During our time in Alabama, one of my favorite teachers was Mrs. King. She was a great teacher, who knew how to maintain order. But she also had a fun side to her, and she felt that she could be herself around me. One day, I set an alarm clock and put it in the garbage can near her desk, and covered it with paper so that it wouldn't be seen. About a minute before it was set to go off, the principal came in and started talking to Mrs. King. He was standing right over the can when the alarm went off. Mrs. King calmly asked me to come and turn off the alarm. She had no doubt in her mind whose clock it was.

I liked to have fun with my teachers. One day, I was visiting with Mr. Cole, our speech teacher, and he asked me to go and get him a cup of coffee from the cafeteria. While I was there, I told the lunch lady that it was for Mr. Cole, and I also asked for two pieces of pie. When I came back to class, I brought him his pie and coffee... but I had also brought a piece of pie and a cup of coffee for me! Who knew, all these years later, I'd still be serving up pie and coffee in Larry's Country Diner!

This is something that would never be allowed today, but it is completely true: when I was in high school, I also drove the school bus! At the age of seventeen, I applied to be a part time bus driver, and got the job! I picked up all the kids and drove them to school, and then when they got off at the school, I also got off and went into class with them! I had to get up very early each morning in order to pick up everyone, and then of course I would drive them all home after school.

I was a fill-in driver during my senior year. No one even questioned it back then. We were in the country, and most kids on the farm had been driving tractors and trucks since they were nine or ten, so it really wasn't a big deal for a seventeen year old to drive a school bus.

During my junior high years, I tried out for all the school plays... I was always passed over. Since I was so stout, most people thought that I would talk with a big, deep voice. But at the time, I had a very high, girlish voice. And as I failed yet again to get a role in the school play, the drama teacher loudly announced, "I don't have any parts for big guys with small voices!"

But my "small voice" would start maturing in high school. It finally caught up with my body! In January of 1960, we moved back to Mobile, Alabama, when my dad was named pastor of the Moffett Road Assembly of God; and in the middle of my eleventh grade year, I walked into Semmes High School. I'd like to say that I was also a good student in school. I'd like to say that, but I seemed to spend a lot of time in the principal's office! But that also gave me and the principal time to get to know each other, and he seemed to like me.

When my Physics teacher, Mr. Hawkins, caught me making fun of him, he sent me to the office. The principal asked why I was there, and when I told him, he just let me sit with him. He never punished me. I became so close with the principal that he would pass me in the hall and ask what I was doing, and I would answer, "Skipping class." He'd just laugh and walk on.

After my significant voice change, I excelled in my Speech class, which later put on a school play, called "The Truth, The Whole Truth and Nothing but the Truth". The boy who was the lead actor quit the play two weeks before it opened, so the teacher, Mr. Cole, came to me and asked, "Larry, would you consider taking the role?" I said, "Of course, absolutely!"

I learned all the lines in a short time, and I did a very good job in the play. That really established me in the school. As I look back at my acting career, I credit my speech teacher, Mr. Cole, for being the first person who ever saw any potential in me.

When I did the play and it was a huge success, I soon became a "personality" in the school. Even though we had just moved there, and I was brand new to all the other students, I was elected vice president of the senior class. They chose me over everyone they had been going to school with since they were in kindergarten! That class play gave me the very first feeling of popularity that I had ever had, and being accepted so well was really a turning point for me.

Another life-changing moment came on the day that our band instructor, Mr. Posey, asked me to do the narration for the halftime show. So, as the band did its marching, I talked over the PA system. The next day, my algebra teacher, who was a retired Navy Admiral, came up to me and said, "Larry, have you ever thought about doing radio?" It was at that moment that the lightbulb (or in my case, the "On Air" light) came on for me. From that moment, I began thinking about how I might be able to get a job at a radio station.

OH BROTHER

My brother Richard is almost two years older than me. He was a great brother as we were growing up, and he is still a great brother today. But we could not be any more different!

Richard was good-looking, talented, slender and very athletic… and I was none of those things! I was pudgy and I was homely. I wore glasses, and I had a flat top haircut from the time I was a little boy up until I was in college. I had red hair, and freckles… lots of freckles. In some of my early photos, I look kind of like a raccoon. The freckles were everywhere my glasses weren't!

Mom tried to make me feel better, as she told me there were very few redheads, so I was extra special. That worked for a while, but on another occasion, I went crying to mom, saying, "People don't treat me as well as they treat Richard. All of the girls love Richard. But no one likes me because I'm homely."

After that, mom went to all the girls we knew, and she told them what I had said to her. They were all twelve and thirteen years old then, and for the next couple of weeks, all those girls just fawned over me. They really poured it on. But I knew they were only doing it because my mom had talked to them. They weren't doing it because they really loved me.

I had a need to be accepted. And I knew I couldn't be accepted for my sporting abilities, because I didn't have any. The only times I was picked to be on a sports team were when my brother was a captain of the team, and he would always choose me. When he wasn't captain, Richard was always chosen first to be on any team, and then he would tell the captain to pick me. I would have been picked last every time, if it wasn't for my brother.

We both played football in a Pee Wee league in Mobile. Well, Richard played. I mostly held down the sideline bench. But I was able to make one memorable play! The coach had put me in, just as the other team was kicking off. I silently prayed that they didn't kick the ball toward me. And of course, that's exactly where they aimed!

But through some divine intervention, the ball somehow fell right into my arms. I was so shocked when I caught it that I had no idea what to do or where to go next! Richard yelled, "Run!" And I did… until I saw some big guys zeroing in on me! Then I tossed the ball to Richard. He took a couple steps, and got crushed by three of the biggest players on the opposing team. Yes, it was yet another time that he "took one for his little brother".

Our Pee Wee team also got to play at halftime of the big Senior Bowl game in Mobile. I didn't get to start the game, but in the second quarter, the coach called me up and told me to play center. He also sent me with the play that he wanted to give the quarterback. I hustled into the huddle, gave the play, and then got ready to snap the ball.

But in my excitement for actually getting to play, I forgot what number I was to snap the ball on. When the quarterback yelled out the number, everyone sprang into action. Everyone but me. I hadn't moved the ball. As the refs called off sides on our entire team, I was called back to the sidelines, where I would watch the rest of the game.

My brother Richard could do everything. He could ride a horse bareback! When our parents needed someone to watch us, they usually took us to the older man and wife who lived on a pig farm not far from our house. The couple also had two horses, and after seeing Richard ride one bareback, I thought that I could do it just as easily as he did.

Well, when I got on, I grabbed the horse's mane. That horse took off, and I fell off right under it! But as soon as I hit the ground, the horse stopped immediately. It didn't step on me. But I was so embarrassed. I wasn't the horseman my brother was.

Richard and I once went from Mexico to Cuba... on a train! Yes we did! This was when we lived in Slater, Missouri. When I was in the third grade, we had mom and dad put us on a train in Mexico, Missouri, and then we rode to Cuba, Missouri. Then we took the next train back. I have no idea why we wanted to do it. Maybe it was so I would have another paragraph for this book!

One of the best Christmases I ever had was the year when Richard and I both wanted English Racers, a model of bicycle that had three speeds. We knew there was no way in the world that mom and dad could afford those, but they somehow managed to surprise us on Christmas Morning with those bikes. I rode my bike to school, carrying my trombone on the handlebars.

I'm happy to say that my brother and I never had a fight. Although we came close a couple times. In Slater, Richard got mad and threw his trumpet at me. In Mobile, we were washing our car, and I sprayed him with the water hose. He grabbed the hose and pulled me to the ground. Right when he was getting ready to jump on me, our dad yelled, "Richard!" I was never happier to hear good ol' Dad!

I always tried to keep up with my big brother, even during times when I shouldn't have. One day, we were with two other boys, walking by a construction area. Richard and the other boys stood against the wall of a window encasement that had been dug out by the construction crew... but when I went to do the same thing, I couldn't get off of the wall! I was too small. I started crying and yelling for my brother to come get me. And as always, he came to my rescue.

When Richard and I visited my Grandma Vivian in South Dakota, we were expected to "earn our keep" by helping on her new husband's sheep farm in Pierre. The farm had no running water, and an outhouse for the bathroom. But when you're young, that's kind of an adventure.

We had great fun helping cut the hay, but there was another job we had to do that was a little less fun... shearing sheep. I later found out that this was the reason for our visit. It was sheep shearing season, so my dad, brother and I were there to help them do the shearing. Since I was only twelve, they had to instruct me on how to do it. If you have never sheared a sheep, let me give you a quick lesson!

You grab them by their front legs, and set them on their rear end. Once they are on their rump, they are as docile as anything. You can shave off their wool fleece with no trouble. But when I went to shear the biggest, really huge bull sheep, I grabbed him, but I didn't get his back legs. He was able to scramble, and he got me on the floor and drug me all through the urine and poop. That sheep drug me all over the floor. I was covered!

During my freshman year of high school, I took Typing as an elective. So did my brother, and we were the only two boys in the class. Before the end of the year, Richard and I could both type faster than most of the girls in the class. That class really served me well, and I went on to type all of my college papers.

In 1958, at age fourteen, I was living in Fort Lauderdale, Florida. On New Year's Day, Richard and I thought we would celebrate by scuba diving off of Pompano Beach, thirty miles up the beach from Fort Lauderdale.

He and I rented some scuba equipment, even though neither one of us was certified. We just stuck the tube in our mouth and breathed. Two other guys and two girls went along with us. None of us had rubber wetsuits; I just wore a sweatshirt, and that January 1st water was cold!

As we swam out beyond the surf, we towed a huge truck tire inner tube with a mesh netting in the middle behind us, and we threw all of our scuba gear in there. Once I went underwater, I never wanted to come back up. It seemed like I was in another world. I ended up staying under so long, that when I finally came up, I saw that all of my friends and my brother were up on the beach... a long ways from me.

I had to swim in, pulling that huge truck inner tube by myself. It had my aqualung and everything thrown into it. When I finally got to the beach, a girl asked me if I wanted a cup of coffee. To this day, that was the best cup of coffee I've ever had. I was so cold and exhausted. But it was so much fun, that we did that exact same thing the next New Year's Day!

A few years later, I wanted to see exactly how good my scuba diving skills really were... a new pool was opening, and I wanted to see how long I could stay underwater. Richard helped me, as I put on my scuba lung and swam to the bottom of the pool. We put weights on me to hold me down. Richard had great lung capacity, and he would dive down there and play checkers with me! He could stay underwater for a long time, on just one breath of air. And when my air would run out, he'd bring me another air pack, and I was able to stay down there for four hours!

When he was only in the ninth grade, Richard got a scholarship offer from the University of Alabama. But he chose not to go there. Richard could have played professional baseball, but three different times when he had a tryout, he'd get injured just before the big day.

So God had a different and more important plan for him. My brother spent the next 35 years as a choir director at a church in Biloxi, Mississippi. He is an incredible worship leader, and today, Richard lives in Lakeland, Florida. Last year, he surprised me when he came to one of our Diner tapings! I had no idea that he was there until I looked out into the audience and saw him smiling at me.

LORD, MR. FORD

Like most teenage boys, I dreamed of the day when I would get my first car. In my dreams, that car was a 1932 Ford. When I was sixteen, we took our summer vacation to South Dakota, and on the way back home, we stopped over in Springfield, Missouri, where we stayed with Ward Williams' family. My father knew Ward, who would later become the dean of the college I attended.

During our visit, one of his sons told me that he had seen a car I might like.

It wasn't a 1932, but it was close. It was a 1930 Ford, and the couple who owned it wanted $225 for it. My mom told me, "I will give you the money, and when we get to home, we'll sell our Plymouth to get some money, until you can pay me back yourself." I would drive the car home to Mobile, while my parents followed close behind me.

It turned out to be a very long trip, however. This car had not been driven in more than a year. The first time I filled it up with gas, all of the sediment that had accumulated at the bottom of the tank over the past year went into the gas line, and came in through the cab of the car. Then it would go back into the engine, and when those little bits of rust went through the line, they caused the car to backfire as I was driving.

Every thirty miles, I had to stop the car and run a coat hanger down into the line to clear it up, and then empty the settling bowl. That was a major pain... but then things got worse. We had just made it to West Memphis, Arkansas, when the water pump gave out, and the radiator busted. Dad jacked the car up, and pulled off the radiator and water pump. He called around to get replacement parts.

My dad was an old farm boy. If you gave him some bailing wire, a pair of pliers and a screwdriver, he could fix almost anything. Once he replaced the water pump, the car's timing started jumping, so then he had to find a remedy to that problem. While dad worked on the car, the rest of the family slept at a truck stop.

We finally made it home to Mobile, just in time for dad to preach on Sunday morning. I'm sure he had to wing most of his sermon. There's no way he could have written anything. He had been too busy helping his son.

But I had my first "dream car", and it was quite identifiable. When the other kids saw that 1930 Model A Ford coming down the road, they knew it was Larry Black! I drove that car until I graduated high school in 1961! I eventually traded it for a boat motor and trailer. I should have kept the car!

To pay for my new car, I took a job at The Burger Castle. How ironic that my career started out selling hamburgers, and now, all these years later, I am still selling them on Larry's Country Diner!

After a short stay at The Burger Castle, I moved on to a job at Gayfer's Department Store, a chain based in Mobile. Charles

Chadwick was the guy who did the hiring and firing at Gayfers. I carried items out to the cars for customers, and Charles told me that I was the first white boy they ever hired to do carry-outs.

I was also in charge of helping the cashiers with anything they needed. The first night that I was there, they told me to change all the light bulbs that were out. So I got a tall ladder, and as I was changing a bulb, I looked down - and I was right over the women's changing room. I could see a woman in her bra and underwear. If they would have looked up, I don't know what would have happened. But I came down that ladder a lot faster than I went up!

Back then, people used to walk or drive by storefront windows to look at all the mannequins. They would really study the windows. A few of my co-workers and I thought it would be fun to get up in the window and act like mannequins. And when someone looked in, we'd all suddenly wave at them.

Charles Chadwick later went on to work at Castner Knott in Nashville, and I've been able to get reacquainted with him. He's now in his 70s too, and it was fun to get to know him again after we had palled around together back when I was just sixteen.

I guess you could say my sixteenth year was one for many firsts. When I was sixteen, I got my first car, my first job, and my first kiss. I didn't kiss a girl until I was sixteen years old. I was always too self-conscious. I saw myself as homely and chubby. And my confidence dipped even lower when I continually compared myself to my over-achieving brother.

But while my brother Richard could have had his pick of almost any girl, he always seemed to stick to just one. He never dated that many different girls. It was a philosophy I did not agree with! While my brother fell in love with just one girl and dated her exclusively, I told myself that I would not be doing that.

When I finally started dating, I guess you could say that I tried to make up for lost time. At the age of sixteen, I made up my mind to date as many girls as I could. I made a list of all the girls in school that I wanted to go out with. I would date a different girl on Friday, Saturday, and Sunday nights.

In an effort to never get too attached to anyone, I made a point to never date the same girl on back-to-back nights. Even if I really liked a girl, and we had a great date, I always went out with someone else the next night. If I dated a girl on Friday night, I would not date her again until I had dated someone else on Saturday.

Using that method, I ended up dating 57 girls in one year!

Yes, I had turned into a very unlikely ladies' man. I would ask girls out that I didn't think I had a chance with, and I never got turned down! The closest I got to a girl saying no was one who said, "I can't this weekend, but please ask me again."

But I never did. I didn't need to. I already knew she would go out with me, and that was the most important thing to me: just the challenge of getting the date, not the actual date itself! So, to any chubby, homely kid reading this… there is hope!

SCHOOL DAZE

In September of 1961, I enrolled at Southeastern Bible College in Lakeland, Florida, where, in my free time, I would work at a Woolworth's Department store. I worked in the receiving area, and helped clean the store.

Then I took a job at the Holiday Inn, where I was the night desk clerk, and worked from midnight until 7:00 am the next morning. All the other college students had a 10:30 pm curfew, but since my shift started at midnight, they excused me so that I could work. But you can imagine that staying up all night did not help me with my studies the next day!

To try and get at least a few minutes' rest, when things were slow at the front desk, I would sometimes go and take a nap in the janitor's closet. I had a little cot in there. But when you work the overnight shift at a hotel, things are rarely boring. One night, an 80 year old woman came down to the lobby... completely naked. She just sat down on the couch. After I had watched her a few minutes, I called up to her room and got some of her family members to come down and get her.

One night, a female guest called the desk and told me she would be in another room, if anyone called for her. Sure enough, a few minutes later, she got a call from her husband.

So I dialed the room number that the woman had given me... but a man answered. The husband hung up and called me again, saying I had connected him with the wrong room. I knew I hadn't, and I dialed the same room again. This time, the woman answered. She had been in there with a traveling salesman, and with her teenage daughter! When the woman's husband found out, he called my desk phone and said he was on his way to kill all of them. I went to the room and told them he was on the way. They all checked out, and were gone before he got there.

During one particularly slow evening, I thought that I would add a little excitement to our dinner hour. The hotel swimming pool was across from a little patio where people sat, and I decided to jump from the hotel roof into the swimming pool. I took off running, and made my giant leap. I flew over the people eating below me, and I made a perfect splash into the pool!

My stunts continued in college. I was always pulling pranks. People would park cars on the edge of the football field, and huge posts served as a fence to make sure those vehicles didn't get onto the field. In the middle of the night, a couple of my friends and I loosened those posts, enough so that we could pull them up out of the ground. Then we pushed all the cars onto the football field, put all the posts back in place, and then the next morning no one had any idea how their car got on the field... or how to get it off!

I saved another midnight joke for the college president's house. I had found some huge banners from a car dealership, and I strung them all over the president's yard in front of his cars. And everyone who went by saw these big signs that read "Used Cars! Cheap!"

On another occasion, when the college president was going to speak in our chapel, I put an alarm clock up in the choir loft, just before the service. I had set it to go off in the middle of his sermon. Of course, I was sitting downstairs during the service.

As I watched the minutes tick down, I started having second thoughts, but there was nothing I could do at that point. I couldn't get up in the middle of his sermon. And when that clock went off, the president just came unglued. He was not happy... but the students loved it.

The president had a habit of leaning forward to grab his mic stand and then leaning forward on it. After watching him do that a few times, I decided to loosen his mic stand one day, before he got there. When he grabbed it, that thing broke right in half. I just loved to disrupt things. I liked to have fun.

In our college manual, I had read that it was an expellable offense if you were ever caught with fireworks. Well, when I went to college, I had a briefcase full of fireworks! I loved to throw cherry bombs down from my second floor dorm room. I'd throw them into the courtyard where the girls liked to gather.

One day, I got a couple cigarettes from one of the bellhops I worked with at the Holiday Inn, and I went down to the college post office, on the first floor. I took two firecrackers and stuck them all the way into the cigarettes, lit them both, and laid them down in front of the post office window. Then I walked back up to my room, got into bed, and waited for those cigarettes to burn down and ignite the firecrackers.

About the time I started thinking that I probably shouldn't have done it, I heard the first one go off. I heard teachers and girls screaming. Then I heard the next one explode. My roommate was a very serious guy, who had a very good reputation. And he was talking to a teacher near our room when the first one went off. I heard him yell, "Larry!"

He came running to our room and saw that I was in bed, and he was standing right next to me when we heard the second one go off. So when they started looking for who had done it, he was my strongest defender, as he swore that I was in bed when everything happened.

One of the guys I went to college with also worked at the local WTWB radio station. He did the news there, and told me they needed another newsman. So I applied for the job, and they gave me some copy to read. I sounded just like my friend, and I could do his voice better than he could. But they didn't hire me.

I went back to the dorm, and my friends said, "Man, you really sound like that guy."

So, of course, I thought up a good practical joke that I could play. We got the phone number of the guy's girlfriend, and I called her and pretended to be him! I asked her to meet me in front of the boy's dorm, and we'd go get a Coke. Sure enough, just a few minutes later, here she came. She got pretty irritated as she waited for her no-show boyfriend.

As I watched her, I started thinking that it might be time for me to get a steady girl. For a time, that girl was Sandy, and I really thought that she was THE girl. She was from Clewiston, Florida, and she reminded me of Doris Day.

Over our Thanksgiving Break, I decided to surprise her, and I drove to Clewiston.

But when I got there, I found her with one of her former boyfriends who had just gotten back from the Army. She wouldn't even talk to me. She had a friend tell me that she was dropping me for her former boyfriend.

I cried all the way back to Lakeland. And I cried for the next day or two. She really broke my heart. I listened to Ray Charles' "I Can't Stop Loving You" quite a bit during that time. Then, I finally came to my senses and started dating as many other girls as I could! I was making up for lost time when, guess who showed up?

Sandy! She told me that she wanted to date me again. But I told her I wasn't really in the mood.

A few months later, though, I moved to Eufaula, Alabama. Sandy had a friend in Eufaula, and when she came to visit her, we started dating again. My brother married a girl who was a friend of Sandy's, and we were all in the wedding together. Later, I moved to Mobile, where I dated some other girls, while Sandy moved from Florida to Bay Minett, Alabama, where my dad pastored a church. And even though we were no longer going steady, Sandy started staying at my parent's house. That created some friction when I went to see my mom and dad, and she finally moved back to Florida.

On the morning of my wedding day, Sandy called me and said, "Larry, you are making a mistake." I said, "No, I don't think so," and hung up.

I left college after my first semester. I just was not college material. The following January, I moved back to Mobile, and took a night desk job at the Albert Pick Motel. And while I was doing that job... I got my first break into radio.

When my hotel shift ended each morning, I would go over to a nearby country music radio station, WAIP, in Pritchard. The station sold time each morning to different artists who came in and sang live on the radio. Every fifteen minutes, a new group would come in, set up, and do their show. Many other stations across the country did the same thing during that time.

Jack Cardwell was the program director at WAIP, at the time. He also worked the morning shift there. Jack would later go on to write the hit song, "The Death of Hank Williams". He let me hang around and watch him do his show. One morning though, he decided to introduce me to his radio audience, and then he gave me a commercial to read... live on the radio!

I can still remember the excitement of reading my first commercial. I just knew the entire world was tuned in! As I read the copy, the level of my voice elevated several decibels. I also flipped around one line of the ad. One listener even called in and said, "The kid is not bad, but tell him it's not 'eggs by the pound and meat by the dozen'!"

When the radio station was sold, Jack asked if I would like to fill in on the morning show until the new owners took over. He told me they wouldn't be able to pay me, but that I'd get a lot of experience. Of course, I said I would love to do it. I worked there for three months... for FREE! No pay, but it gave me all the experience that I needed to get a "real" radio job. While I was on the air, I recorded my show to make an 'air check'. That's a tape that you can send to potential employers to let them hear what you sound like and what kind of personality you have.

W.O. Smith, an Assemblies of God pastor from Eufaula, Alabama, knew their local radio station needed a DJ. He played my air check for them and they offered me $40 per week to do a show from 9 AM to Noon and again from 4 PM to sign off. It made for a long day, but I was making $8.00 a day! During my break from Noon to 4:00, I could sell advertising time.

Part of the deal with Brother Smith was that I would also help with the youth program at his church. I taught junior high boys Sunday school class and lead the Youth. One day I decided to take the Sunday School boys swimming at a local rock quarry. The swimming hole had been created when they were using dynamite to clear an area. Jackie Williams, my assistant teacher, had taken the boys earlier and they were already swimming. I put my bathing suit on in the car and headed to where I heard voices coming from. It was a ledge overlooking the swimming hole. The boys looked up at me (about 20 feet up) and yelled "Jump!"

I looked down and determined I could probably clear the edge, so I backed up and took a running leap. I cleared the edge and hit the water. Normally that would be good, but…when they dynamited out the area, they did not clear the trees that had been in the hole. I hit the water and landed on a jagged tree stump. When I came up, my nose was bloody and my bathing suit was ripped off! I wish the cameras had been rolling that day. You might think I'd learn my lesson about crazy stunts, but as you will see in this book, that is not the case.

After two months in Eufaula, the station owner sent me to Atlanta to Elkins Radio Institute so that I could get a first class license. They wanted me take a two-month course so I could become a licensed engineer. If a DJ was also FCC-certified as an engineer, then the station wouldn't have to pay the salary of a separate engineer.

Once I had received my license, the boss moved me to another station he owned, WMGY, the country station in Montgomery, Alabama, where I did mornings from 9-Noon... and then later each day, I would go across town to the Top 40 WAPX, where I used a different radio name, playing rock and roll music from 9 to Midnight. A short time later, I landed at WBGC radio in Chipley, Florida, where I made $85 a week.

At age eighteen, I had never had a sip of alcohol. Shortly after I arrived in Chipley, I began having voice trouble. But I continued talking on the air until I had completely lost my voice. The wife of the station owner brought me a little vial of clear liquid. She told me to take little sips of it throughout my show.

When I took a drink, it burned all the way down my throat. But it seemed to help. By the end of my show, I had drank that entire vial, one tiny sip at a time. Then I found out that it was straight vodka! My voice was almost as good as new, but for some reason, the listeners couldn't understand a word I was saying... maybe because I was slurring so much!

As soon as my voice problems cleared up, I left Florida for a job back in Mobile, where I worked from Midnight to 6 am at WABB. I had to take a five-dollar-a-week cut in pay, but I liked being back in my hometown. I was still just eighteen, and I wanted to show all of my friends what hot stuff I was.

I went by the radio name of "Larry Lee" while I was at WABB. I didn't use my full name. My dad was pastor of the Michigan Avenue Assembly of God in Mobile, and it took most of his congregation a long time to realize that I was his son. But my father's very good reputation around town might have saved my job one day, when I got a case of the giggles.

One of my DJ friends had been joking around, making faces at me just as I went on the air to read the news. The first story was a very serious and very sad one, about First Lady Jackie Kennedy losing her son. I was reading about the President's newborn son dying, but I started laughing and could not stop. The harder I tried not to giggle, the more I laughed. But the boss was not laughing. He warned me that the next time that happened would be the last time.

When we got new records in at the station, the DJs always got to pick their "Hit of the Week" and their "Bomb of the Week". Of course, the Bomb was the song that we thought was the worst new song that we had heard. Roger Miller came out with "'Dang Me", and I actually chose that as our Bomb as the Week. Shows you what I knew about country music. It turned out to be one of his all-time biggest hits!

Our station format called for us to always play the number one song at fifteen minutes into each hour. At the time, The Chiffons had a huge hit, with "He's So Fine". That's the one with the line, "Do lang, do lang, do lang".

I worked from Midnight to 6:00am, so I would have to play "He's So Fine" five times each and every night. And I worked six nights a week, so I played the song 30 times a week. And that song was number one for six weeks, so I had to hear "Do lang, do, do lang" 180 times! When I would go to bed, I swear I could still hear that song!

One night, Richard was going to stay with me as I worked my Midnight to 6 am shift. We were headed to the station, with Richard driving my dad's 49 Ford, and on the way there, we got a flat tire. Since we weren't far from the station, however, we just started walking from there. A couple minutes later, a cop car pulled up to us. And for some reason - I have no idea why - I yelled to Richard, "Let's run!"

We both took off running, and the cops started chasing us! We hadn't even done anything! We ran all the way to the radio station. We ran from the police for no reason whatsoever. I was just being stupid.

I loved doing unique promotions and live remote broadcasts. One of my favorites was when they put me high up, on top of a 20-foot telephone pole. They had built a little platform up there, with a box similar to a doublewide telephone booth. We even had a porta-potty inside, so I wouldn't have to come down when I needed to go to the bathroom. So I did my radio show from high above, and our listeners would come by and look up at me. I tried to stay awake as long as I could.

That remote was for the Green Lincoln Mercury dealership. While I was doing my broadcast, I was looking down into the showroom floor from the top of the pole, where I saw a baby blue 1963 Comet convertible, and I thought, "That is a beautiful car!"

From that distance, I totally fell in love with that car. I told a salesman that I wanted to buy it, even though I had never driven in it. I had never even sat in it!

But we arranged all the financing while I was up in the air on the radio, and when I finally came down, I had a brand new car; and it was a gorgeous automobile. Our special marathon broadcast ended when I finally came down, after 86 hours and 46 minutes. The fact that I hadn't slept in almost 90 hours might have played a role in me buying the Comet!

Purchasing a brand new car without taking it for a test drive might not have been my smartest move, though. And it was made worse by the fact that I was already making a monthly payment on another car.

I already had a 1959 Austin Healey Sprite. People used to call them "Bug Eyes". It was like a go-kart. So here I was, nineteen years old, with two cars. I tried to sell the Sprite, but I just couldn't find a buyer in Mobile. That's when my dad really went the extra mile for me.

He said he was confident that we could sell the car in Fort Lauderdale. So, he took three days off, took the car there, and stayed there until he was able to sell the car. When he came back home, he gave me all the money. My dad really cared for me, and this was just one of many ways that he showed it.

While dad was in Florida, I kept doing my normal shift at the radio station. But with each shift, it seemed that there was always something abnormal that happened with me. You've heard the saying about, "Everything he touches, turns to gold"? Well, during my time at WABB, it seemed that everything I touched... I destroyed. I was always breaking things at the station. To say that I was accident-prone would be an understatement.

I broke a turntable while I was on the air. Then I broke a long metal railing that was on the roof of the station. How did I even manage that? It was a handrail that kept anyone from falling over the side, and another DJ dared me to try to walk across the railing. The roof was made of tar, and when I stood on that railing, it just collapsed into the tar. Luckily for me, it fell onto the roof, and not over the edge of the building! When our station owner, J. W. Dittman, found out what I had done, he wouldn't talk to me for a month.

A short time later, I took WABB's news station wagon to cover a story. On the way there, the drive shaft fell out of the car. When I'd finally made it back, I went to open the newsroom door, and the handle came off in my hand.

One day, I was walking down the hallway while the program director was on the air. I wanted to try to make him laugh, so I somehow managed to climb up the control room door. I had to balance myself between the door and the wall. When I got to the top, I opened the door and looked at the program director. He couldn't believe I was way up on the door. It was such a funny gag that I tried it again the next day. But as I climbed the door, I accidentally put my foot through the wall! I kicked a huge hole into the sheet rock.

I knew J.W. would surely kill me this time, so, in a panic, I found a huge map of Mobile and taped it up over the hole. When the boss came in, he asked, "What's that map doing there?" I answered, "The DJs need to look at the map as we talk on the air, so we can think about all the people we are serving."

But of course, they found the hole, and they made me fix it. After I had broken all those things, one day, J.W. was heading out the front door when he met me coming in. Jokingly, he said, "Larry, these steps have been here for ten years. We need some new ones. See what you can do about it."

I was at WABB for a year before I moved to WACY in Pascagoula, Mississippi. I was twenty years old then, and had already worked at a half-dozen different radio stations... before I had completed a single year of college!

In 1964, my parents asked me to go with them on a trip to South Dakota. On the way there, we stopped in Springfield, Missouri, where my father wanted to visit with his friend, J. Robert Ashcroft.

Brother Ashcroft was the father of John Ashcroft, who later became the Attorney General. My dad knew him from their time with the Assemblies of God.

J. Robert was a marvelous gentleman. He was President of Evangel College in Springfield. Evangel was an Assemblies of God Fine Arts College.

As we visited, I told him I had only completed a semester at Southeastern Bible College, and casually added, "It would be nice to be able to go back to college."

Then he asked me about my radio work. That seemed to intrigue Brother Ashcroft. He was also in charge of Public Service Announcements for Evangel College. He had some scripts with him, and he asked me to look them over.

After a quick glimpse at them, I said, "I will need to re-write all of these. You talk to your listeners like they are all seminary graduates."

The copy read: "Under the auspice of the Assemblies of God", and I asked, "What does that even mean? You need to talk in plain language."

I re-wrote all the PSAs for him, and I was shocked when Mr. Ashcroft asked, "How would you like to go to college? I will give you a four year scholarship, tuition, books, everything." He added, "All I ask in return is that you be in charge of getting our Evangel show on the air in Springfield."

I couldn't leave my job in Pascagoula fast enough! I jumped in my '63 Comet convertible and moved to Springfield.

LUANN

Since I was now a "college man", my parents bought me a brand new suit for school. I had never washed a load of laundry until I moved into my own dorm. I went to the laundromat and threw all my dirty clothes, including my new suit, into the machine. I poured a big cup of detergent on top, and hit the "ON" button. Sure enough, when I pulled everything out of the machine, my brand new suit had big bleach spots all over it. Those then turned into large holes. I had ruined it.

While I attended Evangel College, I also worked full time at KICK radio in Springfield. We had a ball each day there. One afternoon, I pretended the control room was filling with water. I had a sound effects record, and it sounded like I was sloshing around in the studio. You could get away with stupid things like that back then. Radio was a playground of the mind.

There were five different colleges in Springfield. One day, I was on the air and I invited all of those colleges to meet downtown for a water balloon fight. When I went outside, there were people lining all the roofs in downtown Springfield! They all had water balloons. The police had blocked off a two-block area, and let all of the college kids have a very wet night of fun.

I MC'd many events and live radio remotes around Springfield. One of those events was at a local theater. I knew that Assembly of God folks didn't go to movies back then, and when the school dean heard about my upcoming movie remote, he called me in and told me that I couldn't do it. I said, "Yeah I can, and I'm going to. I've already been on the radio, promoting the event. I gave the sponsors my word that we would do it, and they have already paid for it."

So the dean told me that I would have to get permission from the college President. I went down to Brother Ashcroft's office. I had always called him J. Robert, like my dad did. I explained everything, and Brother Robert assured me, "Don't worry. It's no problem."

Our live broadcast came during a twin bill showing of "The Pajama Game" and "Bedtime Story". I told my listeners I would give them free tickets if they wore pajamas. When I came out onstage to host the movies, I was wearing a bathrobe. Then I dropped it, to show that all I was wearing was a diaper! I had a huge baby bottle, and was wearing a sheet for my diaper. Now that is a mental picture I'm sure you will not be able to get out of your head!

I asked for everyone who was in their PJs to stand up then, and there were a bunch of students from Central Bible Institute and Evangel College! None of them were supposed to be there... and not only were they at a movie, but they were wearing only pajamas!

I played tennis with my Evangel Psychology professor. I usually skipped his class, and he didn't care. I didn't even have my own book! The Professor lent me his own, in which he always had the important stuff underlined, so I knew that was what I needed to remember.

We were going to meet for a tennis game one day, when I saw him drive up in an old Morgan. It was an English car. As we played, we started talking about money. I told him what I was making at the radio station, and he informed me that I was making more than he was even getting paid as a college professor!

He asked me, "So, why are you in college?"

"That's a very good question," I replied. At the end of the year, I didn't even bother to take any final exams - I just left, and never went back.

In all honesty, my dropping-out of school shouldn't have been any big surprise. I had always given my radio job much more of my attention than I ever had given my schooling. But while I only attended Evangel for one year, it was a year that changed my life.

I had a good job, making good money at the radio station. My only real expense was putting gas in my car. I was footloose and fancy free! Those were some of the best days I ever had... and then, my days got even better. I met Luann.

One night, shortly after school began, some of the guys from my dorm met up with a few freshman girls. We challenged them to a football game, two-handed touch anywhere. It was mainly an excuse for us to be able to put our hands on the girls! The main signal call our quarterback used was "36-24-36, hike!"

As we played the game, I immediately noticed the beautiful girl quarterbacking for the other team. Her name was Luann Rouse. She was also a freshman at Evangel. And before our football game was over, I asked her to go out on a date with me.

As I mentioned before, movies were taboo at our Christian school. And if a girl went to a drive-in movie, she was committing an even bigger sin! So of course, for our first date, which happened to be on a Sunday night, I asked Luann, "Would you like to go to church… or to the drive-in?"

I was quite surprised (and very happy) when she quietly smiled, "Let's go to the drive-in."

I don't remember what movie we saw. We just spent the entire night talking, getting to know each other. At the end of the night, I asked for a good night kiss.

She said no. I jokingly shot back, "That's it! I'm not going to kiss you for six dates." That turned into a game that we played, as I refused to kiss her over the next few dates, and I found that that made her want to kiss me!

For one of our first dates, I wanted to impress Luann, so I borrowed a motorcycle from a friend. I knew the faster I drove, the harder she would wrap her arms around me. I did my best to scare her to death! Not long after our date, though, I actually wrecked my friend's motorcycle. It would not be my last accident.

Luann had a love for science and the medical field. She was always reading medical stuff. She still does. That love helped save my life many decades in the future, which I'll talk about later.

Luann had planned to get a medical degree. But then she started thinking that, with her experience caring for her three younger sisters, teaching might be a good career too. While she considered a possible major, I did as little schoolwork as I possibly could.

I cut classes whenever I could; I also tried to get out of Chapel. I was walking to the beat of a different drummer. Luann and I both had a good group of friends, and we hung out a lot with all of our pals. There was a piano in our school cafeteria, and you could often find me there, entertaining the lunch crowd... at any hour of the day.

I brought Luann into my act as we sang together. I played the piano, and we sang gospel songs together. We entertained at parties, events and different meetings. In the 1940s, there was a popular radio show about a quarrelsome couple called "The Bickersons", so Luann and I learned some of the Bickersons' routines, and we would do those at different events.

Luann and I even helped our dormitories build a float for the school's homecoming parade. We came up with the unique idea of creating a huge electric mixer, and on the side of the float, we put, "Beat 'Em". Like most floats, we covered it in colorful tissue paper. Unfortunately, right in the middle of the parade, our float somehow caught fire, and it burned to the ground!

They served chili each Friday night at school. Since I hated chili, and since I had money from my job at the radio station, I liked to take Luann out for a nice meal instead. We usually went to Dillon's Steakhouse in downtown Springfield. We would get the cheapest steak dinner they had, but it was better than the school's chili!

To say that Luann and I had a whirlwind romance would be an understatement. Our first date was on October 25, 1964. Less than three weeks later, on November 9, only a few hours before my 21st birthday, I told Luann that I loved her.

Six weeks later, I gave her a little engagement ring.

For Christmas, I took Luann to meet my parents in Mobile, Alabama. My mom and dad were happy for us... but Luann's family was a different story. Her father, Robert Rouse, had joined the Air Force when he was in his late teens, and he had even ended up working as a chef on Air Force One when Lyndon Johnson was President. Mr. Rouse traveled all over the world.

But Luann's parents had gotten divorced when she was just a little girl. Her mom remarried Bill Cowan, who was a manager of a box plant for Plough, Incorporated. I liked Bill. He was a real down-to-earth guy. He had huge muscles, and looked like he lifted weights all the time, even though he didn't.

Bill was a great athlete. A few years after we first met, I asked him if he wanted to play tennis with me - I played tennis all the time, and Bill had never even picked up a racket, but we went down to an asphalt court. I wore my usual tennis outfit and tennis shoes, but Bill had on dress shoes! He had never played tennis before, and knew nothing about the game. But he beat me all day long. I finally gave up, saying, "I've never been beaten by a guy wearing wing tips!"

When I told Bill that I wanted to marry Luann, he said it was okay with him, if that's what Luann wanted. But Luann's mom was totally against her getting married... especially to me.

We set our wedding date for October, just a year later. Luann's mom totally freaked out. Looking back, I can understand why she felt the way that she did. Luann was only eighteen years old, and the last time her family had seen her, she was heading off the college. Now, just a few months later, not even halfway through her first year of college, she was coming back home engaged! That past September, their little girl had headed off to school, and now in January, she announces that she is getting married? No, her mother was not happy about it.

Luann was the oldest of four girls. When she took me home to meet her family for the first time, Carol, one of her sisters, was standing at the window, looking out. When she saw me, with my flat top haircut, hush puppy shoes, an orange shirt, and a ukulele strapped to my back, she yelled, "Oh no! What has she done?!"

I don't really blame her.

I had just completed my first year of college when I got a job offer at a radio station in Charlotte, North Carolina. And being the scholar that I was (said sarcastically), I dropped out.

Ed Dean, a guy I used to work with in Mobile, was now the program director of WIST, and I was one of the first people Ed hired in his new position. WIST was owned by Henderson Belk, of the Belk Department stores. With her fiancée headed to another state, and with her wedding just a few months away, Luann also ended her college career, after just one year.

Our plan was for her to go back home to Memphis and prepare everything for our wedding, while I got settled into my new job, so we drove from Springfield to Montgomery, where she boarded a bus to Memphis. When she stepped onto that bus, I could see her through the window. And I knew the next time I saw her would be at our wedding, four months later. This was the first time we were going to be apart for an extended time, and I just cried my eyes out. Luann was also crying. It broke my heart to see her pull away on that bus.

In the meantime, Luann's mother made it very clear that she would not help with the wedding in any way. Her mom would not pay for anything, because she was so against her marrying me. Not only did Luann have to pay for her own wedding, but her mother basically disowned her.

She told her, "Once you leave, we are done."

I was fine with that! But it crushed Luann.

As soon as she got home to Memphis, Luann took a new job at a finance company. She wanted to earn as much money as she could, so that she would be able to pay for our wedding. To save money, she would go hungry all week. She allotted herself a food budget of just 70 cents a day! Each day, she skipped breakfast. At lunch time, she took the bus to the Britling Cafeteria in downtown Memphis, where she could get a corn muffin and vegetable soup. That meal cost 70 cents. She also skipped dinner. She did that day after day, for months!

IF AT FIRST YOU DON'T SUCCEED
...then skydiving is probably not for you.

IN 1966, while Luann was trying to save every penny she could, I was getting settled in Charlotte, preparing for my new job as a disc jockey at WIST Radio. My new bosses all wanted to make a big splash with their new hire, so they had planned a big promotion to introduce me.

At the time, the James Bond movies were very popular, so someone came up with the idea that I would go around town as "Secret Agent 1240". I would give hints of where I was, and if someone found me, they would win $1,240.

And since James Bond was always doing such impressive stunts, like jumping out of airplanes, the station management asked if I would be willing to parachute out of a plane myself. I jumped at the chance! I had always wanted to skydive, and the station said they would pay me to make a jump. I was supposed to do the skydive on July 5th, and I would broadcast live on the air as I came down. What could go wrong?!

I was supposed to do a practice jump on July 4th, and then do the 'real jump' on air the next day. But I never got to jump on July 5th... because I almost died on the 4th of July.

These days, they would have you do your first jump as a tandem, attached to a more experienced parachutist - but back then, you took a "crash course". Poor choice of words.

They gave me an 8-hour lesson that included me jumping off of a little platform. They told me not to look at the ground, and to roll when I landed. The instructor showed me a little box that would sit on my chest as I came down, which had a CO_2 cartridge in it. If I happened to lose consciousness and couldn't pull my chute, then at a certain altitude, that CO_2 cartridge would fire, bringing out my reserve chute. They told me to be sure to turn that box off as soon as my chute opened.

The next day, I was a little nervous, as I prepared to make the jump. I should have been. If I had known what was about to happen, I would have stayed home. To try and calm my nerves, I told the other guys in the plane, "You don't need a parachute to skydive... you need a parachute to skydive more than once!"

A few seconds after I'd stepped out of the plane, my chute opened perfectly. That was the last thing that happened as we had planned.

I remembered that they had taught me to turn off the CO_2 cartridge as soon as my chute deployed... but when I flipped the switch for the cartridge, the switch came off in my hand. I pulled out every wire in the box, to make sure it didn't go off.

As I came down, I spotted my instructor on the ground. I could tell he was yelling something, but I couldn't quite make it out. Then he went out of sight. As I frantically looked around, I pulled down on my right riser, so I could look to the right. But when I did that, it collapsed part of my chute! It also turned me directly toward a barbed wire fence.

"This isn't good," I said to myself.

I had big, heavy boots on, so I thought maybe I could catch the top rung of barbed wire and tear it down with my boots. I put my feet straight out in front of me. I managed to clear the fence, but came down in a sitting position, right on my rear end. It was a hard hit. I knew immediately that I was seriously injured. The impact had crushed my first two lumbar vertebrae.

Our program director loaded me into his convertible Thunderbird and drove me to the emergency room, and I spent the next ten days in Charlotte Memorial Hospital. But I never missed a day of work! I did my whole radio show from my hospital bed. They brought in a microphone and mobile unit for me, so that their brand new DJ could host his show. The local newspaper even came in to do a story on me. Yes, I had made a big splash. We all got a lot of publicity from it.

The first airplane ride Luann ever had was when she flew from Memphis to see me in hospital. Hearing that her fiancée had broken his back, Luann was beside herself with worry. Thinking I was on my deathbed, she rushed to my side. But she began to question her concern, when she walked off the hospital elevator and could hear laughter coming out of my room.

When she walked in, she saw me entertaining a room full of candy striper nurses.

I laid there doing my radio show from my bed, and I was surrounded by the young nurses. Luann couldn't believe it, and she was not happy. After a very short stay, Luann told me, "I will see you in three months… at our wedding."

She left me and my candy stripe friends all standing speechless.

I never skydived again. I would have, but Luann wouldn't let me. The one jump I did make was great fun. The dive was fine, but that sudden stop got me. If I weren't married, I would have probably skydived again, just to prove that I could do it successfully.

After a week and a half in the hospital, the doctors put me in a an aluminum back brace that kept my back straight, and told me I would have to wear it for the next three months.

On the morning of October 2, 1965, our wedding day, I was playing a game of football with my groomsmen in the parking lot of our motel. Luann's sister Carol saw me out there playing while wearing my back brace. When she told her, Luann was infuriated.

Luann's mother did eventually buy our wedding cake. It cost $25.00. But other than that, she kept to her word of not helping us at all. That made the entire ceremony so hard on Luann, but she did get a lot of help from her best friend, Anita. Thanks to their hard work, we had a large wedding at the First Assembly of God in Memphis. It was Elvis' church. Being raised in Memphis,

Luann was always an Elvis Presley fan. She joked that she could have made Elvis happy… if he would have just let her!

The Blackwood Brothers went to First Assembly of God in Memphis, and Terry Blackwood sang at our wedding. Luann's dress, which she paid for all by herself, was beautiful… just like my new bride.

We stayed in Memphis the night of our wedding, and the next day, we started out for Charlotte. I had to be back on the air for my 9-Noon show on Monday. That's when the realization of our new life really began to set in for Luann. She had just turned nineteen. Now she was moving to a new state, with a new husband who she barely knew. As I drove, she sat, quietly thinking, "What have I done?!" She began thinking of all the hateful things her mother had said about me. Maybe her mom had been right all along.

As she second-guessed herself, Luann became very upset. I tried to calm her down.

I tried to be sweet and gentle, quietly saying, "Everything will be fine, babe."

Suddenly, she screamed at me, "Talk like a man! I don't need a baby. I need a man for a husband! Talk like a man!"

Yes, it was a fun trip to Charlotte.

Our new home was in a place called Radio Center Apartments, where our rent was $65 a month… for the smallest apartment you have ever seen! We had a king sized bed, that filled the entire room. We couldn't even walk around the bed! We just fell into it as soon as we opened the bedroom door. Our kitchen was even smaller, and also served as our dining room, featuring a small table and four chairs. We didn't have a full set of plates for the table; we just made do with the few plates I had from before we were married.

We had been married for only a few weeks when Luann received a surprising call from her sister Carol. She told her, "Luann, mom and dad are on their way to see you. I wanted to warn you!"

Luann yelled to me, "We don't have enough plates for our table, and my mom is headed here!"

We quickly ran to Sears and bought a set of Formica dinnerware for $8.00. We still have one of those plates, now more than 53 years later.

"I thought your mom wasn't going to have anything to do with us," I said to Luann on our way back home. But sure enough, they came, and stayed a couple days. I know they wanted to check on Luann to see if she had totally ruined her life.

Her mom ended up taking back her vow to disown Luann, but she was still not okay with me. I learned to ignore her mom, and I tried to stay away from her. Many years later, Luann's mother's dislike for me would reach an all-time high, when Luann asked me to accompany her for a visit to her mom's house.

For some reason, Luann told her that we would spend a week there. Her mother had just had her kitchen cabinets freshly painted right before we arrived. And, using my voice to make my living, I could not be around paint fumes. Varnish or paint can mess up my throat and voice. If I'm around fresh paint, I lose my voice, and I get a cough that lasts two or three months. As soon as I opened the door, I said, "I can't stay here."

Luann understood, but it royally offended her mom. She didn't care why I wouldn't stay at her house, even though she didn't even want me there in the first place!

Did I happen to mention that Luann's mom never accepted me? To make things even more interesting, I eventually married her other daughters! Yes, as a minister, I performed the marriage ceremony for Luann's sister, Carol, and then also for her sister Cristy! I wasn't able to officiate her sister Lisa's wedding, because our son Jared had just been born, and we couldn't be there. But none of that won Luann's mother over. To the day she died, she didn't think that her daughters were really married, because she never believed I was a real minister!

Luann and I helped oversee the local Youth for Christ Club, and we wanted to do something special that would help bring attention to our club; so we came up with the idea of creating the World's Longest Banana Split.

Since I worked at Big WAYS Radio, I was able to make a deal with Chiquita Bananas. We held the event in a gymnasium, where we covered the floor with rows of rain gutters and lined them with tin foil. Then we added hundreds of pounds of bananas, ice cream, whipped cream, cherries, nuts, lots of chocolate sauce, and walnuts with simple syrup.

We served that record treat after one of the football games. We had planned for everyone to use spoons to eat it, but when the football players and cheerleaders all came in, they thought it would be more fun if they didn't use a spoon. Instead, they knelt down at the rain gutters and just dove in face first! Pretty soon after that, someone threw a little bit of ice cream at one of their pals... and in just a couple seconds, the event turned into a huge ice cream and banana food fight. The sugar and water from the walnut syrup got all over the basketball floor, and everyone started falling down. No one could stand up.

At the end of the night, after everyone had left, we worked for four hours trying to clean the syrup off of that gym floor. It was so slick. We mopped it and re-mopped it, and mopped it again. My World's Longest Banana Split idea turned out to be a pretty messy deal. But it was a lot of fun.

Youth for Christ held events called CAT, which stands for "Campus Action Time". On Halloween, they called it Black CAT. And Luann and I would drive around in a hearse to promote the Black CAT. We even had a casket in the back of the hearse, and we drove it to different restaurant drive-ins.

The Black CAT event was held at a lodge, which had a lot of little cabins on the property. And every building would have something scary in it. Luann's role for the night was to be in a casket that was inside one of the cabins. The lodge also had a lagoon, with a shaky bridge traversing over it. And everyone had to walk across that bridge, to get from the main lodge to the cabins. We warned the kids that when they crossed the little bridge, they might encounter a troll underneath it. Guess who played the troll? Yep, me! It was very cold that night, and I wore a wetsuit with a scuba diver's air tube and mask. I was underwater, under that bridge. When I would hear kids walking across, I would reach my hand up out of the water and grab their ankle! It was great fun.

One of our first major purchases as a married couple was a new car. Or at least, it was new to us. I bought a 1932 B Model Ford, chopped and channeled with a full-blown V-8 motor. It had headers with huge racing slicks on the back, and suicide doors that opened from the front to the back. The first time I took it to be serviced, the dealership said they would have to keep it overnight.

When I picked it up the next day, it had a blown rod. I found out later that one of the young mechanics had taken my car out on Interstate 85 and raced it until he'd blown the motor. I should have sued them, or at least made them fix it. But instead, I had it towed to Charlotte. I sold it to a boy who was getting ready to go to Vietnam, and he said to me, "This car will give me an incentive to come home."

I hope he did.

While I was at WIST, two of my coworkers, Rick Fite and Mel Harrison, came up with an idea… which sounded like a really funny stunt at the time, so I went along with it. We interrupted the broadcast with a special news bulletin, saying that an Amoeba had been found in West Charlotte. A half hour later, we interrupted programming again, saying another Amoeba had been found. And as the day went on, we started building on it, more and more. By early afternoon, the local Volkswagen business had sent all their people home early, and then the local schools let out early, because of this "Amoeba scare"! The city fire and ambulance phone lines were tied up with calls from panicked residents. The sheriff's department finally came to the radio station and told us to go on the air and tell everyone that it was all a joke. But it was no laughing matter when we were given a reprimand from the FCC.

Right after we had gotten married, Luann worked at Household Finance, before landing a job at City Chevrolet in Charlotte. I spent eight months at WIST Radio, and then I landed my first job in television. Yep, the cameras were officially rolling...and I didn't care! WCCB was a tiny UHF station, owned by Cy Bahakel. Cy was a State Senator in North Carolina, and later on he owned a lot of TV and radio studios throughout the South.

To say the least, WCCB was not the big time. I was basically the entire staff! I did news, sports and weather on camera for our 6:00 newscast. But we didn't even have a news department, so I just ripped the stories off the teletype wires. I also had to be my own cameraman.

One night I needed something to focus the camera on, so I took a piece of gum, and stuck it onto my name plate on the desk. I zoomed in and focused on that gum, and then I zoomed out. Then I sat myself down in front of the camera and waited until I was on the air. I started to read the news, and when I looked up and saw that gum still stuck on my name plate, I started laughing, and laughed through the entire segment.

I cracked myself up almost every day. I knew no one was watching. Anyone who wanted to get the news was already watching Peter Jennings on the national network. I didn't take myself too seriously.

WCCB was small, but it got a very big break. At the time, the national ABC network was airing "The Man from U.N.C.L.E." and "Batman"… but for some reason, the local affiliate passed on those programs, and my little station, WCCB, was able to pick up those shows - which became so popular that they really put WCCB on the map. People were going out and buying converters so that they could watch this tiny UHF station. Everyone just had to see the adventures of Batman!

But Batman had nothing on the adventures that were ahead for Larry and Luann Black. Over the years, Luann and I have moved a total of fourteen times. From one apartment or house to another, from one city and state to another… fourteen times. Unbelievably, thirteen of those times came in the first twelve years of our marriage!

I started out making $95 a week. If another station offered me $100 a week, I'd quit my job and go with that station. Many stations had such a high employee turnover that they had trade outs with moving van companies. They'd give them free ads on the air, and they would move the DJs from one town to another.

I worked at some stations for just a few months, but I stayed at others for a year or two. The only way you could make more money was to go to a larger station every time you moved, and then hopefully you ended up in a big city somewhere.

When I think of our marriage, one thing that I will always be thankful to Luann for is the fact that she was always willing to put her own life on hold and start over every time I wanted to move to a different job. Luann didn't like the moves, but she was always willing to go. She just loaded up our little Pekingese dog, which I gave her the first Christmas we were married. She always followed me as I followed my dreams. Many women would not do what she did.

Luann followed me to Spartanburg, South Carolina, where Bob Brown owned the WORD radio station. Bob was a young guy, but he was a master motivator. He sold recordings of different motivational speakers, and I loved them. One day, he came into the office and I had my head lying on my desk, and I told him I was tired, and that I was resting. Any other boss would've probably gotten angry if they caught an employee with their head on their desk, but he didn't. Instead, he told me that I needed to write a daily "to do list", and I should include "rest" on it!

Bob suggested that I read the book, "Think and Grow Rich". I did, and it was a major step forward in my thinking. I was also happy that it didn't conflict with what I knew the Bible scripture to be. Napoleon Hill made the point of, "If a man's mind can conceive it, a man can achieve it", and "If you plant seeds, good or bad seeds, you will reap a harvest with those seeds". It was totally scriptural.

Bob Brown and I came up with an idea where I could go out and sell advertising on my show. The sponsors would get something called "Larry's Loot", a form of money that had my picture on it. The more ads a business bought, the more "Larry's Loot" they would get in return. Then we would auction off different things during the week, and you could only use "Larry's Loot" to make a purchase.

While I was at WORD, I learned a lot about radio production from our program director, Bob Canada. But one thing I absolutely never learned anything about was fishing. I once had to read a story about crappie fishing, and I'll give you one guess of how I pronounced crappie. Yep… "crappy"! I wasn't much of a fisherman.

After having a good time in Spartanburg, I decided to return to Charlotte, where I joined Big Ways Radio. Jack Gale was the man who hired me. Jack also did mornings, and he was just phenomenal. I followed him from nine to noon. I thought I was a clever disk jockey, and thought that I was funny. But I never felt that I was a great DJ. I never planned my shows in advance. Later in life, Jack Gale wrote his autobiography, and he wrote that he was really proud of me. He loves Larry's Country Diner, and Country's Family Reunion. He spoke very highly of me in his book. I was quite surprised and honored. I never knew he even thought I was that good.

Big Ways was a popular station, and that was very visible throughout the area. We were always hosting fun and unique events. Some of those allowed me to rub shoulders with a few of the biggest athletes in the world.

Our radio station put together a team that took on the Harlem Globetrotters. Of course, I was a horrible at basketball. So of course, the star of the Globetrotters, Meadowlark Lemon, immediately picked me out to be his comic foil for the entire game. I first got Meadowlark's attention when I somehow swatted the ball away from one of the dribbling Globetrotters. Meadowlark stopped the game, took me to the foul line, and told me to shoot the ball. He went back to the half court line, and just as I started to shoot, he flew down from half court in about four steps. Just as the ball left my hand, he jumped up and swatted it away.

I had similar luck when I switched courts to play tennis with the great Björn Borg and Bobby Riggs. They had brought in some pros to play against local celebrities (and having seen none, they chose me!). Björn Borg had won Wimbledon five years in a row, and here I was, on the court, playing doubles with him! It was almost surreal. He probably thought the same thing, as I prepared to serve the ball. Björn was standing up front, near the net, when I hit the ball and nailed him right in the middle of his left shoulder! He just stood there and shook his long hair. I'm sure he was thinking, "Why am I on the court with these clowns?"

I also played against Bobby Riggs. The tennis legend hit the ball over the net, and it looked like there was no way I could get to it. But I somehow swatted at it, and when I hit it, the ball sliced down. It barely cleared the net, and with a back spin, it went away from Bobby. He couldn't reach it. He muttered, "Nice hit." That was the highlight for me, as he just annihilated me. He showed no mercy. I quickly found out that you didn't try to show up the professionals.

I might not have been a great athlete, but there was someone else on our staff who was. He was, and still is, a legend. Jim Beatty was the first man to ever run the mile in less than four minutes. He was superhuman-fast, but Jim had to make a living just like the rest of us. He served as Sports Director at Big Ways Radio.

Charlotte had a hockey team called the Charlotte Checkers. Their cheerleaders were called The Checkerettes. Our radio station staff put together a hockey team and, in between periods of the Checker's games, we played the cheerleaders.

We also did a promotion at a local go-kart track. As I put my helmet on, I asked the manager, "How fast can I go without turning it over?"

"You can't turn these over," he replied.

So I hit the gas and pushed my foot to the floor. When I came to the first corner, my go-kart slid up and over the hill. They found me lying under it when they came to get me out!

Years later, when I was working at WSM in Nashville, a similar incident happened when I raced a stock car, as part of a "celebrity race" at the fairgrounds, where I raced against a couple other local TV and radio guys. My biggest competition was Rudy Kalis, from WSMV-TV. The last instructions they gave us as we put on our helmets were: "Just drive around and try to go as fast as you can, as long as you are being safe. We don't want you to dent up any of the cars. Remember, no wrecking! Wrecked cars cost us a lot of money."

Almost as soon as the green flag dropped, Rudy Kalis ran into me, and my hood flew up. I couldn't see anything, but I kept the gas pedal mashed to the floor. Then the hood flew off the car. Rudy's initial hit had also cut one of my tires, but I didn't know it. I just kept going until the tire blew out. The owner of the car was not pleased.

I didn't have much better luck with my own automobiles. When we lived in Charlotte in the 60s, I had two cars. One was a Corvair, and the other was my Comet convertible. I loved that car, but it was not safe. I wrecked it six times. It would change ends on you in a second, as the rear end would start coming around the front. It was unsafe at any speed, and boy could it speed. That car was fast. Too fast. I got so many speeding tickets that the state of North Carolina suspended my driver's license. Luann hadn't driven before, but she had to learn how. She got her license so she could drive us both to work.

At the time, Luann was working for City Chevy in Charlotte. They made her a notary public and at the age of nineteen, she was the youngest notary public in North Carolina. One of their salesmen liked to tell the customers, "Our notary public sleeps with one of the disc jockeys at Big WAYS!" He never told them that she was married to me. Luann worked at City Chevy for two years, while I worked at Big WAYS.

When I wasn't getting speeding tickets, I was having wrecks. I had six wrecks in six months. My accidents led me to become our insurance company's most valued client. I got their title, "Assigned Risk". I wrecked my Comet so often that I finally traded it and my Corvair for a 1968 Volkswagen Beetle! It had an automatic transmission, and I had mag wheels put on it. I also had it painted red, white and blue, and I topped it off with a Rolls-Royce grill! It was a one of a kind, and it was my pride and joy.

During our time in Charlotte, we attended the Garr Memorial Church in Charlotte, North Carolina. It was a Pentecostal Charismatic church, which Alfred Garr and his wife Lillian had founded. Alfred died in 1944, but his wife was still very active in the church when we were there. She liked me because I played trombone, and her husband had played trombone. We had a huge tabernacle, and one Sunday, Mrs. Garr was in the pulpit, talking about the new Celotex insulation that had just been installed. In front of the entire congregation, she bragged, "We are soundproofing the sanctuary, and if you look up, you can see that we have put hundreds of feet of Kotex in the ceiling."

No one corrected her.

One of my favorite parts of my job at Big Ways Radio was my MC work. Many legendary stars of the late 60s performed in concert in Charlotte, and I was the guy who got to introduce them on stage! I MC'd concerts by The Beach Boys, The Lettermen, Tom Jones, and Bobby Vee.

But my most memorable concert was one where Jimi Hendrix opened the show for The Monkees! Jimi walked onstage with his pants unzipped, and a security guy was banging on the edge of the stage, trying to get his attention. That infuriated Jimi. He walked over to the guy, and when the policeman told him his fly was down, Jimi threw his guitar up in the air, and it landed on the ground. He walked offstage, zipped his pants up, then came back, picked up the guitar, and went on playing like nothing ever happened. He was not a happy camper. He was also probably not happy with being the opening act for The Monkees. But their TV show was such a huge hit at the time, they were hotter than Jimi's burning guitar. But Jimi's star rose shortly after that show.

One of my big regrets from those times was that I never took any photos! I could have gotten pictures with all of those great stars. I would love to have a photo today of me back then, with Tom Jones, The Monkees or Jimi Hendrix.

One day, Mike Green, another DJ, came into the studio, and he told me that I should send a tape to a "headhunter" he was using. A headhunter is someone who seeks out and tries to place disc jockeys with different radio stations around the country. Once they find a job for them, the headhunter is paid a fee, or even a percentage of the DJ's income for a time. Mike was confident that we could both land great jobs.

Just a couple days after I had sent my tape in, I came in to a note on my desk, which said I needed to call WBOB in New Britain, Connecticut. I went to Mike and said, "This is the kind of jobs that guy will get you. I've never even heard of this little station!"

But when I returned the call, I found it was actually WPOP in Hartford. It was a huge station! When I told Mike Green about the job offer, he said, "Man, I haven't had even a little station call me."

WPOP was a place to be. It was also the first place where I said to myself, "I have made it." I knew that if I was going to make it big in radio, I had to be in Boston, Philadelphia or New York, and that WPOP was a great market to move up from. Once you were there, you were just one step away from the big time.

Danny Clayton was the program director who had offered me the job over the phone. I would be on the air from nine to noon, making one hundred dollars more than I did at Big Ways. Two weeks later, Luann and I loaded up our Volkswagen and headed to Hartford. We had never even visited there before!

On our way, we had to go straight through New York City. The only thing I knew about New York City was what I had read in David Wilkerson's book, "The Cross and the Switchblade", which detailed all the gangs in New York. As we drove our little VW into that city, we were both so scared.

But we made it safely to Hartford and checked into a motel. That evening, we went to a restaurant for dinner. As we finished our meal, I started to write a check, but they informed me that they didn't take checks from out of state. I didn't have a credit card or any cash.

A man, sitting at a table near ours, was listening. He said, "I'll take your check." I wrote it out to him, and then he paid for our meal with his credit card. But he never did cash our check! I didn't have a clue of who he was, but he paid for our first meal in Hartford. What a blessing it was for us.

Hartford was great fun. The local radio station was very active in the community. Dickey Heatherton was one of the DJs, and the brother of actress Joey Heatherton. The best thing about WPOP was that the station got free tickets to everything. They called it "Script". Mohawk Airlines gave us script that the DJs could use to fly anywhere they wanted. Sheraton Hotels gave us script for rooms. And since we were only an hour and a half from New York City, the record people who did the songs for Broadway musicals would even give us free show tickets. So Luann and I would fly to New York, stay in a nice hotel, and then go to a Broadway play, all for free! Luann and I did that a number of times. We saw Sammy Davis, Jr. in "Golden Boy", and we also enjoyed Steve and Eydie Gorme in a Broadway musical.

During our time in Hartford, we lived in a one bedroom apartment in Rockville. And in addition to my radio job, I also enjoyed a very successful side venture… which presented itself when I met an entrepreneur named Richard Dugan, who was running an "Under 21 Club". It was a place that young people, under the age of 21, could go for a fun time. And while they didn't allow drinking there, Richard brought in popular, big name bands from New York City for entertainment. I recorded some commercials for him, and Richard and I really hit it off.

Eventually, we decided to rent a building in Manchester, Connecticut, so that we could open another teenage hangout. We called it "The Scarlett Dragon". I managed it on weekends, and between The Scarlett Dragon and my radio job, I was taking home $300 a week… good money, in 1968. Our apartment cost $125 a month, and our car payment was $65 a month. We were doing real well in Hartford. For the first time in our lives, we had no worries about paying our bills.

Luann also had a good job as a secretary at Gerber Scientific Instrument. That was her last "outside job". Once our boys came along, she devoted her time and energy to taking care of them. While she was working at Gerber, Luann also applied to go to the University of Connecticut. She wanted to go back to school - and she got accepted. But then I got an offer to move to upstate New York, so she never got the chance to attend U-Conn.

As my wife rolled her eyes, I began to load up our car again.

Vermillion, S. D., ___November 17_____, 194_3_

Edwin Black_____

___118 Elm St., Vermillion, S. Dak._____

Patient___Mrs. Edwin Black_____

IN ACCOUNT WITH

DAKOTA HOSPITAL

	Amount

7½ days hospital room and care @ $4.00 - - - - $ 30.00
Delivery Room - 12.00
Medication - 1.60
Dressings - 1.10
Birth Certificate - .25
Portable Telephone - .40

TOTAL* $ 45 35

Loren La Black's Hospital

IN PAYMENT:	
Room Board and Nursing } 7½ da	$30.00
Surgery, Obs.	$12.00
Dressings	$1.10
X-Ray, Treatment	$
Medicine	$1.60
Laboratory	$
Birth cert.	.25
Telephone	.40
On Account	$
Total	$45.35

DAKOTA HOSPITAL
Main and Plum Streets

Vermillion, So. Dak., _November 17_, 194_3_

RECEIVED OF _Mrs. Edwin Black_

Acc't in full

Forty-five and 40/100 _____DOLLARS

With Thanks

DAKOTA HOSPITAL.

Patient's No. 6562. By _Margaret Alne_

My mother's original hospital bill. When she gave birth to me, she spent more than a week in the hospital. It cost a grand total of $45.35! Her medication cost $1.60!

Larry Lee, One year
old in Paris, Texas

Two year old Larry. Taken
in Reeds, Mo

First photo shoot with my big brother

While my dad was in the service in France, I had my brother Richard to look after me

My loving family. Edwin, Orpha, Richard, me

Celebrating my dad's return from World War II

Watching
Grandpa Grose
play his fiddle

With my dad

The Black Family coming to a church revival near you!

My mother wrote on the back of this photo, "The church God helped us build in Morrisville, Mo."

Dad, Mom, Richard, Larry, in front of our church in Slater, Mo.

Richard, Dad, Mom and me (already accident prone), with a bandage
on my elbow.

With Mom,
1951 in
Slater, MO.

Enjoying a
visit from
Charles Cross

5th grade, 1954.
Did you ever see
so many freckles.

SCHOOL DAYS 1955-56
MAE EANES JR. H.S.

SCHOOL DAYS 1956-57
MAE EANES JR. H.S.

Jr. High
Photos

High School. Eat your heart out Drew Carey!

GIRLS DATED BY LARRY BLACK SINCE DEC. L(%'A**--1958

Paulette Browder	Pat Brown
Ruth Barraco	Sharon Parry
Janet Phillips	Jnaet Murray
Connie Crawford	Daren Bechtohemery
Vriginia Odum	Diane Peterson
Cecile Bryant	Carol Jarrmen
Barbara Holliman	Judy Allan
Carol Weaver	Bobbie (pasagoula)
Linda Sumlin	Bettie Teague
Murlean Elliott	Brenda Harrison
Eleanor Levick	Kay Browley
Essie Rigney	Elaine Kyser
Charmion Boone	Verna Bethea
Donna Holland	Jo Ann--Married
Ruth Dossett	Sandy Gann
Margo Compton	Dianne Barwick
Rita Replogal	Connie Creel
Barbara Maddox	Helen Hicks
Linda Mann	Jani Burkholder
Mary Myers	
Pam O'Rooke	------------
Helen Smith	Ann Taylor
Jeannie Terrell	Sharon Zink
Leary Young	Betty Barnhill
Raye Ownes	Carol Criso
Betty Jo Carter	------------
Bonnie Falk	Carol Criso
Sylvia Favors	Linda Boyd
Pat Langley	Carol Lancaster
Sandra Moor	Betty White
Sinda Starkey	Donna Carol
Joyce Miller	Jonette Barefield
Eleanor Ware	Shiela Toler
Ann Newbill	Faye Cutts
Carol Mullen	Jo Ann Spence
Tonya Honodel	Carol Butram
	Glenda Lambert
	DOROTHY JOHNSON

The things a teenage boy will do!
In 1958-59, I typed a list of every girl I dated that year!

Student band conductor, 1958.

With my brother Richard in March, 1959.

Taking part in the
Orange Bowl
Parade, 1959.

I was chosen Wittiest in the
class...or maybe Most Likely
to be a Shoe Salesman!.

High School graduation day, Aug. 1961.

Family portrait including Mom, Dad and Richard and his first
wife Linda.

With my prized 1930 Model A Five Window Coupe.

Showing off my car with brother Richard, May 1961.

Leaving Southeastern Bible College, Jan. 1962.

My most treasured autographed photo.

Our engagement,
1965.

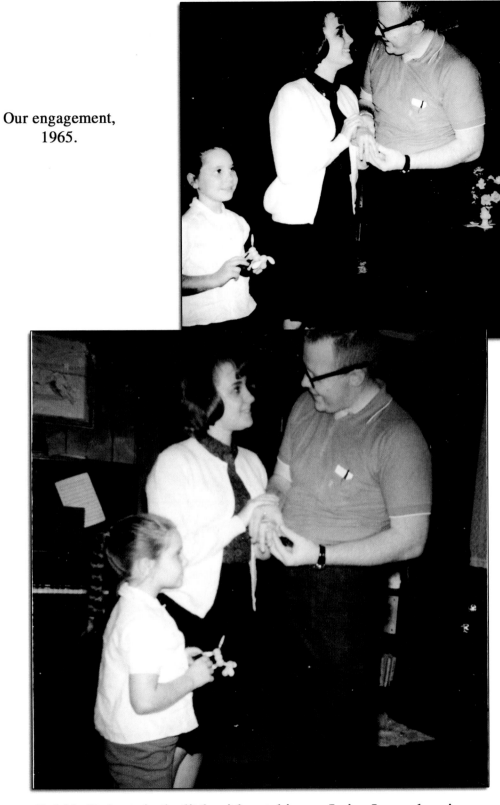

Debbie Roberts is the little girl watching as I give Luann her ring.

Building the World's Biggest Banana Split, Nov. 1967.

Our Banana Split stunt turns into a chocolate syrup riot.

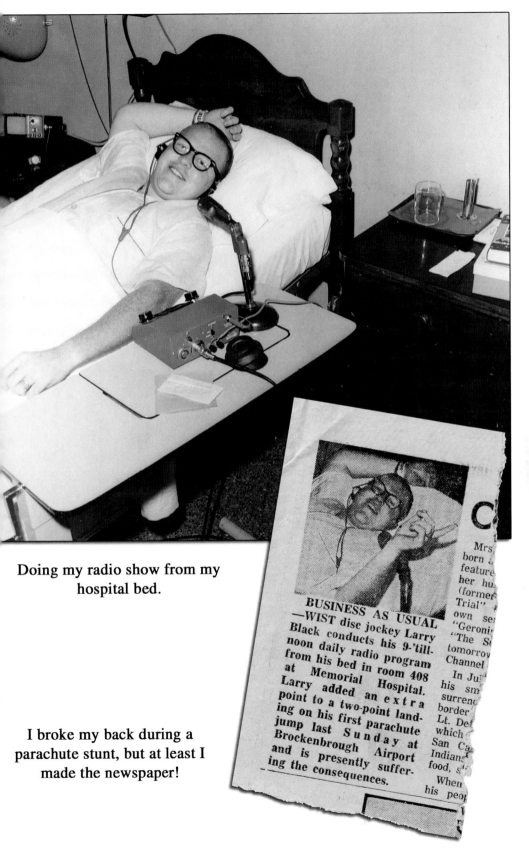

Doing my radio show from my hospital bed.

I broke my back during a parachute stunt, but at least I made the newspaper!

BUSINESS AS USUAL
—WIST disc jockey Larry Black conducts his 9-'till-noon daily radio program from his bed in room 408 at Memorial Hospital. Larry added an extra point to a two-point landing on his first parachute jump last Sunday at Brockenbrough Airport and is presently suffering the consequences.

With my fiancee Luann,
August 1965.

My beautiful
bride Luann

Mid 1960s with Luann. Over the next 13 years,
we would move 12 times!

Our wedding day, October 2, 1965.

The on air staff of WABB. I'm third from the right.

MCing at a station event.

I was the good guy in the lower left.

WABB

JIM TABER

DAN DIAMOND

ED DEAN

BRUCE HAZE

LARRY LEE

BUDDY STAR

"HOME of the GOOD GUYS"

Taking a request, April 1964.

Larry's Loot. Funny money with my photo on each bill for a WORD Radio promotion.

Turntables, 45 records, carts...the good old days of radio.

MC of the Jr. Miss America Pageant.

Heading into the 1970s with Luann

Acting as an airline captain in the play Sunday in New York.

Luann's hair was so long!

MCing another radio event.

Eat your heart out Michael Jordan! I bring the ball up for BIG Ways' team.

A game with the WABB staff. That's me way up in the air on the right!

Playing tennis against the legendary Bjorn Borg. Bjorn is second from the right. I'm to his left, wearing the headband!

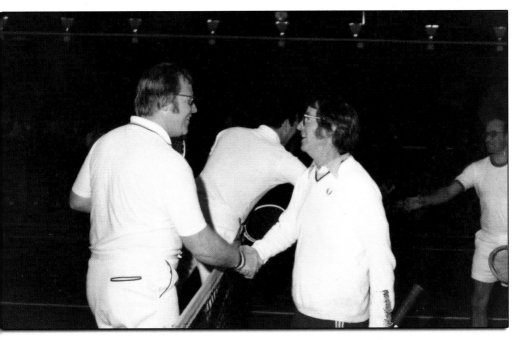

Surviving my match against tennis legend Bobby Riggs.

Rochester Mayor Steven May presents me with the City Doubles Tennis Championship.

Helping my teammate Mike Green during a charity hockey game.

GET INTO
THE BLACK...

Advertising
Piece for The
Larry Black
Show.

Black is bright

The
Larry Black
Show

6 am - 10 am on WAXC

1972 Newspaper
ad for my show
on WAXC.

Gary, my engineer, poses with my red, white and blue bug. Notice the Rolls Royce grill!

Family Photo including Richard, his wife Linda and son Kevin, Dad, Mom, me, Luann and our son Ian.

With my son Ian

Olan Mills Family
Portrait.

Our sons Ian, Adam and Jared.

Family Photos
from May of
1981

Luann is beautiful. My mustache is...interesting.

Spinning the
latest hit.

Larry — Thanks for the kind words but I felt we were blown out of the water by a super star playing Neb News.

Eddie

BLACK and White

WSM postcard promoting our Black and White radio show.

With my radio co-host Liz White.

The listenors can tell if you are smiling.

Interviewing comedy legend Phyllis Diller.

With Maury Povich on the WSM morning show. Photo by Jesse Wayne.

Ed McMahon pays a visit to WSM.

One of my first print ads for Johnson's Show Store.

One of the first Big and Tall models!.

t. 1987 ad for
tner Knott Co.

Modeling
Arrow shirts.

ner Knott Co.

I found I could portray a variety of characters to sell almost any product

Playing the coach of The Team That Can't Be Beat

LARRY BLACK

FOLLOWING GOD'S PATH

Ithaca, New York was destined to be the next stop on our "World Tour".

It's funny how some of the people we meet as we go through life end up affecting our entire future. Just a chance meeting with a stranger turns into something that totally changes the path you end up following. At the time, we don't realize the important role that certain people will play in our life. I'm sure it's a God thing.

Back when Luann and I were working on the Youth for Christ events, we met a man named Dave Boyer. Dave's dad was a Pentecostal pastor, but Dave was a singer. He was also in the mob. Dave also turned out to be one of those people who led Larry Black to where he is today.

When he sang onstage, Dave used the stage name "Joey", and he was a Frank Sinatra sound-alike. He was a great singer, and a great saxophone player. He performed at a nightclub in New Jersey, and he eventually ended up running the club.

But one day, Dave found the Lord, and completely changed his life. He started a ministry and recorded a Gospel album. We booked him for an event in Charlotte, and I got to spend some time with him. During our visit, Dave asked for one of my air check tapes. Then he took that tape to Pat Robertson, and told him that I would be a good disc jockey for the new stations Pat was buying. Pat was just starting his Christian Broadcasting Network. Yes, I was introduced to Pat Robertson by a former mobster who sounded just like Frank Sinatra!

I wasn't playing much Frank Sinatra on my radio show. During that time, music was changing, and not for the better. It had become very heavy metal, and I just didn't like it. I loved the old time rock and roll from the 50s and 60s. I just wasn't interested in the music I was being made to play, and for the first time in my life, I was thinking about leaving radio.

That opportunity came when I got a call from a man I had worked with at WORD Radio in Spartanburg. He was now with the Atwood Richards advertising agency in New York City, who produced radio station jingle packages. I thought the chance to work on Madison Avenue sounded like fun. When I said I was interested, the man informed me that I would have to wait two months before I started work.

But I never made it to the Big Apple. A separate call from Pat Robertson changed my plans... and my life. He had just listened to the tape I'd given to Dave Boyer.

We were having friends over for dinner, sitting at the table, when the phone rang. It was Pat Robertson, who asked me to come and work for him.

I told Pat I was thinking of getting out of radio, that I had received an offer from the Atwood Richards agency, but they had delayed my hiring for two months.

Pat replied, "Good! When can you come work for us?"

Without taking a breath, I answered, "Two weeks."

I accepted his offer right then, without even stepping back to the table to talk it over with my wife. As I hung up the phone, I quietly announced, "We are moving." I saw Luann roll her eyes. Then I added: "And we're moving for less money."

My wife let out a deep breath.

So if you're keeping score of the first few years of our marriage, we went from Memphis to Charlotte, North Carolina. Then we moved to Spartanburg... then back to Charlotte, followed by Hartford, Connecticut... to Ithaca, New York... back to Hartford, before we headed to Rochester, New York, and then back to Ithaca! I had been bringing home $300 a week, and now after all those moves, I was going to be making the grand sum of... get ready for it... $150 a week!

When I went to quit my job at WPOP, Danny Clayton, the program director said, "If it's more money, I'll give you more money."

"Danny," I said, "it's not about money. I'm taking a 50% cut in pay. Pat Robertson is going to pay me $150 a week."

Danny laughed, "I'll give you $145!"

Leaving Rochester also meant that I had to say goodbye to my SONUS Recording Studio. It had been in business for three years when I told Dave at the bank that I was going to sell the company, or just close it and take the loss. Dave didn't want to hear that, and he said, "You are doing fine! Don't close it down."

I gave myself one month to sell it. But at the end of the month, with no buyer in sight, I closed everything. I pulled all the equipment out and took it to Ithaca. A guy who was our engineer at the radio station came down and bought new equipment for the studio, and started operating in my place. He continued the business for another 20 years.

Out of all of our moves, this was the toughest one for Luann to make. Luann was totally against the move. She did not want to do it. As we drove away from Rochester, I know that she left her fingernail marks in the interstate all the way.

But I truly felt that this was a move God was leading me to make. When I was listening to Pat Robertson offer me the job, I didn't hear Pat's voice. I was hearing God's calling. I felt that I was supposed to do it. It was a move that did not make much sense at the time; taking such a severe cut in pay to go work for a Christian radio station seemed like a pretty idiotic decision. But it ultimately led us to moving to Nashville many years later. I know it was a God thing. God was directing us. I was just driving the car… back to Ithaca.

As it turned out, Pat Robertson was very instrumental in what we did with Country's Family Reunion many years later. I'll get into that in a bit. But at the time, Pat's radio stations were pioneering what would become known as "Jesus Music". Andy Anderson was the manager of Pat's five stations, which were all based in Ithaca. In 1969, I was hired to be a disc jockey on WEIV from noon to six - but almost as soon as I went on the air there,

94

Pat knew that my style was a little too hot for Christian radio. I really wasn't all that wild. I was like most radio DJs at the time, but in that Gospel format, I came off as a crazy man. I only lasted three months and I was fired!

When Andy fired me, I had nowhere to go. We had no money. I had been making $150 a week, and we were barely able to pay the rent when I had a job. Now that I was unemployed, we were really hurtin'.

It was during those challenging times that we received another challenge: Luann was pregnant. Luann became very sick as her due date neared. The doctor threatened to put her in the hospital because she wouldn't eat. She couldn't keep any food down. But she managed to get through the nine months.

When our first son Ian was born, I felt a tremendous responsibility for the first time. I also had a love that I had never had before. Ian was born in Ithaca, but we were living in Rochester, New York by the time he started first grade. Our other two sons, Jared and Adam, had also come along by then.

I tried to find some commercial work. I went to Bill Cook Cadillac Oldsmobile and began voicing ads for them. They let me have a nice, used Cadillac convertible as a trade out for the spots. I also did some voice work for WTKO in Ithaca, where the very popular radio personality Jerry House was also working. I didn't know him then, and I didn't find out he had also worked there, until we had both moved to Nashville!

One DJ I did meet during that time was one who became one of my dearest friends. His name was Scott Ross. Scott had worked at WINS in New York City with "Murry the K". When the Beatles came to town, Scott hung out with Paul McCartney and John Lennon! During that time, Scott also met a gal named Nedra Talley. Nedra was part of the group The Ronettes. When The Ronettes played in London, they were so popular that The Beatles were their opening act! The Beatles were so impressed with them that, when they came to the U.S. in 1966, they had them open all of their concerts.

Scott and Nedra fell in love. They were an exciting couple. Nedra was performing on stages all around the world, and Scott was MCing at similar events. He even MC'd a Rolling Stones concert in New York City! But there was one major problem. While he was hanging around groups like The Rolling Stones and The Animals, Scott was also getting heavily involved in drugs. Keith Richards of the Stones became a drug buddy of Scott's.

But Scott was able to kick his drug habit, and once Scott came to the Lord, he was very good about ministering to all the artists and performers he knew. He was friends with Eric Clapton, and I still have a tape where Eric tells Scott, "I asked the Lord Jesus to come into my heart."

Scott and Nedra came to the Lord at a revival meeting in Maryland. In 1993, they both appeared on the Rock and Roll Graffiti Series we did. It was a rock and roll version of the Country's Family Reunion shows.

After all of his rock music days, Scott ended up working for Pat Robertson at the Christian Broadcasting Network in Virginia Beach. Scott was one of CBN's most popular personalities.

While Scott was having great success, my job prospects also brightened - at least momentarily - when I got a call to go to

Toronto for an audition with the rock station CHUM. It was a monster station, with a huge audience. As I sat with the program director, I knew he was going to hire me.

But as we visited, I still got a strong feeling that God wasn't through with me in Ithaca. I ended up talking the program director into hiring somebody else! I told him, "This other guy would be a much better fit for you."

I'm sure he thought I was crazy to come all the way to Toronto and then pass on this great job.

My wife probably thought the same. Six weeks after I had been fired, we were down to no money at all. Zero. Scott and Nedra brought us a big bag of groceries. We got everything out of the bag, and at the bottom was a roll of toilet paper.

I yelled, "Yes!"

Scott laughed, "I told Nedra not to put that in."

I said, "That toilet paper is worth more than a can of soup to us right now!"

It was.

After they left, Scott went back to Pat Robertson to tell him how bad off we were. Pat immediately called, and said he would like for me to come work in the sales department for his radio network. I did... and I couldn't close a sale if my life depended on it! I was a horrible salesman! I didn't sell one thing.

Since I worked on commission, based on my sales, we just died financially. Only thanks to Luann's money management were we able to survive. She often went to the grocery store with just six dollars, knowing she had to feed our family for the entire week on that. Without coupons, she couldn't have gotten the milk and peanut butter. But if she had eggs and milk, she could make almost anything. There were some really tight times, especially after we had kids. But we just had to find a way to make it work.

While Luann tried to stretch our food money as far as possible, one year I even struggled to afford a Christmas tree. We took our entire family to pick one out. We piled into our only car, my El Camino. Once we agreed on the perfect tree, I put it in the back of the vehicle. I didn't tie it down, I just laid it in the back of our shallow pickup truck.

As we were going down a hill, the tree flew out. I stopped, ran back to get it, and threw it back in. Before we got home, that tree flew out of the back three times! The third time, a semi ran over it before I could even get to it. But once again, I threw it back in the truck. Luann started crying, but I was angry. I said, "We are still using this tree!"

Then I received another call from Pat Robertson. He had been on a retreat in Brazil, where he said God had spoken to him about reaching the young people of America. He would do that with a syndicated religious rock and roll radio show with Scott Ross. Pat asked Scott and me to come down to Virginia Beach for Thanksgiving. Harald Bredesen and Bob Slosser were also there. Pat looked at me, and said, "Larry, you know the rock and roll market. I want to put you in charge of this."

I was hired to be manager of CBN Productions.

There's a scripture that says: "If a man sets in his heart to do something, God will go before him and establish the path." I always thought if I chose to move my family to Alaska, God would be telling the angels, "He's moving again! Let's open some doors for him and keep him safe."

Through a grant Pat received from the Lilly Foundation, we bought a recording console, and we rented space in the old Parks Broadcasting building in Ithaca. Roy Park owned the building, which was also the home of his Duncan Hines offices. Roy had bought the rights to Duncan Hines' name, and made a fortune licensing it to food-related companies. All of that eventually led to the Duncan Hines cake mixes.

I produced and directed the Scott Ross Show. I was also responsible for getting it on as many radio stations as we possibly could. The first station that bought the show was WMAK in Nashville. Joe Sullivan was the program director. I flew to Nashville and talked to Joe, and he agreed to put it on. We ultimately got the show on 250 stations.

To add those stations, though, I had to do a lot of traveling. I was flying all over of the country, meeting with program directors and visiting their stations. At the time, credit cards were a fairly new innovation, and Pat Robertson preached against them. None of the folks at the Christian Broadcasting Network believed in credit cards. They also didn't believe in giving me any money in advance for all of my trips. I had to pay for everything myself, and then turn in all of my expense receipts.

I got tired of the hassle, so I applied for an American Express card for the company. It didn't take long for Pat to find out about the card. He had been so dead set against them, but I explained, "Pat, it's not a credit card. It's a charge card. You pay it off every month. If you're going to function in the world of business, fly and rent cars, you've got to have a card."

Mine was the first card that CBN ever had.

Pat Robertson had earned a pilot's license when he was in college. Someone gave CBN a single engine plane, and Pat loved to fly it himself. We were supposed to fly to Syracuse for a Full Gospel Businessmen's luncheon, and Pat said, "Let's take the plane."

Minutes later, we were jumping into the plane. Walt Wadsworth, a salesman for CBN, went with us, and Scott Ross also came along. He would soon start to reconsider that move. As we taxied onto the runway, Scott asked Pat if he had filed a flight plan. Pat flashed his big smile and said, "You can literally fly the interstate, it's a straight shot from Ithaca to Syracuse. I can look down and see the road, and just fly along it."

Pat took off, with me sitting in the copilot seat. About 40 minutes into the flight, I glanced over at him, and could see that he had a very concerned look. Ten minutes later, he admitted, "I can't find the airport."

I immediately thought of Patsy Cline and Jim Reeves, who had both died in plane crashes. Scott Ross was reading a book, not paying attention, but Walt started sweating profusely. I started sweating too, when Pat announced, "We need to start looking for a place to land. I think we are very low on gas."

As we all said silent prayers, we searched for a soft spot to crash. But Pat finally found a landing strip, and he was able to get us safely to the ground.

When we traveled, to save money, Pat and I stayed in the same hotel room. We also played tennis on a daily basis. I knew that Pat read and absorbed Forbes Magazine and the Wall Street Journal, so I started reading them as well. When Pat saw that I could also talk, or at least listen intelligently, when he would speak about financial deals and his dreams and goals for his future, it had a bonding effect for us. That stuck with him, and he knew I was loyal to him through the years.

Pat always had an open door for me. I think the thing Pat liked about me was that I never allowed him to take himself very serious. Everyone knew Pat was an important religious leader and an important media mogul. He was not someone that many people joked around with. But I was not like most other people!

In the early days of CBN, we would have board meetings, and everyone would always be so serious. But I would always crack a joke, and Pat liked that. But I always treated him with respect, as well. When I listened to Pat, I knew that I heard the voice of God through him.

I was great at my job at CBN. Everyone loved me. Then, as seemed to be a regular occurrence with me, right when everything was going well, I got bored and left! After spending two years there, I felt that I had completed what I had been asked to do.

Before I gave my notice to CBN, I wanted to let Pat Robertson know about it. But for some reason, he wouldn't take my calls.

When he wouldn't answer, I thought I would just go and see him in person. I knew that he was flying to Atlanta, so I arranged to be on the same plane.

I was flying with that new CBN American Express card, and the only seat available on the flight was a first class seat. As I was walking through the airport, I saw Pat walking up ahead of me. I knew he only flew coach, and I was going to be flying in first class... with his money! I started walking slower and slower, thinking that I would get on last. I would then find the person sitting next to Pat in coach, and I'd ask them to change seats with me.

But Pat spotted me... and he also spotted that red first class boarding pass sticking out of my pocket. He asked, "Oh, you're flying first class too?"

He explained that he had felt God tell him to change his ticket to first class so that he could have a meal and get some rest. When we both boarded the plane, we were seated side by side!

After our first class meal, I told Pat that I thought I should leave my job. He asked if I would move to Atlanta and start a production company for him there.

I answered, "Pat, I know you like me, and you don't want to see me leave. If you can tell me that the Lord has told you that I should do this, I will. But if it's just you trying to keep me, you need to let me go."

He thought about it for a moment, and finally said, "You can go."

I left Ithaca for Hartford, where I did weeken
continued to have a close relationship with Scott ?
recent years, I have said many prayers for Scott as he ⌣
cancer. He was very near death, but had a miraculous recovery.
To celebrate our 50th wedding anniversary, Luann and I traveled
to Virginia Beach to visit with Scott and Nedra. We have all
stayed very close for many decades. We have a bond that will
never be broken.

Some of the best years of my radio life were spent in
Rochester, New York. I did mornings at WAXC in Rochester for
two and a half years. One of the first people I met there was
Richard Funke, our news director. Today, he is a State Senator in
New York.

WAXC was located on the fourth floor of the Catholic Youth
Organization building at 50 Chestnut Plaza, the same building
where Bishop Fulton Sheen, who did the signoff for hundreds of
TV and radio stations around the country, had his operations.

On my way up to the fourth floor to do my show, I noticed
that the third floor was completely empty. It had been Bishop
Sheen's private chapel, where he performed marriages and
baptisms. It had beautiful, stained glass windows. As I walked
around the empty floor, I thought that it would be the perfect
place for a recording studio.

So that is just what I did. I rented half the floor, and began
building a studio that I called "the SONUS Sound Corporation".
We were the only recording studio located downtown. We were
right in the middle of all of the ad agencies, and there were two

TV stations and three radio stations within walking distance of us. Our location was a huge advantage.

But I had one disadvantage: once I had paid my rent, I didn't have much money left over to buy the equipment I needed for the studio! I was able to put in a little two track system, but I knew I needed more. So I went to the bank to get some money.

Luckily for me, the man who owned the bank also owned the building that I was renting! He said he wanted to see my studio succeed, so he loaned me $40,000. That was good for a start, but I eventually needed more. Thanks to lax banking regulations at the time, I somehow managed to borrow $100,000. Six months later, a bank examiner looked at my loan and flagged it.

But my banker assured him, "He's okay. Trust me on him. If you want to look at it the next time you come through, we can, but give him six months."

The examiner came back six months later, and he had forgotten the name of my Sonus Studio. My banker played dumb, and didn't help him come up with it; and so, my loan continued.

One of my favorite parts about the building was the athletic facility and swimming pool down in the basement. I would do mornings on the radio on the fourth floor, then I'd go and work in my recording studio on the third floor. Later in the day, I'd go play racquetball in the basement of the building. Sometime after that, I'd go back to work at my studio, and I'd be all sweaty from playing racquetball.

For the next couple of years, we built up a very good recording business. We used our new studio to record commercials for Xerox, Kodak, and a bunch of other companies.

I filmed a series of TV ads for Flanigan Furniture, who had a tag line of "It's a Symphony of Savings". In the ad, I played a musical conductor, wearing a tuxedo and holding a baton, as I acted like I was directing a symphony. But I was standing on a bed!

Then I came up with the idea that, at the end of the ad, they could pull back on the camera, and it would be revealed that I wouldn't have any pants on! I only had boxer shorts on. We did one ad where it was straight, as I wore my entire tux, but in another cut, I didn't wear pants. They rotated the two ads on the air, and people always watched, hoping it would be the spot where I wasn't wearing any pants!

My deal with Flanigan stated that, instead of paying me in cash, they could give me furniture. But I did so many ads for them, we ran out of room in our house for all the furniture they kept sending! As it continued to pile up, we started giving furniture to our friends. I made the same deal with a leather store, and got so many coats that I could never wear them all. I just gave them away.

One day, I was walking in downtown New York City, and I found myself standing in front of the huge "American Bible Society" building. Without an appointment, I walked in the front door and asked to talk to the person who was in charge of promotion. For some reason, they let me go right up to see him!

I knew they were releasing a new thing called "The Good News Bible". I told the manager that I would like to produce some unique radio spots that would promote the new Bible. To my surprise, they said yes!

The most unique aspect of my idea was that we would sell the spots as Public Service Announcements, and not as actual ads. Radio stations were required to air a certain number of PSAs for free, and that allowed the American Bible Society to promote their new product without buying commercials. I wrote six scripts, all straight out of the Bible, and I ended each spot with "This Public Service Announcement is brought to you by the American Bible Society and the Good News Bible."

I brought in Jefferson Kaye, who was a big voice of WKBW in Buffalo (and would later even become the voice of the NFL), to record the spots. The ABS paid me $22,000 for the six spots. I then sent those to every Christian radio station in the country, and they repeatedly aired them as free PSAs, even though it was really an ad for the Good News Bible!

Many years later, when I moved to Nashville, I would do a similar promotion with the Thomas Nelson Company. They were releasing a new King James Bible. I went to Ed Light, and I presented him with the idea of getting different artists to each read their favorite verse from the new Bible. I brought in Amy Grant, Bill and Gloria Gaither, and a bunch of people. We turned that into another PSA that ended with "This PSA, brought to you by Thomas Nelson and the new King James Bible." It spread the word about their new Bible, but they didn't have to pay for the ad.

I hired a man named Bob Whyley to be an engineer for my SONUS studio. Bob's life would make an amazing book. Bob eventually left my company to work for Pat Robertson in Virginia Beach - and from there, he joined up with Bill Gaither in Indiana. Then he went back to Pat Robertson at CBN and the Family Channel. Jerry Falwell then hired him to do sound engineering work at Liberty College.

After another stint at the Family Channel, he would move to the PTL Club, where he ran audio. The guy just couldn't keep a job! (Sound familiar?)

Finally, Bob moved to Los Angeles… where he really made his mark as the greatest sound man in the history of The Tonight Show! He worked for Jay Leno for seven years. He ran the audio for all the big country acts who came onto the show, and they loved it when he mixed their sound.

Bob Whyley was in charge of making sure all of our remote broadcasts made it onto the air. He also had a great voice, and he could mimic my own voice exactly. Bob never forgot that I was one of the first people to ever hire him. He also never forgot one unusual request I made of him.

I had an El Camino, and for some reason, I wanted a phone in the car (who would have thought of such a crazy thing?!) No one had a phone in their car back then. But Bob could rewire anything, and while he was able to get me a car phone, he didn't like it. He called it my "Golden Calf". Today, Bob and his wife Laura live in Prescott, Arizona, and we remain very close friends.

While I was doing my morning show, I also met a man who would become one of my dearest friends. Walt Blackburn was the hottest real estate person in Rochester, New York, and he had me do some radio commercials for his "Town Cryer" company. Walt was, and still is, a creative marketing genius. He developed many items and techniques that are used by other realtors today.

Luann and I lived in apartments for the first eight years of our marriage. Then Walt took us under his wing. Thanks to all of his help and advice, we were able to purchase our first home.

Walt had a habit of working all night. I went on the air at 6am, and had the wild idea of suggesting that my listeners call his number. I instructed them to just say "Waxcey loves you!" when he answered. His office phones began ringing almost immediately, and they didn't stop until later in the morning.

That was the beginning of a friendship that is still going on. We became so close that Walt told me where he kept the key to his boat on Canandaigua Lake. I took full advantage of his offer to use the boat, and I was sleeping on the boat in the middle of the lake, the night that Elvis died. I wouldn't find out about his death until I docked the next day. I will always remember that day. But there is one other day that I will also never forget… the day I sunk Walt's boat.

The boat was a cabin cruiser, complete with a small kitchen and a bathroom, or "head", as boat people call it. The deck was a private place, where I liked to do creative writing. When I went to take the boat out, it was in a slip, and I saw that the engine was being worked on and had the intakes off. Since I couldn't take it out, I decided to change clothes and just sit on the back deck to do my writing. Several hours later, I decided to get some food, and I opened the door leading down to the cabin below. When I did, my shoes floated to me! The lower deck was flooded. While I had been sitting on the boat, the combination of my weight and the tide coming in had caused the lake water to come in the open intakes.

I put on my wet shoes and walked to the Marina at the end of the slips. When I told the attendant that I thought we had a problem, he walked back with me to Walt's boat. As we got closer, the young man saw the listing boat, and yelled, "It's sinking!" I got back on Walt's Titanic, and the attendant jumped in a small boat with a 7 horsepower Evinrude outboard motor. He yelled for me to throw him a rope.

It was quite a day on the lake, as this wannabe sailor threw a rope to a wannabe tow boat captain in a row boat with a small outboard motor. When he revved the little engine, his boat stood almost perpendicular to the water... but Walt's boat slowly started to move out of the slip. When we finally got to the marina and lifted it up, water began to pour out of the boat. We would have been much safer just leaving the boat where it was, since it had been on the bottom in the slip. We could have easily lost it completely, when we pulled it into the middle of the lake.

I made a quick call to Walt, saying, "I have some good news and some bad news."

"Give me the bad news first," he said.

"I sunk your boat."

He chuckled and asked, "What's the good news?"

And I answered, "We know where it is."

If you're ever going to sink a friend's boat, it needs to be a friend like Walt Blackburn.

In Rochester, I was in a play called "Sunday in New York", where I played an airline captain. I was doing mornings at WAXC, and many of our listeners came to see me in person. It was fun, but it was an awful lot of work for an hour and a half onstage! I decided I didn't want to do anymore stage work.

While I was at WAXC, I received a call from Paul Drew, program director at the big WIBG in Philadelphia. Paul had heard a tape of me, and called to ask if I might be interested in coming to Philly.

Would I?! That was the big time!

When Paul flew me out to Philadelphia, I knew I was more than halfway to the job. They didn't pay for just anyone to fly in and see them in person. But as soon as I walked into the station and said, "Hi Paul. I'm Larry," his first words were, "I thought your voice would be lower."

Paul took me into a studio, and I did a live audition for him. When it was over, I got in a cab, went back to the airport, and flew home, all on WIBG's dime, and I never heard from them again! I guess they weren't very impressed.

As you might have learned by now, I have had a lot of jobs. I also had quite a few jobs going at the same time. In Rochester, I had my radio job and I ran my recording studio. I then added more to my workload when I became Promotions Manager of the Eastview Mall. The funnest promotion I came up with was the time when I brought in young women dressed in different

110

costumes. We had them be the "game pieces", and they moved along a huge Monopoly board we had built around a water fountain. It's too hard to describe here, but it was very fun.

Here I was with three jobs. So, what did I do next? I got another one! I was never afraid of work. I became the Associate Pastor of Bethel Full Gospel Church. It was the first time I had been named Associate Pastor of any church. I also served as youth leader. Bethel Full Gospel was an Assemblies of God church in downtown Rochester, not far from WAXC, where I was the morning rock and roll disc jockey. But no one in the church seemed to mind about my "day job".

Luann and I also taught a Sunday School class of young adults. With the workload I tried to handle all week, by Sunday, I truly would need a day of rest. During our Bible study class one week, I just fell asleep right in the middle of everything. My body shuddered and started to shut down, all because I just wasn't getting enough sleep.

For our Sunday School class, Luann and I were using a book that David Wilkerson had written. He fathered the "Teen Challenge" movement, and had a tremendous ministry. One Sunday, during his sermon, our Pastor shouted, "If you are going to a Sunday School class and they are teaching anything other than the Bible, if they teach things out of Dave Wilkerson's books and not the Bible, you need to get up and leave!" I couldn't believe my ears.

After the service, I went to the pastor and asked, "What are you doing? You know we are teaching from David's book. The kids get a lot out of it."

He said, "I'm wrong. Next week I will tell the congregation I'm wrong."

The next Sunday, he didn't say anything, and he never did say anything. But it ended up making our class stronger. We all said, "We know what the pastor is saying, but what is God saying?"

A short time after that, the pastor was in the pulpit, and as he was preaching, he just dropped to the floor. I was one of the first to get to him. We got him to the hospital, and he survived, but he left the church a short time later. I filled in for him a couple Sundays.

The congregation and church leaders had some interest in me becoming their main pastor, but I told them that I was not a pastor. I could speak well, and give a sermon, but there is a distinction between those who are gifted to speak, and those who are pastors. A pastor is a shepherd. They care for the flock, and they are willing to leave the herd to go out and get the one lost sheep. That's not me. If you come to me for counseling, I can give you my advice from what the Bible says. But if you don't follow through with that, I am no help to you. My dad and mom were pastors. They loved the sheep, and the sheep loved them. My parents would be there for anyone at any hour of the day, but I couldn't do that. It was just not me, and I never considered myself to be a pastor. My parents died when I was in my 60s. They were very proud of what I did with my life. They were not disappointed that I didn't become a pastor.

Our life in Rochester was great. My good jobs allowed us to buy a home for our growing family. All of our sons were born in upstate New York. Ian was born in Ithaca, and Jared and Adam were born in Rochester. We had a good church, and we had good friends. After four years, I knew that Luann was content enough to never want to move again.

Then I asked her to move again.

In 1976, my friend Scott Ross called to tell me he was going to stop doing The Scott Ross Show. He said the only person they wanted to take over his spot was me... but they wanted me to move back there.

The Bible says: "If God asks you to give up something, he will restore that to you in a double portion and overflowing." I leaned hard on that scripture as we prepared to make another move.

At first, I just filled in for Scott. It was still called "The Scott Ross Show". But eventually, we changed the name to "The Larry Black Show". While most other syndicated shows were just a half hour long, both mine and The Scott Ross Show were three hours. Our organization was a faith-based non-profit that relied on money from listeners to keep it going. Our friends from Scott's "Love Inn Ministry" were also big contributors.

The Larry Black Show aired on 125 radio stations around the country. It featured rock and roll music, the exact same music all the other stations played. But we also played contemporary Christian music. We played all the latest "Jesus Music". Some churchgoers didn't like that I had chosen to include secular rock music on the show, but they didn't understand that this was my way of also getting some Gospel music heard on Top 40 stations, who would have never played it on their own.

We also spread the Gospel in between each record. All of my comments, all of my talk was of a religious nature. Because of that, the FCC said that stations could count it as a religious show. Back then, the FCC required all stations to air a certain amount of religious programming, so our three hour show was a great fit for many, because they could still get their religious credit without breaking their station music format. It was on the air in Los Angeles, and also in the Big Apple. WOR in New York City was the biggest station that aired The Larry Black Show.

I was supposed to promote The Larry Black Show on the PTL Club with Jim and Tammy Faye Bakker. I had known Jim from back when he was at CBN, and I had already been on the Jim and Tammy Show a couple times, with some recording artists I was helping. When I arrived at their studios, I was taken to makeup and then told to wait in the "green room", where all the guests killed time before their segment. I waited and waited, and eventually they ran out of time on the show. They apologized, and asked me to come back the next day. I agreed… but even the next day, I could tell they were going to run long again. With just 60 seconds left in the show, Jim Bakker commanded his crew, "Let's get Larry on!"

But I said, "No way. I'm not going on for less than a minute." I refused to go on the set, and they killed the last minute, probably by asking for a donation.

We put the Larry Black Show on big, reel to reel tapes. Each show consisted of six huge reels, and we had to ship those to each radio station that carried my show. We had to do that every week. Shipping out all of those tapes was much harder than doing the actual show.

I used a variety of talented people to record jingles and cut promos for my show. One of those people was Gary S. Paxton, who was known for his work on the huge novelty hits "Alley Oop" and "Monster Mash". Janie Fricke also sang on some of my commercials, long before she started having number one country songs. And the great drummer Larry London played drums on some of those.

I was once asked to do an in-person interview with televangelist Kenneth Copeland. He was known for preaching his "prosperity gospel" at large rallies all over the world. They flew me out to Texas to do the interview with him.

When I arrived, one of his guys picked me up at the airport and drove me to the interview. On the way there, he gave me a list of everything that I was not allowed to ask! Well, by now, you know me pretty good. So what do you think I did? Yep, as soon as we sat down in the studio, right after the tape started rolling, I asked, "Why are there some things that I can't ask you about?"

He was taken aback and said, "You can ask me anything you want to."

I did, and he answered every question I threw at him.

For a short time, I also added the title "Magazine Publisher" to my resume. I started the LBS Magazine, which was devoted to Christian music, but we only published a few issues before it folded. All during the run of The Larry Black Show, I was still making monthly payments on the $100,000 worth of studio equipment that I had not even set back up in Ithaca. Then things really got challenging. "The Love Inn Ministry" shut down their support of The Larry Black Show.

In 1975, as I considered where I should go next, Bob McKenzie, the owner of Paragon NewPax, called me. I had gotten to know Bob through Gary S. Paxton. Bob told me he would give me a job, if I moved to Nashville, Tennessee. He told me he'd pay me $18,000 a year to work two days a week for Paragon, and to also do The Larry Black Show from there.

I didn't know if I should take the offer. I wanted to ask my friend Bob Mumford for his advice, but I couldn't reach him. I was doing a project for the Thomas Nelson company at the Christian Booksellers Association Convention in Denver, Colorado, as I worried about my next career move, and I couldn't sleep. So I decided to go take a walk at midnight.

As I walked the streets and paths of downtown Denver, I ran into Jamie Buckingham. Jamie was a pastor, author and magazine publisher. I had never met him before, but I immediately recognized him. I introduced myself and told him what I was going through. He told me that I should listen for what God was telling me to do. He also told me to follow my heart. I knew it was God talking to me through Jamie. And as I headed back to my hotel, I thought, "What are the odds of me running into someone like Jamie Buckingham at midnight in Denver, Colorado?" It had to be God's intervention.

I called Bob McKenzie and told him I was heading for Nashville.

Bob was in the process of joining up with Bill Gaither to form Paragon Associates, a publishing company and record label, at the time. Bill invested his royalties from all the songs he wrote, including "He Touched Me", into the company. One of my first duties on my new job saw me accompanying The Gaithers to New York City.

They were going to be doing a concert at Madison Square Garden. To get attention for the show and sell some tickets, I planned to try and get the group an interview on one of New York City's most popular TV shows.

Joe Franklin was a television legend, and everyone in the Big Apple watched his show. Of course, I was just coming out of the rock and roll world, and I had no idea that getting a Gospel music act on TV in New York City was just never done... but since I didn't know any better, I went knocking on Joe Franklin's dressing room door! To everyone's surprise, he said yes to my request of having The Gaithers on his show. They did a great job on his program, and Joe loved them!

One of my most memorable record promotions was for a song called "Special Delivery". The man who wrote it was promised by Word Records that it was going to be Evie Tornquist's next single. But when Word decided later not to release the song, it absolutely infuriated the writer. He called Bob McKenzie, and Bob told him that Richard Roberts would record the song, and then they would release it.

I was supposed to promote that song, so I had my son Ian design a package that had the record wrapped in brown paper, tied with twine. Me and three other guys filled huge mail bags up with those records, and we flew to different radio stations all across the country. When we arrived in every new town, we always made sure that we took press photos of us delivering the record to each program director, and we turned Richard Roberts' "Special Delivery" into a major hit.

When I wasn't promoting records for Paragon, I was doing my Larry Black Radio Show. At first, I taped the show at WKDF in Nashville. Then I turned a room of my house in Bellevue into a studio. I installed all the equipment that I had bought in Ithaca - and while it took me almost a decade, I was finally able to pay off that $100,000 note.

After each show I recorded, I would take the tape over to Dixie Pressing, where they would convert those into record albums. And after each record was pressed, we'd send it out to radio stations across the country.

Pat Robertson was a huge financial help to my show. I asked him if he would give us $20,000 for the first three months we were on, and he did that. But he then continued to support the show for the next three years! My brother in-law, Bill Bass, was making really great money working in stocks and bonds in New Jersey, and he would tithe his money to our show. There were times when his tithe really kept us afloat.

God always provided for us. The elders of The Lord's Chapel also embraced my show. They made me an elder of the church, and they also supported my show financially. We hosted a couple "Jesus Music" concerts at The Lord's Chapel.

The Larry Black Show had quite a following. We received lots of fan letters. We also heard from a few folks who weren't big fans. One woman wrote me a letter that was just horrible! It lambasted everything we did on our show. I wrote her back and said, "You need to be aware that someone is writing really stupid letters and signing your name to them."

One of the biggest fans of The Larry Black Show was a man named Steven Weyhrich. Steven is a doctor in Omaha, Nebraska. He started listening to my radio show when he was a college student, and continued listening after he'd gotten married! And he ended up being the last person ever who donated money to my show. We relied on financial help from loyal listeners like him, and he stayed with us until we went off the air.

Many years later, I was totally shocked to discover a website Steven had created, called "Great, Great Joy". On that site, he went into great detail about my show, and the work we had done over the years. Steven and his wife came to meet me in person in Nashville, and we enjoyed the time we spent together. He was such a devoted fan, and such an expert on the Larry Black Show, and he even has some of my air checks that people could listen to. You can still hear them at his website, at www.greatgreatjoy.com.

But after seven years of doing the Larry Black Show from Nashville, I finally got burned out. I was especially burned out on sending out letters asking for money. I just got to the point where I didn't want to send out any more newsletters begging my listeners for money. So we ended the show.

I began to think that might have been a mistake, as I waited for my next job offer. I had a wife and three boys to support, and no money coming in at all. My boys were all going to Brentwood Academy, and that wasn't cheap.

During the next year and a half, I continually prayed, asking God where he wanted me to go next. I had a tape of all the radio commercials I had done, and I sent those tapes out to every advertising agency that was in the yellow pages. I sent one to the President of Word Records, one to the President of Sparrow Records, and one to the boss at Thomas Nelson.

I wanted to make sure my unsolicited package got their attention and reached each person, so I tried a rather unique approach: on each one, I wrote on the outside of each envelope: "Herpes Test Results. Personal and Confidential"!

Well, my mailing did get their attention. Every high-up person I sent a tape to tore into those envelopes! I'm sure they were a little perturbed, but also tremendously relieved, when they saw that it was just my pitch for a job with them! They all thought it was hilarious... everyone but one... the PTL Club.

At that time, I was in the running to run PTL's record company. I had lived in Charlotte before, and we liked it there. But when the Vice President of PTL received my "Herpes" envelope, he called and yelled, "Larry, you don't know what you've done!"

"It was a joke!" I said.

He explained, "They put it in a special sealed package, and everyone was freaking out."

He had to take it into Jim Bakker and explain that it was from me, and that it was all a joke. Less than a month later, Jim Bakker's sex scandal broke. They never offered me the job.

As we continued to struggle to make ends meet, I knew that God was with us the whole time, but it was not easy. It was rough. We were ninety days behind on our mortgage for almost eighteen months. Luckily for me, my wife was very understanding. She always had the attitude of "we are going to get through this, someway and somehow". That attitude was needed on many occasions, especially during one blazing hot summer in Nashville.

With the outside temperature searing at over 100 degrees, our air conditioner quit working. Our bank account was empty, and I didn't have enough left on my credit card to get the air conditioning fixed. But I did have just enough on the card to take one of the first ever "stay-cations".

I told Luann to load the kids into the car, and we headed to a local motel. It wasn't anything fancy, but at least it was cool, and our boys just loved it because it had a pool. We swam and enjoyed the cool air for two days. Then we went back home to the real world.

As we drove into the driveway in our purple van, as soon as we all piled out, I heard a "pop". I saw steam coming out of the radiator, and I knew something had burst. Luann had just opened the back door to our house, and she screamed at me, "Larry, there is water everywhere!"

At that exact moment, I lifted the hood on the van and said, "Yeah, a pipe burst."

"No," she screamed, "there's water in the house!"

A hose to the washer/dryer had broken, and there were a couple inches of water over the entire house. I guess our "vacation" was officially over.

Luann and I both started laughing at that point. Sometimes you have to laugh to keep from crying. As we laughed, we talked to the Devil and said, "Okay, you've had your fun. You've done your best, but we are still here and still laughing."

HORRAY FOR HOLLYWOOD!

A year and a half after I ended The Larry Black Show, I was hired by WSM Radio in Nashville. I started out doing weekends, and I would also fill in for anyone who called in sick or took vacation.

Bill Winters was hosting the morning show on WSM, but the Gaylord management thought that he was a little too risqué for the morning. One day, the program director called and asked me to meet him at Shoney's, where he told me they were taking Bill off the morning show and were going to conduct a nationwide search for his replacement. He asked if I would fill in for a few weeks while they looked for a permanent host.

So I did the morning show for the next couple of weeks, for the huge salary of $5.00 an hour. After two weeks though, they asked me what kind of salary I would need to become the permanent host. I asked for a huge amount of money, and they said "No way. We'll just keep looking."

But I continued filling in every day, for the next two months. I finally went to the boss and said, "You are paying me $5.00 an hour, and I've been here every day for almost three months." So they agreed to double my salary.

At the time, the Tennessean newspaper was doing a survey, asking their readers who their favorite radio personalities were. I bought a bunch of papers and voted for myself! But a lot of other people voted for me too. I wound up in the top 3, and I wasn't even a permanent host! With that showing, WSM's management asked me once again what it would take for me to be their full-time morning man.

The deal I made with them was amazing. They agreed to a big raise, and I also talked them into making my pay increase retroactive to when I first started filling in. I ended up getting a $5,000 check for the time I'd already worked! It was a huge blessing. When you ask my boys what their favorite Christmas was, they will name that one, because they all got everything they wanted. Ian wanted a fancy keyboard, Jared wanted a motorcycle, and Adam wanted drums - and they each got them, thanks to my money from WSM.

When I first moved to Nashville, I really wasn't a big fan of country music. I grew up in the 60s with rock and roll. Luann's father loved country music. He always had it on in his car. But when I joined WSM, I really got into country. Of course I love it now, and I love all of the people who make it. I love the artists.

My WSM morning show got even better when they brought in Liz White from New York. Her real name was Elizebeth Flamhaft, but she married Gary Louizides. With either of those last names, "Liz White" sounded better for a radio name. Liz was a Jewish girl from Long Island, New York. She was in her late 20s, very smart, and so delightful to work with. We had good chemistry. They initially brought her in as a newsperson, but the more we worked together, the more it became "Black and White in the Morning", and that's what we named our show. I never once got up in the morning not wanting to go to work with her. We did that show for two and a half years.

This might be hard for people to believe, but even though I was working full time at WSM, we just could not keep our bills paid. I was a popular radio personality on one of the biggest stations in the world, but we still had more money going out than we had coming in. After doing everything we could possibly do, we finally decided to declare bankruptcy. When we filed, most of our friends had no idea. We filed under our real names of Loren and Jette Black... but almost everyone knew us as Larry and Luann, so they didn't know it was us.

After talking to our bank, mortgage and car loan people, we found that there were certain things they couldn't take from us when we filed for bankruptcy. We sold off everything we could, and then our bank agreed to give us a loan for an affordable, used car. We found a little Jimmy GMC. A short time later, we borrowed a thousand dollars, and we paid that back very quick, so we started improving our credit rating.

Our financial situation started looking much brighter, when I started getting requests to do some commercial work again. One of the first offers came from Don Roy with the Ad Mark Company, who produced automobile ads that aired all over the country. Don told me that he wanted me to play the role of a coach in a 60 second radio spot. With each new dealership that signed on, I would come in to voice a custom spot where I gave their name, and they aired those ads in 50 markets around the country.

The ads became so successful that they asked me to be the face of the coach for a billboard campaign. I was excited to see my face up on a huge billboard! But I was even more excited when Don called back to say they were going to turn the radio spots into a TV commercial! It would be my first major television exposure. I filmed six commercials where I played the coach of "The Team That Can't Be Beat".

That opened up the "video" door for me. Up to that point, I had thought I could only do radio ads. One of the first businesses to use me on TV was a Cadillac Oldsmobile dealership in Paducah, Kentucky. They asked me to do all of their television ads, and it made me very good money, which I used a lot of to reinvest in myself. I paid to have tapes made of all of my commercials, and then sent them to everyone who might be interested in hiring new talent.

The ad campaign for "The Team That Can't Be Beat" also included newspaper ads featuring photos of me as a coach. I had never even dreamed that I might become a model. But that's exactly what I did! I always thought that every male or female model had to be beautiful... and that was one thing that no one had ever called me! But I was wrong. I found out that models come in all shapes and sizes.

I became a model for "Big and Tall" ads. I modeled for the Castner Knott department store in Nashville. When I expressed my surprise at being a model, one ad photographer told me, "When your face is friendly, it doesn't have to be pretty."

I laughed. "I guess I'll take that as a compliment."

He explained, "You don't have to have a pretty face. But you do need a friendly face, and you have a friendly face."

I did a whole series of print ads for different products and companies. One was for the Robert J. Young Company law office. I also did a fun photo shoot for a hot dog company. People used to tell me all the time that I looked like a younger Ned Beatty, or an older John Goodman!

While I continued on the air at WSM, I also wanted to expand my outside commercial work. I signed with Betty Clark at Talent Model Land, and she got me an audition for the movie "Ernest Goes to Camp", starring Jim Varney, who had already become typecast as the funny character of Ernest P. Worrell. I auditioned for the role of the owner of the camp, Mr. Tipton, and I got the part!

The movie was filmed at Montgomery Bell State Park in Dixon, just outside Nashville, so I was able to work on the set for six weeks and never miss a day of work at WSM. I always did my morning show, and then I'd head straight off to film the movie.

Being in "Ernest Goes to Camp" was a wonderful experience. Me being in the movie got WSM and our morning show a lot of good press. But the best part about the entire thing was that it gave me enough material for a film reel that I could show to people who were looking for actors for other roles!

Jim Varney went on to play Ernest in more than a half-dozen other movies. In 1991, when they were getting ready to make "Ernest Scared Stupid", I wanted to play the role of the town mayor. John Cherry, the producer of the movie, didn't think that I could play the serious role. Buck Ford, Tennessee Ernie Ford's son, was an actor I had worked with on a number of different things, and Buck told John that I could do serious roles; so John let me read for the part, and I got the role of mayor.

Jim Varney was a marvelous guy. He was so funny, but he didn't act like a big star. He was down to earth, even though he was making millions. He could have made even more, but Jim didn't own the character of Ernest. It was owned by an advertising company.

After the first "Ernest" movie, Jim tried to get away from the character. He had studied Shakespeare. He was also a stand-up comic, and even worked in Vegas for a short time. When he couldn't get other work, he went back to the Ernest character, and he did about ten more Ernest movies. Jim lived in White House, Tennessee, a small town located north of Nashville. In 1999, Jim got lung cancer, and he died the next year, at the very young age of 50.

In addition to my first movie roles, I continued to make a quite a few TV commercials. I did an industrial video for Shoney's. I shot a few for different medical products. I tried my best to sound like I was an expert on whatever new hospital thing I was promoting!

Shooting a commercial for TV is not always as easy as it looks, though. One of my toughest was for a bank in Knoxville. The script had some banking terms in it, and some words I had never used before, and I had asked for cue cards... but they refused to let me use them. We did 20 takes, and I blew it every time. Finally, the director came over to me and said, "Give us a few minutes and we'll write up some cards."

But my most challenging day came when I was scheduled to film commercials for two different companies... on the same day... one in Nashville, and one in Memphis! Both were important, national ads, one for Kroger and one for Auto Zone.

I told both directors that I couldn't do both on the same day, but they insisted. They agreed to fly me to Memphis to do the Auto Zone commercial after I had finished doing the Kroger spot in Nashville. Of course, I couldn't even start that shoot until I was done with my early morning shift at WSM! The Kroger shoot took all day, and I arrived in Memphis that night, just in time to get my script for the Auto Zone spot.

As I tried to memorize my lines, I realized they were not going to start filming until after midnight. By then, I was going on almost 24 hours without any sleep. My brain was fried. They wouldn't let me use cue cards, and I was worn out. We did more than 30 takes before I was finally able to get one where I hit every line all the way through. The entire shoot lasted until almost 6:00 am. But can you believe that thing aired for two years, in different markets across the U.S.? Both spots paid very well, and every six months, I'd also get a sizable residual check.

I decided to spend some of that money on a new car, and I found one on a Friday afternoon at Reed Chevrolet. It was a gorgeous Camaro that had been ordered by the Georgia Highway Patrol - but for some reason, they had cancelled the order. It had a supercharged Corvette engine, and a special suspension that would have allowed the highway patrol to drive it almost like a go-kart.

Doing everything he could to make a sale, the salesman told me that I could leave my car with them, take this one home, and drive it for the weekend. That night, I got a call for an audition that was set for the next day in Wilmington, North Carolina. And the dealership where my own car was parked was already closed, so I drove my "test drive" car all the way to Wilmington and back!

On Monday morning, when I brought it back to the dealership, it had 2,000 more miles on it! The salesman wasn't real happy with that, and he got even less happy when I told him that I really couldn't afford their asking price. I told him what I would be willing to pay, but he said it was much too low. Then I reminded them that the car was now pretty used (thanks to my weekend test drive)! He went to the general manager, and they agreed to lower the price… and I bought the car.

I had barely driven my Camaro when my son Jared came home from college and asked to take it for a drive. Fifteen minutes later, I saw him walking up the driveway, with no car in sight.

I opened the door, and he whispered, "Dad, I wrecked it."

He had missed the first turn he came to, and blew out two tires. He was more upset than I was. I was just thankful he wasn't hurt.

I got the car fixed, and it was so fast. On my way to Atlanta, I got the car up to 140 miles an hour, and drove at that speed for about fifteen minutes on the interstate. I loved driving it. I would get it up to 100mph on a daily basis on I-40 outside of Nashville, but I knew I was being much too dangerous. I thought that if I kept the car I would kill myself, or kill someone else because of my fast driving. So I traded it for a Suburban. The guy who bought the Camaro took it to dragstrips and won a lot of races with it.

I eventually got some help in paying for my "car habit" when I became the announcer on Hee Haw. I did that for two years, during the last few seasons of the show. I was on my way to New York for a job, when they asked me to come out to The Nashville Network to audition to be the Hee Haw announcer. They let me know that, if I got the job, I would have to do some actual spots for the show later that day. I told them I had to go to New York at 4:00, did the audition, and left. But as soon as I got home, they called and told me I had the job, if I could come right back and record everything that they needed. And every six months, they would ask me to come in for a few hours and voice some new intros.

I introduced the show's cast and the guest stars for each week, and for that very minimal work, they paid me $18,000 each year! Since it was AFTRA-controlled, and a national show, it was crazy money.

That money would definitely come in handy, as my radio career was about to come to a screeching halt. Two and half years after we had started our "Black and White in the Morning" show on WSM, Liz White got a job offer from a radio station in New York City. She didn't really want to go there, so she asked the WSM bosses if they would give her a raise. Our ratings had always been very strong. But they wouldn't even try to offer her anything comparable. They wanted her to commit to staying, before they would offer her a raise. So she left. It was so stupid of them to let her go to New York, when she wanted to stay in Nashville.

Ted Cramer was the Program Director. I went to him and asked, "Now that Liz is gone, do I need to be looking for a job?"

"No, No," he assured me.

Two weeks later, they let me go.

To be honest, I was a little sad and a little angry at being fired. I was certainly surprised. But most of all, I was relieved. I knew that I now had the time to pursue my acting career. I immediately called my agent and told her I was available for anything.

My first major television role came in 1989. My agent had me meet with Shay Griffin, who had the Chez Studios and Griffin Casting in Atlanta. They were currently looking for new actors for the series "In the Heat of the Night", starring Carroll O' Connor. They filmed the series in Georgia, and they had already gone through the pool of actors based in Atlanta after the first several seasons of the show. They asked for my picture, and then they brought me in for an audition.

When I got to the audition room, I recognized everybody! They were all people whose faces I had already seen on television. They were all about my age, and they all had similar body shapes to mine. I was given part of the script for one of the scenes. In acting, they call those small parts of the script "the sides". It has only one character's "side" of the story. I read it, and Shay put it on tape. I told her afterwards that I was going to go get something to eat, and then head back home to Nashville.

But before I had even left Atlanta, I got a call from her, asking if I could go out to Conyers, Georgia to meet with the show director. Conyers was 30 minutes down the road, and they were going to do a callback that very day.

When I arrived, I walked into a doublewide trailer, where three other people waited inside; they were also up for the same part. The director called us, one by one, into the back room of the trailer. And when I walked into the back room, I saw Carroll O' Connor sitting there with the director. A couple other people were also in the room. I was carrying my script in my hands, since I hadn't had time to memorize it.

"Let's run through the scene," they announced.

I delivered my lines, and they said, "Thank you very much. We'll call you if we need you."

Before I started driving home, I called Luann. She asked me how it went. I said, "Who knows. It was a good experience. It gave me a little understanding of what to expect next time."

She then asked me if I thought I would get the part. I said, "Babe, I don't know. I read the part, and did as well as I could. If they want me, they'll call."

Two days later, Betty called and yelled, "You got the part!"

"In the Heat of the Night" paid "scale", which was $400 a day. My agent got 15% of that. I was booked for two days, so I thought I'd make an easy 800 bucks. They also paid for my mileage.

When I arrived on set, I found my dressing room in a little trailer. My name was on the door, and all of my lines from the script were waiting for me. The "sides" also included all the scenes that I would be in. I also found a suit they had given me for my wardrobe. I looked at my watch, and saw that it was exactly 10:30… in the morning. After getting into my suit, I read over my lines. Then I waited.

At noon, they called us to lunch. It was a big, sit-down lunch with the cast and crew. After lunch, I continued to wait. I read my lines again for an hour or so. I was bored sitting there in my little trailer, so I walked onto the set, where I could watch some of the taping. I met Carroll O'Connor again, working with a standup desk in the middle of all of the sets. Any time he was not acting in a scene, he would go to that desk and work on the script for next week's show. He did a lot of writing for all the scripts.

Then I went back to my trailer… and continued to wait. A couple hours later, I went over to Craft Services and had a snack. But they finally called me for my first scene, at 11:30pm… at night! 13 hours after I had put on my suit for the part!

My first scene was with Carroll O'Connor, Howard Rollins and Alan Autry. Carroll played the police chief, Alan was a deputy, and Howard played Detective Virgil Tibbs. Virgil was black, and my character was kind of racist and didn't like him. In the scene, I'm asking the chief for his help. He asks me, "Why me?"

I answered, "I need somebody who is old and white."

Howard Rollins perked his ears up and just stared at me. I had delivered the line real slow. Carroll O'Connor was standing in front of me, and after the scene, he said, "Do the line faster. It will be funnier if you read it fast, and then pause and look at Virgil."

I did it again, the way he suggested, and he said, "That's it! That's it!" His simple advice had made me so much better.

We wrapped up our shoot at 2:00 in the morning. As we left, they told me to be at a local school that morning (which happened to be on a Saturday) at 11:30.

When I got to the set at the school, I found out that I would be wearing a tuxedo for my next scene. I was playing the manager of a beauty contest, and I was quickly surrounded by forty girls in bathing suits!

As the filming dragged on, at the stroke of midnight, just as Saturday night turned to Sunday morning, the entire crew broke into wild applause. I had no idea what they were all cheering about. Then someone told me that we were now making well over "double time" pay… much more.

We finally wrapped at 6:00 am Sunday morning, and I headed home, thinking to myself that I had made a fairly easy $800. But when my check came, I was totally shocked to see that it was for $4,000! It blew my mind. I had to have a more experienced actor explain it to me. It cost them $750, because they hadn't given me 12 hours off in-between my shoots from Saturday to Sunday. That's called a "forced call". Every six hours, they are required to give you a sit-down meal, even though there's food all over the place, all day. But since they didn't serve a meal, that cost them

$200. And all the other overtime boosted everything up to $4,000. I thought, "This is good! I need to do more of this acting!"

The initial money I made for "In the Heat of the Night" was impressive... and then the residuals started coming in. That's money you get from every time they rerun the show somewhere. The residuals are based on your final check from the shoot, so the more they have to pay you initially, the more your residual check is going to be in the future. I still get checks for "Heat of the Night", and most of the other TV and movie projects I've worked on. "Heat" has done well overseas, so I even get foreign residuals. They're not a lot, but it's nice to get any kind of check in the mail.

I ended up doing episodes of "Heat of the Night" three years in a row. After my role as the mayor and as the beauty pageant manager, the next year I played a prison warden; and the following year, I played the owner of a hardware store. They were all totally different characters, but they felt that there had been enough time between my different roles, so they kept hiring me.

I found Carroll O'Connor to be a lovely man. He was a nice guy, and was very encouraging, very gentle. He was a very nice man to me, as he was to most people. Carroll saw it as his show. He was Executive Producer, and he looked at all of us as his family.

Even though I was new to acting, I was very comfortable on the set of "In the Heat of the Night". I was never very good at memorizing lines word-for-word. I like to ad-lib anytime I can.

On "Heat", as long as you knew the scene, and could get most of the words in, they were good with you ad-libbing. You had to make sure the actors you were with knew when you were ending your lines, but they were loose with the script, and they gave you some leeway to ad-lib and use your own words.

They still air my episodes of "In the Heat of the Night" quite often, every week or two somewhere. As I write this, I just had a call from a guy who saw me on "Heat"! I was much younger then, thinner, and had a little more hair. But I think my voice gives it away, and people still recognize me from the show.

After proving myself on "In the Heat of the Night", my agent, Betty Clark, started sending me out on as many auditions as she could find. I landed a lot of commercials, and did a lot of instructional videos. Some of those were serious, and some were humorous. Because of my large size and my "everyday man" look, I could play a businessman or I could play a truck driver. Almost everything I auditioned for, I landed. My agent confidently exclaimed, "Larry, you are on your way!"

In 1990, I would play a school principal in the TV movie "Sudie and Simpson". Lou Gossett, Jr. and Sara Gilbert were the stars of the movie. The movie was shot in Atlanta. Most of my TV and movie stuff was shot in the Atlanta area, an easy drive from my home in Nashville.

And even though I was a grown man, I still had to call my parents to tell them they were going to hear me say a cuss word in the movie. During the first couple run-throughs of the scene, I purposely left the word "damn" out. But the director came over and said, "I need a real good 'damn' right here." She made me say it.

A year later, I appeared in an episode of "I'll Fly Away", a series starring Sam Waterston. I went down three different times to audition for the show. The first time, it was an audition for the role of a politician. I walked in and acted how I thought a politician would act. I was very upbeat, smiling and shaking hands with everyone in the room. But they passed on me. I had a second audition a short time later for a different part, and again, I was very upbeat in my audition, and again they passed on me. The third time I was called for an audition, I decided to be much more reserved, very understated and low-key. And they chose me for the role!

I also played a politician in the CBS miniseries "Grassroots". I played the Governor of Georgia. It was based on a book that I had read. I had no idea that this was the one role that I (and my wife) would never forget!

I was already booked for "Grassroots", and had already committed to it, when they told me that I was going to have to do a nude scene! Of course, "nude" for TV is different than "nude" in real life, but either one can be very uncomfortable!

We had already done most of the filming, all the usual political scenes, a debate, and things like that. I thought that I was totally done, and went back home to Nashville. A couple weeks later, they called and said, "We need to shoot some still photos, and we need to talk about the nude scene."

I said, "Excuse me? You're joking, right?"

But they replied, "No, no. It's something we need to do."

"Can I wear a bathing suit?" I asked.

They said, "Yeah, yeah, that will be alright."

So I headed back to Atlanta, where I met with the great actress Joanna Cassidy. She was playing a reporter who was caught in an intimate act with my character, the Governor. To make things even worse, we weren't filming in a studio, or on a soundstage. We were out in a public park! As we got ready for the shoot, we were both wearing bathrobes. The crew laid a blanket down on the grass. In the movie, my character loses his political race because a tabloid photographer takes pictures of the nude tryst in the park.

As I very uncomfortably sat next to Joanna, I cringed when I heard the director shout, "Okay, lose the bathrobes!"

I knew it had to be done, so we both took them off. At least I had my swim trunks on. It was then that I heard the most dreaded words that I have ever heard.

The director said, "Okay, lose the suit."

I thought, "Oh my God."

Fortunately, I was wearing a jockstrap under my bathing suit. But I knew I was now down to my last layer! I understood that the scene was needed. But that didn't make it any easier.

The things we do for "our craft". Off came my swimming trunks. Joanna tried to make me more at ease. She started kissing me. But I was so uncomfortable. I hugged her, but there was nothing sexy about the entire thing. She continued kissing me. But I was sweating. I was so uncomfortable. I kept thinking about what my wife would think. Oh, and did I say that I was uncomfortable?!

After I had shot the scene, I came home and told Luann what had happened. They had given me a Polaroid picture of the shot, and I showed it to her. I told Luann, "Nobody wants to see a naked, 250 pound, 45-year-old guy."

As she looked at the photo, I'm pretty sure she agreed!

At the time, we were going to the New Hope Church in Brentwood. I was one of their elders! I warned the pastor about the scene, but he just laughed. No one really cared… but my family sure did! As we all gathered in front of the TV to catch the show as it aired, the camera started a slow crawl into the nude photo of me and Joanna. It kept coming in, closer and closer, and Luann started yelling at the TV, "Get it off! Get it off the air, get it off the air!"

My sons were on the couch and they were laughing like crazy. Ian slid off the couch, laughing. Then they yelled, "Don't make us go to school tomorrow! Everyone will make fun of us."

The one saving grace about the entire thing was that, on the night it aired, the CMA Awards were also airing on another channel, so all of Nashville was watching that instead. That was the one and only nude scene of my career. The only other time I came close was for the Mel McDaniel music video for "Real Good, Feel Good Song". I was in a bathrobe for the entire video, but at least I didn't have to take it off!

I was not a member of the Screen Actors Guild when I got my first TV roles, but a short time later, I got a call from Randy Himes, the local SAG-AFTRA office President. Tennessee is a Right to Work State, so they can't prevent you from working on a union job if you are not in the union. They have to pay you union scale, and pay your pension and welfare benefits, even if you're not a union member. But when Randy Himes saw that I might be on my way as a successful actor, he called to say he'd really like to have me join the union.

I was already an AFTRA member. AFTRA stands for "American Federation of Television and Radio Artists". When I was on the radio in New York, you had to be a member of AFTRA. But I wasn't a SAG member. Randy told me, "You know I can't prevent you from working, and the only thing I can do as a director is I can challenge someone's ability as a non-union actor. I can suggest they hire a union actor, because their abilities are different."

But he told me that I had proven that I was able to act and do any job, so he couldn't say they could find someone better. When he invited me to become a member, I said, "Sure, I would love to."

I joined the Screen Actors Guild, and it paid off so much for me, in ways I could not have seen when I first joined them. In fact, it was a lifesaver thirty years later, when the SAG-AFTRA insurance companies paid the bill after I had my major accident in Montana. After my fall off the mountain, my hospital bill was for more than half a million dollars… but between Medicare and SAG-AFTRA, I never paid a dime of it. They covered it all. The

Lord was looking out for me many years in advance, when I signed up with SAG-AFTRA.

But just when I was sure I was going to become a big TV and movie star... I was brought back down to earth. While I had started out getting almost everything I tried out for, six months later, I would only be landing about a half of what I auditioned for. That further fell to about a fourth, when I was no longer the new face. Once all the casting directors had seen me a few times, they started passing me over.

I went many, many months and couldn't get any work. I couldn't get arrested. Luann asked me if she should get a job, but I wanted her to be available to take care of our boys anytime they needed. I just knew that if I could get a little commercial work, we could pay our bills. We prayed that the door would open to my TV and radio commercial work. And we always seemed to get just enough of those things, so that we could pay our bills and keep going.

I was asked to send a tape in for a Chevrolet commercial. I used a little cassette recorder, and once they heard my tape, they called and said they "loved my relaxed feel". I did six Chevy ads, which aired on the Motor Racing Network. They sent a lady from Detroit to produce the spots, and we recorded them at a studio in Berry Hill. When I walked in, they had a rocking chair by the microphone. They had wanted to use my southern accent and laidback feel, and thought I would do even better in the rocking chair.

But as I rocked, it squeaked so much that it took away from my reading! Even without the rocker, though, they said, "It sounds like you're sitting on a porch, telling a story."

I made some very good money from those spots, and every six months for the next two years, I'd receive a similar check from them. That money really kept us alive, until my next job... at a very familiar place.

KING OF ALL MEDIA

A year and a half had passed since WSM decided to let me go. They had gone through a number of morning crews, with none of them lasting long. But I'd continued to be friends with the manager who had fired me. I would stop in occasionally, just to visit with a few of my old pals.

Everyone knew that I had been doing a lot of acting jobs. One day, I drove to WSM to see a friend, and I pulled into the lot driving my 350 Mercedes Coup. It was a used car, but it made me look like I had all the money in the world. As I stepped out of the car, the WSM manager was walking out. He looked at my car, and then at me, and said, "You can't hide money."

He just knew, with a car like that, I was making it big... even though I really wasn't. Then he surprised me when he asked, "What would it take to get you back here?" I didn't even pause, before stating: "I will only do mornings from 6 to 9. You have to give me my original vacation time from when I first worked here. I get paid for all the extra production I do for the station. And you'll let me off to work on any movies I have." I also gave him a high amount I wanted to be paid!

Also without pausing, he answered, "Let's do it."

So, a year and a half after being fired, I was now back in the same chair, making a much higher salary! I later asked them why they hired me back. The program director said that, every time they did rating surveys, people would always mention Larry Black. Many still said that I was their favorite WSM personality, even though I hadn't worked there in a long time.

I loved doing the morning show on WSM Radio. All of the Opry stars listened to WSM every day, and most of them got to know me through the radio. We had so many big stars come on our show. They would all stay at the Opryland Hotel, where we were also located, so it was easy to get them to come down from their room to our studio. Willie Nelson, Marie Osmond and Wayne Newton were all on my show, and some of the more unique guests also included Phyllis Diller, Jerry Springer, Ed McMahon, and Maury Povich.

My bosses at WSM kept their word to me, and always allowed me to be off if I got a call for an audition, or landed a movie role. When I needed to be away, they would get someone to cover for me, and that would usually be Bill Anderson or Johnny Russell. I always thought it was so neat to have these huge country music legends fill in for me! During that time, I got to know Bill Anderson, and after I saw what a great host he was, a few years later, I gave him a call when I was looking for a host for Country's Family Reunion. Bill was my first and only choice.

During my time at WSM, I continued doing some of the more unique radio promotions that I always enjoyed being a part of. One of those was a weeklong broadcast from the roof of the Service Merchandise business in Cool Springs. I had a little tent set up there, inside of which I slept on an Army cot. The one drawback to my stunt was the fact that my wedding anniversary happened to fall during that same week! But instead of me coming down, I had Luann come up on the roof!

We made a big deal on the air, as we had our anniversary dinner catered to us up there. J. Alexander's restaurant brought up our fancy meal, along with a nice table and tablecloth. It was an anniversary that Luann has never let me forget!

One of my regrets about my time at WSM, however, is that I never got to announce the Grand Ole Opry. The Opry used on-air talent from WSM, and I would have loved to host the Opry. At the time, they mainly used Keith Bilbrey and Al Winter. Since I was on the air early each morning, I think maybe they didn't think I wanted to stay out late.

During my time at WSM, The Nashville Network was just beginning. TNN was also based at Opryland. The Nashville Network was a huge part of the Country Music explosion of the 1980s and 90s. Dan Miller was on a show on TNN called "You Can Be a Star". He was the sidekick to the show's host, Grand Ole Opry star Jim Ed Brown. "You Can Be a Star" was a talent show, similar to today's "American Idol". Dan also hosted a lot of the rodeo events TNN carried.

I ran into Dan a number of times, and we quickly became friends. We both liked to play racquetball, so we began playing together two or three times a week. My radio shift ended at 9:00am, and we would meet for a game as soon as I got off the air. Our friendship really grew during those racquetball games.

One day, Dan told me he was going to leave "You Can Be a Star". He was being promoted to daily host of a new show, called "American Magazine".

Dan told me I should try out for his job on Jim Ed's show. I met with the show producers, Allen Reid and his wife, Mady Land. Mady had really loved Dan Miller, and I could instantly tell that she didn't like me at all.

I later asked Dan, "What's not to like?"

And very honestly, Dan said, "Larry, you are overweight, and Mady does not like fat people." Of course, Dan was very thin, so she loved him!

But Mady grew to like me. Once she saw that I was loyal, and I wanted to stay with the show, she started warming up to me. After a short audition, I got the job. I was going to be on TV every day!

I had interviewed Jim Ed Brown at WSM, but we had never really worked together. But he was a hoot. He was so fun to work with. He was a great host, and he was hard to fluster. One day, as a joke, I went on the air, wearing a huge floppy earring in my left ear. Jim Ed always stood on my right side, so he couldn't see what I had on my left ear, until I turned around and looked him square in the face. Once he noticed that earring, he was speechless.

I played "second banana" to Jim Ed for two years. I told jokes and interviewed audience members. We watched so many talented singers come on, all trying to get their big break in Music City. One of those was Trisha Yearwood. In 1988, the show was Trisha's first major television appearance. That same year, Lari White also competed on our show. Neither Lari nor Trisha won the biggest prizes on the show, and they were both eventually beaten by other singers… but almost 30 years later, in 2016, Lari White performed on Larry's Country Diner. She was so great. But less than two years later, Lari would pass away, due to cancer.

"You Can Be a Star" was a half-hour show, and we taped five shows a day. That meant that we could do a week's worth of shows in one day. We filmed the show for four to six weeks, two times a year.

Mike Johnson was in charge of all the music on the show, and he had to write charts for everybody. Mike had been part of Bill Anderson's band before that. After watching him work on "You Could Be a Star", I knew that he could handle pressure. So, years later, when we were looking for the musical director for "Country's Family Reunion", Mike was an obvious choice. He has been the CFR band leader since the beginning.

As I became more known around The Nashville Network, I started getting other opportunities. I became the host of a show called "Road Test Magazine". I did that show with Big Daddy Don Garlits. Don was the father of drag racing. He knew everything about cars, and I knew next to nothing about them! But they wanted me to also sound like an expert, so they put all of the info I would need on a teleprompter, and I'd just read it! I'd read: "Hey Don, what's the compression ratio on this car?" I had no idea what compression ratio even meant! But Don and I got along very well. He was fun to work with. We did that show for a couple years.

I also did a few live remotes for Ralph Emery's "Nashville Now" show. One was with Charley Pride, when he went to the baseball spring training down in Florida. I interviewed Mary Chapin Carpenter at the Wolf Trap outside of Washington, D.C.

I also interviewed Don Williams. Just before we went on, I said to Don, "I'm told you are a horrible interview."

"What?" he said.

"You have a reputation for giving 'yes' and 'no' answers."

He laughed. "Don't worry about it."

When it came time for our interview, he warmed up to me, and we had a nice, fun interview.

I loved my time at The Nashville Network. But then the leaders of the network started making changes, which would eventually lead to the end of TNN. They wanted younger hosts and hipper shows. They got rid of Jim Ed Brown... and his sidekick Larry Black. They also cancelled the other shows I had been a part of.

Oh well, at least I still had my radio job. Yeah... about that...

The second time around, I was at WSM for two and half years. That Christmas, I wanted to take a two-week vacation to go to Virginia Beach with my family. But the boss, Kyle Cantrell, said that I couldn't have the time off, because others with more seniority had already asked off. I told him it didn't matter who was on the air over the holidays. They could have anyone fill in, and no listener would care. But Kyle refused.

So, two weeks before our vacation, I turned in my two-week notice. It was the first time in all of my radio career that I left a job, and then never missed it. I knew it was time to go. My time on radio was over. And I have never wished that I could go back. Bill Cody replaced me at WSM, and he is still doing the morning show, more than 25 years later! Bill is a radio legend.

One of the main reasons I knew it was time to go, was that I had started to get into different television productions. Bud Wendell, the President of Gaylord Entertainment, which owned the Opry and WSM, was very strict about people on the staff doing work on the side that was not a part of the Opry, TNN or WSM. It was considered a conflict of interest.

But for some reason, Bud really liked me, and he looked the other way when he knew I was working on an outside project. But even though Bud allowed me, I still felt uncomfortable about it… so I felt it was time to leave WSM.

My friendship with Pat Robertson continued over the years, and in 2002, he called to say Michael Little, the President of the Christian Broadcasting Network, would like to meet with me in Nashville. When we met, Michael asked me for my help in finding a broadcast and production facility for CBN in Nashville. It was to be their "Disaster Recovery Site". In the event that there was a major disaster like a hurricane or terrorist attack in Virginia Beach, Virginia, they wanted another location they could broadcast from.

I looked at a number of options in Nashville, and found the perfect place at a 120,000 square foot complex sitting on 16 acres. The asking price was $30 million. I advised Pat this was the perfect place, with everything he had been looking for, and he took my word for it. He sent his financial guy, Bill Carter, to town - and by the time the deal was done, Bill had talked down the price considerably.

I also told Pat that we should try and launch another Family Channel, this time with the very best in Country and Gospel music. The Nashville Network had folded, and we could offer just the thing to take its place. Pat agreed.

I had initially thought I was going to run the network facility, but they ended up hiring a new general manager. When we started filming our "Country's Family Reunion" and "Larry's Country Diner", though, I knew that the facility, then known as North Star Studios, would be the perfect place to produce those shows.

Through every move and career change I made, I always continued my involvement in the Youth for Christ organization. Luann and I had been working with YFC since we were in college.

Youth for Christ is an organization that has helped raise up so many of the most important religious leaders of our time. Billy Graham, his music director Cliff Barrows, and George Beverly Shea all went through YFC.

Billy Graham was the first evangelist for YFC. He did his crusades in Los Angeles, and that's where Roy Rogers and Dale Evans came to the Lord. Stuart Hamblin also found the Lord there, and on his way home, he wrote the Gospel standard "It Is No Secret". God used Youth for Christ to build a lot of important groups and organizations.

Robert Pierce, the man who founded World Vision International, also came out of YFC.

Jimmy Durato was a Youth for Christ evangelist, and he asked me to come speak to the students at King's College. I was invited because I was a rock and roll disc jockey, who was also a very public Christian. Jimmy also invited Danny Taylor to come speak. Danny was the drummer for a group called The 28th Dream. They played at the famous Peppermint Lounge in New York City.

Danny was known for being a nightclub drummer, but the King's College students were spellbound, as he talked about his relationship with the Lord. In 1971, I recorded an album for Danny, called "Taylor Made".

I was very honored to be able to help raise money for Youth for Christ. That chance came when I met an extremely talented person by the name of Lynn Doerschuk.

When he was fifteen years old, Lynn had run cameras for Rex Humbard and Maude Aimee's church service. In high school, he got a studio camera job at a local CBS station. A couple years later, he was floor director for all the big TV game shows that were filmed in New York City. And in 1967, he was chosen to be the director of Barbara Streisand's concert in New York City's Central Park. There were 135,000 in attendance!

But after all of those accomplishments, Lynn's heart was always in doing God's work. He came to me and declared, "We want to do a Care-a-thon for YFC!"

After he explained his idea, I had some jingles written for it. He also put me in charge of interviewing a lot of famous people who were Christians, and who understood the value of Youth for Christ. One of the first was Pat Boone.

Our next step was to fly into a city and rent a radio station for a day. We'd bring in the area Youth for Christ directors, and we'd talk about the local YFC program and what all they did. We'd also play all of my celebrity interviews in each town. As the broadcast went on, we asked for donations throughout the day. In just one year, we had raised several million dollars for Youth for Christ.

We held the same fundraiser in a different city, once a week, for 20 weeks in a row. A year later, we came back and did the same thing; then we'd come back and do it again the next year. We went to Tacomo, Washington and raised over half a million dollars in one night. They got so many envelopes full of cash that it took them two weeks to open them all.

The Care-a-thons were very successful for Youth for Christ. But they became too successful in some areas, and it ended up destroying their programs.

Until we came into town, they had relied on monthly giving from local people... but when those people saw that we had raised hundreds of thousands of dollars for the group, they figured Youth for Christ didn't need their money anymore, so they quit giving.

I have always been very proud of my work with Youth for Christ. We raised a lot of money during each event, but my family's own personal checkbook always seemed to look quite meager. We still struggled to pay our own bills at home, but the pay was not what I was doing it for. It was during that part of my career that I felt I was able to use my radio experience to do something that was good, and I felt that I was using my talents for a much bigger cause than just myself.

A strong division of YFC was a group called "Youth Guidance". Lynn got Johnny Cash to do a Youth Guidance TV special. He also talked other huge stars like Paul Newman, Phyllis Diller and Bill Cosby into being on the show. The special raised hundreds of thousands of dollars for troubled children.

The Youth Guidance TV show was such a success that plans for follow-up shows began immediately. But Johnny Cash got sick, and was not available for the next special. Lynn wanted to try to get Glen Campbell to host the show, and he sent me to make the request.

I flew to Las Vegas, where Glen was performing. I didn't know Glen, and I hadn't set up an appointment. I just went in unannounced. As soon as I got to the casino, I saw a man talking on a payphone, and it turned out to be Glen's road manager! I introduced myself, and he took me in to watch Glen's show. I met Glen in his dressing room after his concert. My first words to him were, "My understanding is that you have a relationship with God."

And Glen replied, "Hell, I love God!"

I gave him a tape of the show that Johnny Cash had hosted, and he promised he would watch it. At 3:00 in the morning, my phone rang. It was Glen, who said, "I love the show! Can you meet me for breakfast?"

Glen agreed to host the special, and he was as great as we had hoped he would be. A few years later, Barbara Mandrell took over as host of the Youth Guidance specials. We had no doubts she would be wonderful...and she was.

Then Lynn Doerschuk and I started talking about teaming up together to produce some different TV shows. During my two years at TNN and through our Youth Guidance specials, I had learned so much about Television, and about country music programming. I figured this would be a good time to put some of the things I had learned to work.

Lynn and I formed a company that we named Windyville Productions, and produced a TV special that was a tribute to Minnie Pearl, called "Hats Off to Minnie". We knew it was going to be something very special when Barbara Mandrell agreed to host the show. We also put on an all-star tribute to Ralph Emery. Barbara and Johnny Cash hosted that show.

From there, we bought the rights for the 15th Annual Dove Awards, and sold the broadcast to the Family Channel. Glen Campbell hosted the Dove Awards; it was the first time that a non-Gospel music artist had hosted the Doves. The show did very well in the ratings, and we had an option on the next year. But the morning after it aired, Lynn and I decided that we didn't want to work with the Gospel Music Association anymore. They were very hard to work with. Everybody wanted to direct the show, and no one would take our advice.

Lynn and I knew we could produce very successful TV shows, but we decided to switch from Gospel to Country music. In 1993 and 1994, we taped thirteen one-hour specials, called "Country

Music Spotlight". They were all filmed at the Palace Theater in Branson, Missouri, and they would have been perfect for The Nashville Network, but their management was not interested.

But The Family Channel jumped at them. TNN thought they owned the whole country music market. But Lynn Doerschuk and I were so lucky that TNN passed, because there is no way they would have paid us what The Family Channel did. For those thirteen shows, Family Channel gave us a production budget of three MILLION dollars!

I started going back and forth from Nashville to Branson, as we filmed our shows.

They featured live concerts by artists including Merle Haggard, John Michael Montgomery, Kris Kristofferson, Wayne Newton, Martina McBride, and Three Dog Night. We also did a special Christmas Show, and for the 4th of July, we put on The Star Spangled Branson Special - both of which brought phenomenal ratings to the Family Channel.

The thirteen shows we did were a huge success. So much so, that I went back to the network and sold them on another thirteen! I also tried to talk the President of the Family Channel, Tim Robertson, the son of Pat Robertson, into buying a theater in Branson. I thought it would be great for the network, and they should have done it.

They did get involved with a theater, but they chose one in Myrtle Beach instead of in Branson. Instead, they joined up with Calvin Gilmore, who had three theaters. Calvin had been a very successful real estate guy. He also loved to perform at his own theater. Tim bought into one of Calvin's theaters, and they wanted us to do all of our shows there. But we only did three.

We were contracted to produce thirteen more shows, but we just couldn't get along with the theater owner Calvin Gilmore. I told the high-ups at the Family Channel, "I don't want to do this anymore. The only thing worse than Gilmore's ego is his insecurity. We can't work with him."

Lynn and I said, "If we have to do more from here, we are done."

The network official agreed, and we were able to mutually end our contract, and Lynn Doerschuk was somehow able to put together a proposal… and it actually ended up making the two of us more money by stopping the production. Luann and I took our half of that money, and we traveled the country for the next year and a half.

Then, finding myself with more free time on my hands (again), I figured this gave me one more chance to go after my acting dream. But this time, I was going to give it everything I had. I decided that I would go to Hollywood. I talked with Luann and said, "If there was ever a time to go for it, it's now."

But Luann said, "This is not going to be good for our marriage."

She did not want me to leave our family and go to Los Angeles. I understood that. But I knew that nothing was going to happen to us. I knew our marriage would survive, and I really wanted to try and give my acting career my very best shot.

Luann agreed that I could be gone for two months. So, in February of 1994, I went. It was "pilot season", when they are filming all the new TV shows for the next year. The majority of pilots never get picked up by a network, but they are still good pay and experience for any actor who can get booked for one. Since there is so much activity during that time, if you were ever going to find work as a TV actor, it would be when they are shooting in February and March.

I rented a motel room in Los Angeles by the week for two months. I found an agent there, and that was an accomplishment in itself. Getting a good agent is not easy, but Robert Williams, who was from Nashville, knew an agent, and he put in a word for me.

During that time, I went to two auditions. One was for a Staples commercial. I didn't get it. Then I auditioned for a movie, and I didn't get that. I spent most of my time playing golf and racquetball, because I couldn't get any acting work. At the end of two months, I prepared to head back home to Nashville. As I left Hollywood, I prayed, "Lord, if you want me to be an actor, you will have to make it happen from Nashville. I'm not going to leave my family again."

On the way home, Shay Griffin called from her casting company in Atlanta. She had gotten me a role for an HBO special called "Miss Evers' Boys", and before I had even gotten back to Nashville, I was booked for three shows. I immediately remembered my prayer after I couldn't get anything in L.A. When I got home, I told Luann, "I think the Lord is going to be my agent. He only takes 10%."

I played a taxicab driver in the film "The Thing Called Love". My part of the shoot was supposed to be just two days, but it ended up taking nine. I didn't mind at all, as I knew each extra day was more money for me!

My longest-running acting job came in 1996, with the TV series "The Cape". Corbin Bernsen was the star of the show, and this was the second time I had worked with him. The series was shot in Florida, at Cape Canaveral. They originally booked me for a week; I was to play the boss of the Cape.

I did my week, and as I got ready to come home, the director asked if I would come back the next week. Of course, I said yes. And when the second week was over, they asked, "Are you available next week?"

I asked them, "Is this going to become a recurring character?"

He said, "It could be."

At the end of the third week, they asked if I could come back again the next week. But I told them I couldn't. I had planned a vacation to Montana, and I wasn't going to cancel. But they insisted that they had to have me just for one day, and they ended up flying me from Montana to Coco Beach, Florida. I did the shoot and immediately flew right back to be with Luann.

I did a total of 22 episodes of "The Cape". It was a fun time. Once you get into a character, and you've established who the character is, you can be more comfortable. They also allowed me to ad-lib as my character developed. As long as I stayed true to that character, they were okay with me using my own words.

In 1995, I thought that since I had enjoyed success on the radio, TV and in the movies, where else could I go? I would record an album. Yes, I would become a singer!

We called the album "Rattlesnake Retreat", and it featured some funny songs, a number of them written by Buddy Kalb. We made a music video for the title song, and The Nashville Network aired the video quite a bit.

The album also had a couple serious songs on it that I did as recitations. One was "Creation of Mothers". We had taken it from one of Erma Bombeck's newspaper columns. I called Erma, and asked for permission to put her words to music. She loved Minnie Pearl, and we made a deal that any royalties we received from the piece would go to the Minnie Pearl Cancer Center.

Bill Gaither helped produce the album. He loved another recitation I did, called "The Square". One year, he called and asked me to send him the lyrics to the piece, so that he could do it in his church on Father's Day. But Bill was one of the few who actually heard the album. It only sold 5,000 copies, and my dream of a recording career came to a quick end. If I would have waited 15 years until we had the Diner show, my album would have sold a lot more.

But at least I still had my acting career to fall back on. I played Val Kilmer's parole officer in the film "The Real McCoy", which starred him and Kim Basinger.

In 1999, probably my most unique billing came for the movie "Chill Factor". Cuba Gooding, Jr. was the main star, and in the credits, I was listed in the credits as "Fat Man in Tunnel"!

I've been blessed to work with many, many great actors including Katherine Helmond (who starred on "Soap" and "Who's The Boss"), Linda Purl and James Reed, just to name a few. I always had fun with the serious roles. I have a good sense of humor, but I think I'm better at serious roles than I am at comedy. I played the part of a private detective in a TV series "Savannah", and it was a very serious part, but quite fun to do.

The last major role I did came when I played a judge in "Pardon in the Sand". Ed Bruce was also in it, as he played a defense attorney. We filmed it in Shreveport, Louisiana in August. It was so hot, and we were in a courtroom with lights, cameras and hot bodies. Everyone was in period clothing, and I was wearing a wool suit under my judge robe. At the end of the first day, I asked if it was alright if I didn't wear a suit under the robe. You couldn't see it anyway. So, for the next two weeks, I was the coolest guy in the room. I had a lightweight shirt on under the robe, and I wore shorts! I also enjoyed that role, because I didn't have to try and remember my lines. Since judges have papers on their desk, I just put the script down right there in front of me. I didn't even bother trying to memorize anything.

One reason I don't pursue more film or commercial work is because my brain will not allow me to focus on memorizing lines. I just cannot focus, and it has gotten worse as I have gotten older. I can ad-lib, but I hate trying to say the words exactly as they are in the script, and a lot of directors don't like that.

I think my TV and movie work also influenced my sons. Jared did some Opryland ads when he was in his early teens. Adam also did quite a bit of TV work. His longest-running thing was the Kroger Price Guide television spots. He's also done a lot of instructional videos. He's better at it than I am.

When I was growing up, we weren't allowed to go to movies. Mom said we shouldn't sit next to non-Christians in the theaters. And we weren't supposed to watch TV. So what did I do? I ended up with my own TV show! But my parents eventually came around. They loved me in "Ernest Goes to Camp", and they were proud of everything I did.

Being in the movies and on TV was quite fun, but as my job offers started coming in less and less, I watched our bank account get lower and lower. At the time, I didn't know what my future held. Then I came up with an idea… I wondered what it would be like to be in a small room, sitting with a bunch of country music legends, as they sang their songs and visited with each other.

COUNTRY'S FAMILY REUNION

One of my favorite Bible verses is Proverbs 16:9, that says "A man plans his course, but the Lord directs his steps."

I have no doubt whatsoever that the Lord was directing my steps throughout my life. In 1996, I needed that direction more than ever, when I formed Gabriel Communications.

I had the idea to start Country's Family Reunion... but I had NO money. We were flat broke. I figured it would cost about $350,000 to produce and market the first CFR, but where was I going to get $350,000? I went to my friends.

My first stop was Bill Pratt, who owned Southeast Jeep Eagle. I played racquetball with him, and I knew he had the money to do it. But he didn't give me the money. He did give me some advice however, saying, "Don't get one guy to give you $350,000. Get ten guys to invest $35,000 each."

He said he would be one of those ten investors. As I left, I thought, "Finding nine guys might be harder than finding one big one."

I can't tell you how hard it was to find ten people willing to invest in my dream. And finding a "believer" to invest was next to impossible. I knew my idea would pay off for all of those involved, because I truly felt that God's hand was on it. I just could not understand why all my religious friends would not help.

As the struggle to find investors dragged on, we had to mortgage our house just to have some money and pay our personal bills. But that money didn't last long at all. During that time, I kept a daily journal. As I read back over it today, I can remember how desperate things had become. Here are a few of my journal entries:

"After months of looking for the investors, I still do not have all the money raised. I pick up one or two investors, and by the time I get back to them with news of others, one of the two has gone away."

"The mortgage money is gone. We had $8,000 worth of credit, and we have already used half of that. Then that will be it. No visible signs of income. No additional signs of work."

"I am still so encouraged about this Family Circle (the original name of Country's Family Reunion) because I believe the Lord is in it. It is going to be interesting to look back and see how it all came about."

And it is!

Any time I received money from any projects I had worked on, I always made sure to tithe to the church. It was my number one priority, even before any of our bills were paid. When Luann made out our weekly bills, she sometimes let our tithe slide, or would forget to pay the full amount. I got upset and said I would be in charge of paying our tithe. I wanted to make sure that the Lord knew that I had complete faith in him.

I was excited when two of my racquetball friends agreed to invest $35,000 each with my company. Then I asked a friend at my church to do the same, and he turned me down. I met with another prospect at a bar in Brentwood. I knew this man could easily come up with the $35,000. I also knew that he was not a believer. At the end of our meeting, he announced, "I won't give you the 35. I'll give you 10. If you can put it all together, I'll give you the 35. If it falls through, you can keep the 10. But don't come back to me again."

I really needed that money, but I said, "I won't take it."

From there, I drove to Rome, Georgia for a funeral of my brother-in-law's mother. The entire way there and back, I thought about the $10,000 offer the man had made in the bar. The entire way home, I prayed, "Lord, you know I need the money. Please don't make me take that guy's money. I will take it, but I don't want to. Please give me another option."

When we got home, I opened the mailbox, and there was an envelope with a check inside for $5,000, attached with a note that said: "I've been praying about it. God said for me to give this to you."

I yelled, "Oh. Thank you Lord!"

The money was from Ralph Sonntag and his wife. Ralph owned Telco Research, which was a big digital and tech company. He was the church member who had earlier turned me down, when I'd asked him to be one of my investors. After the show had become a huge success, I returned the money to him and told him to pass it on to someone else.

Then Steve Brumfield introduced me to Joe Rodgers. Joe's construction company helped build hospitals across the country. He also oversaw the building of Opryland USA and the Country Music Hall of Fame. Joe was chairman of the Republican National Committee when Ronald Reagan was running for President. Reagan later named him as the Ambassador to France.

When I met with Joe, he asked, "What will you give me if I raise the rest of the money? Will you give me an extra five percent profit?"

I said, "Sure. But I'd like to make one more call first."

I really felt led by the Lord that I should call Pat Robertson. He had been such a good friend, and I thought he would love the idea of being included in the deal.

Pat and Joe knew each other very well. They had lots in common, since Pat had run for President. When I met with Pat, I told him that Joe Rogers was interested in the deal, and Pat asked me to call Joe. They both had a short conversation, and by the end of it, they both agreed that they would each put in a third of the money. I had the audacity to ask Pat to write me a check on the spot. He laughed, "Send me the paperwork and I will."

Today, as I look back on my life, I can see how the Lord had always been guiding my friendship with Pat Robertson. Decades earlier, I felt that I was following the Lord when I took a 50% cut in pay to go and work with Pat for just $150 a week. But I was rewarded when Pat supported my Larry Black radio show. He was also a great source of strength, and I treasured the faith that he had in me.

Now, as I tried to get my Country's Family Reunion idea to become reality, and after all our years of friendship, Pat was my earliest and largest investor in Country's Family Reunion. And he would continue to invest his money in future CFRs. I can honestly say that, without Pat Robertson, there would have been no Country's Family Reunion. I would have never come up with the money to get it going. And without the CFR, there would have never been a Larry's Country Diner. So country music fans should say a word of thanks for Pat. I know that I do!

After Pat agreed, I flew directly to Joe Rodgers and asked for his money. He pulled out his personal checkbook and wrote the check, but he asked me to wait a week before I cashed it. I know what his original plan had been. He had wanted to get someone else's money to invest, give that to me, and then he would get his 5% extra without risking any of his own cash. But after he had talked to Pat, he felt that he had to keep his commitment to me.

Before I go much farther, I need to explain that the only way my company makes any money on the Family Reunions is when our viewers buy our DVDs. Of course, back when we started the CFR, we were selling VHS tapes. No TV network ever paid us to produce or air the show. In fact, it was always the other way around. We had to pay all the costs to film the shows, and then we had to pay to get them on the air. So, our only income came from the people who bought our shows on VHS or DVD.

Most of the $350,000 budget would go to produce the show and pay all the artists. I had planned to use $50,000 for marketing, but when I heard that we could buy an hour of time on The Nashville Network, I knew that was the place for us to try to sell our CFR tapes. But there was one big problem: that one hour of time cost $125,000!

I went to our accountant, Ken Kraft, and told him that I needed to come up with another $75,000. Ken went to some of his clients and told them that, if they loaned us the money, we would give them five dollars for each tape we sold. The people who took him up on the offer eventually made out like bandits! They got quite a return on their investment.

I had initially planned to call the show "Family Circle". I thought that made sense, as all the country stars were sitting in a big circle while they sang and visited. But when I tried to get the name trademarked, I found out that "Family Circle" Magazine had beaten me to it. My next choice was "Family Reunion".

The first Country's Family Reunion aired on the Nashville Network in 1997. To say that it was a success is an understatement. On that first airing, we sold 5,000 VHS sets! We aired the same show again six weeks later, and we sold another 5,000 units! A month and a half later, we sold the same amount. But each time the Reunion aired, it cost us $125,000 for an hour. So, after three airings, we had spent $375,000 just to get it on the air.

The television viewers absolutely loved seeing all these great country artists (many of whom hadn't been seen on TV in a long time). The CFR was also a huge financial success for my company, and it worked out very well for all of our investors. They loved it!

All of them but one.

Leading up to the first airing of the CFR, Joe Rodgers called me almost every night. He was so worried about losing his money. But when it finally aired, I gave him all of his money back, plus a 29% return on his investment! After the success of the first Reunion, we immediately started planning to do a second one. I told Joe that we would also do a special Christmas show, so we were going to increase our budget, up to $650,000. Before he signed on, Joe sent me a list of twenty questions about the entire production.

I decided that it wasn't worth all the hassle, so I told Joe we didn't need him. He got so mad that he sent a guy over to audit our books. Ironically, his name was Steve Thorn. As soon as we met, I said, "So you're the thorn in my side?"

He went through all of our financial books for two days, and finally said we had paid Joe all we had owed him.

When the CFR kept selling, a year later, I sent Joe another $20,000. I thought he would be thrilled, but instead, he sent Steve back over to audit the books again! Five years later, we started selling the CFR through a national infomercial. It was also a big success, and I owed Joe another $22,000. When I sent it along with a thank you letter, he responded with a lovely note that said, "In my lifetime, I wish I had done more business with people like you. I would have had no idea of knowing that you owed me that money."

When it came time for me to buy everyone out, I offered Joe's widow a fair amount for their stock, and I still have Joe's thank you letter.

Once we had made a pretty big profit, for our next CFR project I went to my friend Mickey McElroy in Biloxi. Mickey was one of my first investors, and I told him, "Mickey, if you're willing to put up half the money, I'll put up the other half. We'll do it all ourselves, without any other investors."

We did that, and on the evening the show aired, we both made a profit! And mine just happened to be the exact amount I owed the IRS!

I probably should have taken some time to enjoy our good fortune... but I decided instead to take our biggest risk yet. I wanted to do a totally different kind of Reunion show, and I knew that it would take a lot of money.

NASCAR was just starting to really get hot, and I wanted to do a stock car racing reunion. So we gathered as many racing legends as we could fit into the room. The only one missing was Richard Petty. But we had Buddy Baker, Darrell Waltrip, David Pearson, Junior Johnson, Bobby Allison, and a bunch more.

We had twenty-two racing legends sharing all of their great stories. They told lots of funny stories, and quite a few sad ones. It was everything I thought it could be. It was also horribly expensive! It cost us one million dollars just to produce the show! We then had to come up with the money to actually air the show, of course.

The Nashville Network told us that we could have just one hour of air time for $145,000. At the time, TNN was airing most of the races, so I bought the hour immediately following the second race of the season. Since it was airing right after the race, throughout the entire race the announcers kept promoting that our show was coming up next. I was gambling that the racing fans would keep watching after the checkered flag had fallen. It was a huge gamble. But it paid off, and we made all of our money back, plus more!

You've heard the old saying, "It takes money to make money". In an effort to expand our company, I knew we would need access to more money. Ralph Sonntag, the friend who had given me $5,000 a couple of years earlier, was now tremendously wealthy. I took Ralph on a trip to Montana, and on the way back to Nashville, he told me, "Larry, I have sold my company for millions of dollars. When we get back home, I'll get you a line of credit at the bank for one million dollars. In return, I'll take 30% of your company."

After the great success we had with the Stock Car Legends Reunion, we knew that there just had to be a similar audience for other sports-related projects. We chose to go with college football first, and we filmed an Alabama Football Legends Reunion, which included Kenny Stabler and thirty-one other Alabama players.

That was followed by an Auburn Legends Reunion, and then Hershel Walker and twenty-nine Georgia players came in for a third taping. When we hosted the salute to Oklahoma football, Barry Switzer, Billy Sims, Brian Bosworth and Keith Jackson were among thirty college football legends.

To try and market the Oklahoma Reunion, I flew to Oklahoma City to meet with local TV sports announcers. But I couldn't get anyone to return my calls. I could only stay for one day, and I wasn't having much luck. Toward the end of the day, a local sportscaster called; and when I told him I was flying out the next morning, he asked me to meet him in the station parking lot at midnight.

At the end of our middle-of-the-night meeting, the sports guy promised he'd share all the info with his news director. As soon as I got home to Nashville, they were calling, saying they wanted to air excerpts of the Reunion on each of their sportscasts for the next week. They also agreed to give out info on how fans could order the entire set from us.

When the station aired highlights from the Football Legends Reunion, it was a huge ratings success. It did so well that they called and asked if they could continue airing clips for a second week! Each time they aired it on their newscast, our phones lit up with people wanting to order the series. It did so well that we paid back all of our investment in that series, and then we gave several thousand dollars to the "Sooner" football program.

All of the players who took part in those Football Legends Reunions were so thrilled to be there. They enjoyed being with their former teammates again. But those shows were so expensive to produce and market, and we lost almost every bit of profit we had made through our earlier CFR projects in the process of making them. With the exception of the Oklahoma City TV station, we were not able to find a good place to air the shows, so that we could, in turn, sell the tapes. It was too expensive to buy airtime in Atlanta to sell the Georgia set, and we couldn't afford to pay the TV rates in New York City to advertise to the Auburn fans.

Our attempt at a sports-themed Family Reunion ended up costing us a lot of money. And then things got even worse. Remember that million-dollar line of credit that Ralph Sonntag had taken out for our company?

Ralph wanted his money back. All of it. Right now.

Ralph had become hard to work with in recent months. He had played football for the Washington Redskins, and I thought all the head injuries he'd gotten during his career might have had something to do with him being a little unstable. One day, he came in and tried to fire everyone in the company for no reason.

Ralph had also been impacted by the September 11th World Trade Center attacks. On September 10, 2001, the day before the planes hit, he had dinner at the top of the World Trade Center in New York City. He had just flown home, and when he turned on his TV, he saw the towers falling. That affected him in a huge way. He decided to totally retire, and he wanted all of his money out of our company. He told me, in no uncertain terms, that he wanted his one million dollars right then.

I called my banker, Jimmy Green, and asked him how close I could get to a million dollars. Jimmy was concerned that, if Ralph wanted out, the company must be in trouble. I assured him that that was not the case. He said I could get $450,000. I had $250,000 in my bank account, so I was still short of the million that Ralph was demanding.

I called my friend Mickey McElroy. He owned two restaurants in Biloxi, and had been one of my investors since day one. He is still a great friend today. Mickey went to the bank and got a loan for $250,000 for me. I finally paid Ralph his one million dollars, but that left us with almost nothing. For the next year and a half, I had to scramble every day just to pay our bills. The bank worked with me so much, but when things started to look even darker, my friend at the bank said, "Larry, at some point, we are going to have to take your land in Montana. We don't want to do that, because we would just sell it for what we can get. You could sell it and make more."

But I was able to work a refinancing of the place in Montana, and finally paid off the bank. After all the bills were paid, we didn't have enough money left to tape any new Country's Family Reunion shows. We were very close to folding our tent. I figured I could try to get a job on the radio someplace.

I've always trusted that the Lord has a plan, and that when he closes one door, he'll open another. As it turned out, that new door was a bedroom door... that my son Adam opened, when he borrowed a bed!

Adam had been teaching at Brentwood Academy, and was having some guests coming over for the weekend, so he needed to borrow a bed. He found one at a friend of a friend's. When he returned the bed, the friend told him he knew someone in Virginia who produced infomercials. That man was Nick Cirmo. He was known for producing cosmetic and medical infomercials.

Adam told him about our College Football Legends Reunions. He also told him it looked like I was going to have to close our company. Then, just as an afterthought, Adam had said, "We also have some old country music shows."

When Nick found out what we had with the Country's Family Reunion shows, he exclaimed, "Your dad isn't closing his company! You are sitting on a goldmine!"

Nick came up with a proposal that had a budget of $100,000 for an infomercial.

"We are just hanging on by a thread! I don't have a hundred grand," I said.

As I looked at his plan, $50,000 of the $100,000 was going for the show host. I told him, "I don't need a host. I've got Bill Anderson, who will work with us, and he is better than any $50,000 host."

We agreed to give Nick a total of $10,000 to produce the infomercial. He would also get a percentage of the sales. Then we spent $25,000 to air the spot for one weekend in different markets across the country. When Monday came, we had broken even, but we hadn't made any profit. Then we spent the same $25,000 again. We took it off the stations that didn't bring in any sales, and we added a few new ones. That weekend, we made a little profit. We did the same thing a third weekend, and then we hired Steve Newton out of Virginia Beach, Virginia to buy some airtime for us. He had worked with the 700 Club, and it wasn't long before we started to make some good money. I told the guy to add another $15,000 to the budget, so we were now spending $40,000 to air the spot.

Each week, I would get nervous as I reinvested the $40,000. I knew if our sales came up short, we would be back to square one. We just didn't have enough in the bank to the point where we had any extra to fall back on. To get my mind off my money worries,

Luann and I went to Montana over the 4th of July. But if you know me, you know that I also took all of my business papers with me!

As I was reading over that week's reports, seeing everything that had already been pre-paid, I was totally shocked when I discovered what we were paying for that week's airing. Instead of $40,000, it showed $75,000! I immediately called Steve, the guy booking everything for us. He knew I was panicked when I asked, "What have you done? We don't have that much money. You have killed us."

He sat there, and finally said, "Well, I have some more bad news. Not only did we spend that money this week, but we did it two weeks in a row. You'll have to come up with $150,000."

But God had a plan. God probably knew that I would never have taken such a huge risk, with money that we didn't have. So he took the risk for me. The next two weekends, we aired $150,000 worth of Country's Family Reunion infomercials across the nation. And those two weekends made our company. Our sales exploded! We made so much money, we were able to spend $150,000 every week. As the orders poured in, we spent a total of two million dollars that year on advertising!

Our Gabriel Communications company was finally a financial success... and it all started when Adam borrowed a bed from someone who knew a man who did infomercials!

When I went to get artists for the inaugural Country's Family Reunion, the first ones I approached were Bill Anderson, Johnny Russell, Jeannie Seely, Jean Shepard, Grandpa Jones, Connie Smith, Little Jimmy Dickens, and Billy Walker. They all jumped at the idea! They were so excited to be able to spend a couple days with their friends.

The night before our first CFR taping, Jeannie Seely was performing a concert in Pigeon Forge, Tennessee. She was also sick. I sent a limo to go pick her up, and she slept the entire way to Nashville. When the taping was over, they drove her back to Pigeon Forge, so she could do another show there.

Jeannie Seely was there for our very first Reunion, and she has appeared on almost every other one we've had, with only a couple exceptions. She is known for telling it like it is... so I thought it might be fun to let her share a few memories of our time together.

"When Larry first told me about his idea of having the country stars all sit in a circle and just visit as they sang their favorite songs, I tried to be nice to him when he asked my opinion, but at the time, I thought it was a really dumb idea! But it turned out that I was the dumb one. Larry's idea turn out to be truly brilliant.

The exposure I got from the Family Reunion and Larry's Country Diner shows made a major difference in my career. I've had thousands of people come up to me over the past two decades and all say the same thing, "We enjoy you so much on the Family Reunion!"

Over the years, my role on the Reunions has grown a little bit. I usually sit next to Bill Anderson, and Bill likes to have me there to bounce stories off me. He knows that I can jump in if he needs to take a breath. Between the two of us, we have more than a hundred years of stories, friendships and experiences in Country Music. When I know I'll be with Bill, I try and do some homework on all the artists who are scheduled to be on. I always want to know as much as I can about them and their songs. And doing that has also helped prepare me for my current radio show on Willie's Roadhouse, on Sirius XM Radio.

Of course, in addition to the CFR, I've also been a part of quite a few Larry's Country Diner shows. I learned pretty early on that any time you step into the Diner, you need to always be on your toes. You never know what Larry will throw at you! With no script, you never know where they are going to go next; and since they don't stop taping, that also adds a little pressure. After Larry's accident in Montana, I was honored to be a substitute guest host on the Diner.

The viewers love Larry on the show. But they're not able to see the kind of man he is off of TV. I was able to see the real Larry when my husband, Gene, was in the hospital. He came very close to dying, and at the time, I was so worried. Larry and Luann called me and they prayed for us. Larry reassured me that Gene was going to survive, and I will never, ever forget how he took the time to pray for us.

We love doing the Diner and LCD cruises. We knew my husband wouldn't be able to walk around the ship, but Larry put us at ease when he told him, 'You bring your electric scooter and I'll bring mine!' They drove those scooters everywhere, and were a riot.

I thank Larry for having the vision of the Country's Family Reunion and Larry's Country Diner. Not only did he have the vision, but he was also willing to roll the dice and risk his own money to make his vision a reality. Larry Black gave all of us artists, and all country music fans, an incredible gift that we will never be able to repay."

– Jeannie Seely

Once filming for the first CFR had begun, the artists all said, "This is like the old package shows we used to do, when they booked a bunch of us together on a concert." The stars ended up enjoying the taping as much as the viewers at home did.

Over the years, we've done more than thirty different Country's Family Reunions. During that time, we've had a couple hundred different artists come and be a part of our Reunion family. You can find a list of all of the CFR series in the back of this book. All of those stars helped lift up our show, and in turn, the shows lifted up the artists and their careers.

In 1990, I came up with the bright idea of filming six different Family Reunion shows over a nine-day period. It was a logistical nightmare. It was also a huge undertaking, and an even larger financial risk.

Jamie Amos, Patrick Kennedy and their staff did an incredible job in handling all the logistics of taping so many shows in such a short time. They had artists landing at the airport, and as they were picking them up, they would be taking others from the day before to fly out. They had to make sure all of those artists got to their hotel, and then to the studio on time. We had limousines driving all over Nashville.

Those Reunion tapings were all quite different. One of them was called "Young 'Uns", but we later changed the name to "Generations". It featured the sons and daughters of country music legends. We did another one called "Grass Roots to Bluegrass" - Mac Wiseman did most of the work in putting that reunion together. He not only found a lot of the artists and asked them to take part in it, but he also hosted the shows.

Our marathon week of filming also included a Reunion we called "Celebration". It featured a rare appearance by Chet Atkins. Bill Carlisle called and asked if we would like to have Chet join us for the next day's taping.

I told him, "Bill, we've been trying to get Chet for a long time."

Bill laughed, "Well, he's eating a bowl of ice cream right now, but he'll call you in twenty minutes."

When Chet called, he said he would love to do the show, but he didn't know how long his health would allow him to stay. He was still recovering from a recent hospital stay.

I said, "Just to have you on the set for a little while would be a blessing for us all."

Chet sat through our morning tapings, and when we broke for lunch, I figured he would have to leave. But he came to me and asked, "If I stay this afternoon, can I sing?"

Of course, Chet was known for his guitar playing, and many people didn't even know he could sing! During our next session, he sang, "I Still Write Your Name in the Snow", and it was one of the highlights of the entire show.

That same week, we produced one of the greatest Reunions we ever did, and it was one that was not Country at all. It was called "Rock and Roll Graffiti"! Of course, with me being an old rock and roll DJ, I was soaking it all up, as we watched almost forty stars from the 50s and 60s all walk into the studio.

The entire mood of "Rock and Roll Graffiti" was so special. It was very, very spiritual. It really turned into a religious experience. As they talked about the highs and lows of their careers and lives, everyone shared how they had found the Lord.

We shot that show over two days, but just before lunch on day one, Len Barry, who had had the hit "1-2-3", quietly walked out of the studio. The floor director came to me and said, "Larry, Len Barry is on the floor in the lobby. It might be a heart attack."

We called the EMTs, and then I explained everything to the group. I told them, "I believe in prayer, and I would like Scott Ross to say a prayer for Len right now."

Carl Gardner from the Coasters said, "Let's all hold hands."

Thirty-six rock and rollers all held hands while Scott prayed for Len's healing. Then Scott and his wife Nedra went to the lobby and prayed over Len.

Len stayed overnight in the hospital, but the next day, the doctors said that he was well enough to leave. He came straight to the studio, and we opened our second day of taping with him, singing his hit "1-2-3".

One of the highlights of that show came from Ketty Lester. Ketty had a huge hit with her version of "Love Letters". Many years later, she starred in the TV show Little House on the Prairie. I was a huge fan of Ketty. When I worked at WSM, I would announce her birthday every year on the air, and I'd always say how much I loved her. One year, someone who knew her had her call me at the station.

When we were planning the Rock and Roll Graffiti show, I invited Ketty. She told me she had stopped singing, and had basically retired, but I told her I'd still pay her if she'd just come and sit in the circle, even if she didn't sing.

Before the tapings, I had been warned that Mary Wilson of The Supremes could be a real diva. But we never saw that, because when Mary found out that Ketty Lester was there, she was just in awe. There was no way she could have an ego when she was a room with her hero. I watched Mary as she watched Ketty, and she could barely take her eyes off of her the entire time.

During one of the breaks, I asked Ketty if she would be willing to sing, and she said she would try. During and after her song, everyone just cried. It was so touching, and was one of the true highlights of all the Family Reunion shows.

The Rock and Roll Graffiti Reunion was just awesome, and it is a piece of musical history. But we lost a lot of money on it. We could never find an outlet to sell the show. I allowed PBS to use it for a fundraiser, and they aired it a couple times.

And we lost even more money on another Reunion that we shot during that period, called "Jesus Music". It has never been seen by anyone. While all of the bluegrass, country, and rock and roll people were very candid about their lives, many of the folks who were on the "Jesus Music" show were quite guarded. They were more focused on protecting their image, and it seemed like they didn't want to share stories of their ups and downs in life. We never released that one.

We had planned to air all six of the new Reunion series on The Nashville Network. TNN was really rocking, with a complete lock on the country music audience. Of course, that was our target audience!

But the TNN audience didn't appreciate (or buy) the "Rock and Roll Graffiti" series, and we didn't even air the "Jesus Music" Reunion. We were starting to get way in the hole. With all of our previous series, we usually sold about 5,000 units on the first airing. Then we would re-run the shows two more times, and each time we sold another 5,000 sets.

But I was so anxious to get the new shows to the fans that I decided we would air each Reunion just one time, and then we'd air the next one. I should have stayed with the business formula that had been working so well, but I didn't. Instead of selling a total of 15,000 units for each series, we sold only 5,000 - or even less. When people thought a new series would be coming out the next month, they held off on buying the current Reunion. It was a costly mistake.

But we tried to learn from our mistakes as we went back to our successful Country's Family Reunion formula. With each new series, we found that our CFR shows lifted the profile of each artist in a way that The Grand Ole Opry cannot do. CFR is on national television every Friday and Saturday. Even if an artist doesn't sing on that week's show, you'll still see them sitting in the room, and that raises their profile to the fans. It reminds them that the artists are still out there.

The fans always love it when T. Graham Brown is on the Reunion. He is so funny and sings so wonderful. The show also helped give his career a second wind.

T. has told me, "Larry, I'm not going to say that my career was in the doldrums, but I had people come up to me all the time, saying, 'I thought you was dead!'"

Connie Smith was one of the first people I asked to do the Reunion. Connie is so popular on the Opry. But she was with her kids overseas when we filmed the first show. When we did the next one, she said she didn't want to do it. She's never done any of them, and I honestly have no idea why. She would have loved it. It is her loss.

There have been some others who always said no when we asked them to be on the Reunion. Porter Wagoner refused to do CFR. One Saturday night, Porter was hosting the Opry Backstage show on The Nashville Network, and live on the air, one of the Opry stars asked Porter why he was not on our show - and he answered, "I've never been asked to be a part of that."

I called Porter a couple days later. He didn't answer, so I left him a message.

I said, "Porter, you know that I have asked you to come to every one of the Reunions. I personally asked you! And if you ever say that 'we didn't invite you' again, I will personally take out a full-page ad in Billboard Magazine that gives the true

Newspaper ad I did for the Robert J. Young Company

Where did your copier salesman go after he sold you a copier?

Hard to believe this was an ad for a copier company!

Don't wait until after you buy a copier to discover a serious problem. You learn that [...] from is unwilling or unable to service and maintain the machines they sell! **Robert J.** [...] **longer than Xerox™ because we are dedicated to pleasing our customers ove**[...] you with award-winning, factory trained service personnel who are computer-di[...] please you with Customer Relations Representatives whose only job is to meet you[...] we'll please you with the quality of the copiers we sell. Robert J. Young is Midd[...] Ricoh and Savin Dealer. We invite you to visit our offices and showroom at 809 [...] in Middle Tennessee.

ROBERT J. YO[...]

Work Safe...Not Sorry

on the WorkSafe System

Photo shoot for the WorkSafe System company. I couldn't strike that pose with my bad back today

ach week, we sent
ut these huge tapes
f the Larry Black
how to radio sta-
ons across the
ountry. Mailing
em was harder than
oing the show.

Interviewing the one of a kind Gary S. Paxton

Supervising Glen Campbell as he hosts a Youth Guidance special

Interviewing Tony Orlando during a show in Branson

With my dear friend Lynn Doerschuk and Branson legend Shoji Tabuchi

Larry, Luann, Nedra
Talley-Ross, Scott Ross

Scott and Nedra Ross are two of our closest friends

Filming Ernest Goes To Camp

Waiting for my next scene

What a trio!
Larry, Jim
Varney and
Iron Eyes
Cody

Enjoying a Mardi Gras event with Luann in 1984

Portraying Gov. Ned McWherter during a 1984 Gridiron show.

No we're not brothers! With sportscaster Eli Gold.

With Carroll O' Connor on the set of Heat of the Night

It doesn't look like a car commercial, but it is! Shooting an automobile
ad in Atlanta

The last time I sang and danced in the back of a pickup

Filming Web of Deceit with Linda Purl and James Read

Playing Gov. Mack Dean in the NBC Mini series Grass Roots with Katherine Helmond

With Lou Gossett Jr on the set of Sudie and Simpson

Filming I'll Fly
Away with Sam
Waterston

With Corbi[n]
Bernsen as w[e]
film The Cap[...]
Photo by Pet[er]
Gualtieri, Th[e]
West Kentuck[y]
News

With a friend between takes of Swamp Thing

Jim Ed Brown and Larry Black

Sidekick to Jim Ed Brown on The Nashville Network

Larry Black playing the judge in Pardon in the Sand

Larry Black and Charlie Monk

Skiing in Montana. Look at how much air I am getting!

On the slopes with
my big brother
Richard

With Luann, 2000

02 cruise with Luann

Larry's Country Diner is on the air!

The cast who would become my second family

Urban Cowboys. Larry, Renae and Nadine

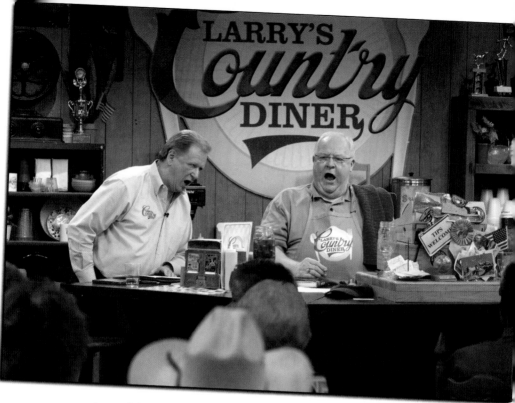

As Keith Bilbrey says, The cameras are always rolling...

And we don't care!

With Bill Anderson during a live Larry's Country Diner show

The Diner cast celebrating our 100th episode

My grandson Sam Bam was a huge hit when we joined me on the Diner

Larry and Renae visit with the great Mel Tillis

Christmas photo with all of our staff

With my friend
Gene Watson.
I thank him for
writing the
foreword for
my book.

On stage in
Branson during
Barbara Fairchild's
Teddy Bear song

Wowing the crowd with my guitar skills!

With the My Pillow man Mike Lindell, and Patrick Gottsch, the founder of
RFD TV

Cover boy for Lifestyles magazine

I loved Jim Ed Brown so much!

John Conlee is always one of our most popular guests

Giving some singing tips to Con Hunley

Cruising with some of our grandkids

Singing on the big finale with Rhonda Vincent

This gang of Cereal Killers crash the Diner

A surprise visit from a couple more grandsons

So much for Gene Watson's serious song!

With Joey and Rory during a live Diner show

State Senator Joe Haynes proclaims me a Tennessee Ambassador of Good Will

Sen. Joe Haynes, Larry, John Greenwood

What it looks like from the stage during our cruise show

True love...now 55 years

Flying home in style, thanks to Gus Arrendale

Back in Nashville after my near death experience in Montana

Luann, Larry, Johnelle and Randy Little

Reading just a few of the thousands of get well cards I received

Bill Anderson surprising me

A few of my friends surprised me with a special tribute-roast

The Diner Cast

Sharing a big laugh with Jean Shepard and Jimmy Capps

A wide shot that shows the Diner is really a TV studio!

The Oak Ridge Boys visit the Diner

Jeannie Seely during one of our first Diner shows

Coming out from behind the counter to talk to The Whites

Keith, Larry, Jimmy, Larry Gatlin and Renae

With Wendy Corr, my longtime friend Dan Miller and his daughter Hannah

With three people who've helped keep the Diner on the air. Ann Tarter, Gus Arrendale and Randy Little

Staff Christmas Party

Hosting Wednesday Night Prayer Meeting CFR with Bill Anderson

Another Wednesday Night Prayer Meeting CFR taping

The stars of one of our cruises

My Saturday morning brunch bunch. (Back Row) Ralph Emery, Don Cusic, Larry, Ray Stevens, Jim Stephany, Buddy Kalb, Norro Wilson. (Front Row) Do Cherry, Bergen White

Another year - another great lineup of artists

Raise your hand if you watch Larry's Country Diner every week!

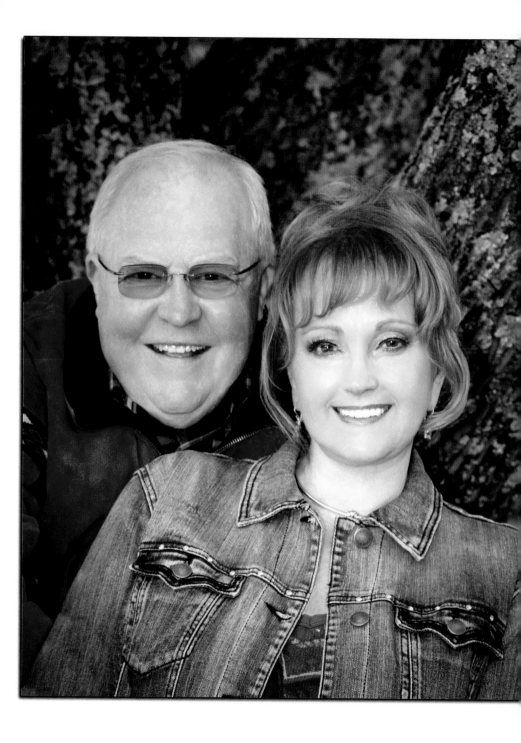

My favorite photo with Luann

Larry,Luann and our grandkids

With our children and grandchildren

Our family joins us on stage during th
Alaska Cruis

One of my favorite photo shoots
with our kids and grandkids

explanation. If you don't want to do the show, that's fine, but don't say we didn't invite you."

Years later, I met Porter in person and asked, "Why won't you do the Reunion?"

"Larry," he said, "I've spent forty years of my life being the star, and I'm not going to start now being second fiddle or part of a cast."

I talked to Bill Anderson, and Bill offered, "Larry, if you want me to sit out and let Porter host the show, I'll be more than happy to do that."

I said, "No. I'm not gonna do that. He's no better than the rest of the people sitting in that room."

"If Porter would come do that show, he would own the room," replied Bill. "He would own it! He would never be second fiddle to anyone."

Ironically, in 2007, we finally got Porter to say "yes". He agreed to do the show, but he got cancer, and passed away before the taping. Later, we had Porter's daughter come on the show, and she did a special tribute to her dad. She told us that he watched every show, and had always wanted to be a part of it. He loved all the Reunions, and he really would have enjoyed it.

We also just missed on another country music legend. In 2015, I told our staff, "Let's do our biggest and best CFR ever. I want to do a tribute to Merle Haggard. And I want Merle to be there to enjoy it all in person."

I had Terry Choate call Ronnie Reno to ask him to see if Merle would do it. Ronnie had been very close with Merle for decades. When he told Merle that I wanted to do the tribute to him, his response was, "Oh yes, by all means. That is something I need to do. I want to be there."

I was totally thrilled with Merle's response, and we started planning our biggest, most expensive, and most exciting Reunion taping. Every star in Nashville wanted to be a part of the show, especially with Merle there. We were actually turning some big-name artists away! We knew this series would lead to us being able to get different and even bigger stars for future tapings.

But in early 2016, just before we taped the show, Merle passed away. We were all heartbroken. But we went on with the tribute. All of the artists who had committed to being there with Merle kept their word and did the taping. It turned out to be one of our biggest sellers and most popular shows.

Mel Tillis had another reason for not appearing on the show: he wanted to use his own band. Even though he knew that we had the best musicians in Nashville, he was always more comfortable with his own guys. When I told him he couldn't bring his own band, I asked him to just come and sit and tell stories, and not sing at all, but he wouldn't. He would have been great.

But Mel loved the Reunion shows. We were doing a live show at the Starlite Theater in Branson, and he came to watch the show from the audience. Before it started though, he came to my dressing room and hopped up on the counter. We had never met before, and the first words out of his mouth were, "Hey L-L-Larry, I enjoy your shows!"

We probably could have talked Mel into coming on, if Grandpa Jones had stayed around. Grandpa passed away after our first tapings. We had planned to have him on our Christmas Reunion so that he could do his wonderful recitation of "The Christmas Guest". Since he died just before the taping, everyone's emotions were very raw. We played a tape of him doing "The Christmas Guest", and just filmed everyone as they sat there listening. Everyone was in tears, as they thought about all of their memories of Grandpa. It was one of the most moving moments in the history of the Reunions.

So many of the artists who were on those first Reunion shows have passed away. Probably 90% from that first show are now gone. When they left this earth, all of their road stories and funny and sad memories also went away. But thanks to the Reunions, we were able to save a lot of those stories. We got them down on tape just in time! At the time we started doing the CFR, we didn't realize that we were capturing true country music history. Now, when I look back at all of those awesome stars who are long gone, I just shake my head and give thanks to the good Lord for letting me play a role in keeping their legacy alive.

In 2008, we filmed a Family Reunion simply titled "Nashville". And it was one of our best series. It had so many wonderful artists, and one very special guest for that show was Patti Page. It was a huge surprise to me that she would even consider doing the show. But she was thrilled to get invited! When she got here, we found out that she had a great love for all of the country artists. She was a country girl at heart. Patti had fallen and hurt her hip the week before, and she had to sit as she sang her songs. Patti sang her classic "Tennessee Waltz", and then Jim Ed Brown led everyone in singing Patti's "How Much is That Doggie in the Window".

I approached John Conlee quite a few times, asking him to be on the Reunion. For whatever reason, he turned down my initial requests. But he finally joined us for one series, and once he did, he never wanted to miss another. He has been one of our most frequent guests. He always sings so great, and he is a fan favorite. A few years ago, as a thank-you for letting him be a part of the show, John gave me a pair of his "Rose Colored Glasses". Whenever I put them on, the entire world looks nicer.

While we sometimes had to invite an artist a couple times before they finally appeared on the show, quite often the stars were calling us, hoping to be on. The William Morris Agency called me and said, "Roy Clark wants to do the next Country's Family Reunion."

I said, "We would love to have to Roy! But you need to understand that this is not for big bucks. We only pay the AFTRA scale."

"He wants to do it," they insisted. "The pay does not matter."

Roy ended up being on quite a few of our series! He was always magical.

John Rich of "Big and Rich" has been on a couple of our Reunions, too. Larry Gatlin asked him to come on, and John really enjoyed being with everyone. Randy Travis also joined, as he recovered from his stroke. He couldn't sing, but he added so much warmth and joy to the room just by being there. He laughs so easily, and he has a huge, beautiful smile. While he couldn't talk very well, he could still communicate through his eyes and his expressions, and he has the greatest laugh.

Before he became the superstar that he is today, Blake Shelton was also on one of our early CFRs. He sang his first hit, "Austin", and "Ol' Red". I'm sure that Reunion was one of Blake's first TV appearances. He had a long mullet and wore a cowboy hat.

One of the biggest stars that has appeared on many of our shows is Vince Gill. Vince dropped in at the last minute for one of the tapings, and when he found out how much fun they were, he came back. Vince has always been a real good guy with us, and with all the other artists. The thing that makes Vince such a great guest is that he is always willing to open himself up and share his feelings. He has cried on the show probably as much as anyone else. His willingness to show how touched he is really touches the viewers.

When we were going to film the "Tribute to Bill Anderson CFR", we knew that Bill couldn't host the show himself, so we decided to ask Vince.

Terry Choate and I met with Vince over lunch. Terry is the man who has always booked all of the artists for the CFR and Diner. We told Vince that we wanted him to host the Tribute to Bill, and he said he would love to, but that we would need to go through his management. Then he added: "They will tell you 'No'."

Just like he said, when we went to them, they turned us down. A couple weeks later, we met with Vince again, and told him his management had, in fact, said "no".

"Good! I'll do it!" he replied.

Vince did a marvelous job hosting the show.

Our Tribute to Bill Anderson Country's Family Reunion came in 2010. That year, and that Reunion, were both big turning points for our company. I'll get to the Bill Anderson CFR in just a bit, but first, I hear some raindrops…

NOAH'S CALLING...

On May 1, 2010, it started raining in Nashville. It was also raining in Bellevue, Tennessee - where we lived, and where our offices were located. The night the rain started, I worked late in my office. Luann had recently bought me an office full of furniture out of the Atlanta Market. She had paid a lot more for everything than I'd wanted her to, but she thought it was pretty. It included a huge, heavy desk, which took up most of the room. I was working on my computer at my desk, when the electricity went off.

I waited a few minutes, and when the lights didn't come back on, I decided that I might as well go home. Just a mile from our offices, our house sits up on a hill. That night, we had eight of our ten grandkids staying with us. Since it was raining so hard, they all had to play inside. The next morning, we were going to take them home, but when we started down the hill, we quickly discovered we couldn't get out, because there was water at the bottom of our subdivision. The power had gone off in that section, too.

We had a grill outside, and I started grilling some chicken to feed all of our grandkids. I thought we could make a party out of it. As we enjoyed our cookout, we had no idea about the destruction that was occurring, less than a mile away from us. I knew our offices were 500 feet above the floodplain, so I really wasn't all that worried.

I should have worried.

The flood completely wiped out the gas station located across the highway from our company. The water also tore through the Shoney's a couple hundred yards up the road.

When we were finally able to get to our offices, there was water up to our knees in the parking lot. When Jared and I walked in the front door, we waded into water. It had actually gone down quite a bit, but at its highest, there was almost ten feet of water inside our building.

But the electricity was somehow back on. I had a furniture piece that looked like a fireplace, and the lamps on top of it were still on and burning. When he saw that all the electrical outlets were underwater, Jared asked, "Dad, do you think it's wise for us to be wading in this water with the power on?"

I said, "Probably not."

We went outside and pulled the breakers to turn the power off.

We had a door that had a life-size painting of Porter Wagner on the back of it, and as we made our way through the offices, that door floated down the hall toward to me! It was upside down, and the painting was on top, and by some small miracle, it was still dry. We still have it on the wall of our office today.

Everything in our offices was floating all over the building, though. The only thing that wasn't floating was my desk, if only because it was so heavy. The papers on my desk and my computer were totally dry… but every other piece of furniture had been turned upside down. I found my checkbook in my desk. I put it and my computer in my car.

Later that day, I was called by a guy who owned a building across the street. He told me there were some men from Chicago who were going to do rehabs on the buildings. When they saw images of the Great Nashville Flood, disaster recovery companies started coming in mass. The crew from Chicago started clearing our stuff out that night. By the next morning, they had all of our damaged furniture and appliances out in the parking lot. All the local waste removal companies were totally booked, so I called a friend who owned a dump truck. He said he would bring in all of his trucks, if I'd let him rebuild our buildings.

Unlike thousands of people in Nashville, we didn't lose our power for very long. Since we had electricity, our air conditioner was always running, and that really helped the drying-out process. It also helped us keep away any mold. But we ultimately had to replace the air conditioners, as well as all of our furniture.

We had all of our legal contracts from Country's Family Reunion and Larry's Country Diner stored at the office. They were signed by all of the artists who had been on our shows. Every one of those contracts had been underwater. I called the Robert J. Young Company, and they came out and picked up all the papers that were water-soaked, dried them all out, and digitized each and every document. They also gave us back the originals too, so we didn't lose any of those important items.

We knew we wanted to rebuild our offices, but we also knew it would not be cheap. It was going to cost us $300,000 to rebuild, and we only had $40,000 in the bank. But FEMA told us to go ahead and rebuild, and that they would pay for it. At the last minute, however, FEMA decided against helping us. We would be on our own. I'm sure we were not the only ones.

I met with Renae Johnson ("Renae the Waitress" on the Diner) and asked her, "What should we do?"

She answered, "Let's do what we always do when we're in trouble... let's expand!"

My brother-in-law, Bill Bass, took over the daunting task of overseeing the rebuilding our two office buildings. Bill had the ability to keep the rebuild flowing while the rest of us gave our attention to planning a new reunion and raising the required cash to continue going forward. I couldn't have asked for anyone better than Bill. He is just the best, in so many ways. We couldn't have done it without all of his help.

We hoped our next Family Reunion would help pay some of our rebuilding bills. We sent out a letter to all of the people who had bought videos from us over the years, asking them to 'pre-order' the Bill Anderson Tribute CFR. We were putting our trust in our viewers, and they were putting theirs in us... as they sent in their full payments for a show we hadn't even filmed yet!

We had a mailing list of 70,000, but we could only afford to send out 5,000 at a time. As the money came in from those, we could afford to send out another 5,000. We did that for a couple months; and in each letter, we told them all the artists we hoped would be on the show. We didn't have a firm promise from anyone except Bill, but we hoped that most of those we asked to do the show would be there.

Thanks to those loyal viewers, we had almost one million dollars in the bank before we walked into that studio! It totally blew our minds! We got $980,000 in the bank in less than two months! That money not only paid for the production cost, but it also allowed us to rebuild our offices. After that huge success, we began offering all of our Family Reunions for pre-order. That took a lot of stress out of us trying to borrow money to pay for each show.

Over the years, we've had so many requests from people who wanted to sit in on a CFR taping. I understood the requests. Who wouldn't want to be a fly on the wall as all those country legends shared their songs and stories? But the Reunion tapings were always closed to the public.

In an effort to give the viewers a little taste of what the tapings are like, we decided to do a live, onstage version of the show for two nights in Branson, Missouri. It took place in the RFD Theater, which had been Ray Stevens' theater. The theater had 2,000 seats, and we sold it out both nights. But we lost money on it! RFD made money, but we didn't.

It was hard to do a live CFR. People came expecting to see 30 different artists, and there was no way we could afford to pay all of those acts. If you have an audience of 2,000 people, there's just no way that you can also pay 30 artists. Even if you could, they all wouldn't have time to sing even one song each. When we did the television tapings, we filmed for eight hours a day, over the course of two days!

As I was wrapping up writing this book, we booked another live version of the CFR in Branson. We had a half-dozen artists on the live show, and did two nights at The Mansion Theater. So, who knows what the future might hold.

I get asked "What was your favorite CFR series?", or "Which Reunion are you most proud of?" That's pretty easy. A couple years ago, we did the "Wednesday Night Prayer Meeting", and then followed that with "Another Wednesday Night". Those were so special. Everyone who was part of those knew that they were in the presence of the Lord. Ricky Skaggs told me, "This is a little bit of what Heaven is going to be like."

It really was an anointed day. It touched the lives of so many people.

We might like to think that we are in control of everything in our lives, but we are not. I always try to remind myself that everything happens for a reason; good, bad or in-between, it happens for a reason. I still don't know the reason I had that horrible accident four years ago. I think maybe our Wednesday Night Prayer Meeting Family Reunion is something that I was supposed to do, that maybe I wouldn't have done without that accident.

But I'm not sure I handled the Wednesday Night Prayer Meeting Reunion right. As I look back at them, I wonder if I failed God with those two series. I think I should have tried to reach more people with those. I should have gotten them on every Christian TV station in the world. I truly regret that more people didn't get to see them. I think we should have possibly done a live version of that as well. It would have been similar to the Gaither Homecoming shows. But again, only the Lord knows what the future holds.

THE DINER

Larry's Country Diner premiered on RFD TV on August 3, 2009. As I am writing this, we have just celebrated our 11 year anniversary. Back when we first went on the air, I had no idea if we'd last 11 episodes, let alone 11 years!

People often ask me how I came up with the idea for the Diner. So I guess I'd better tell the entire story right here.

I had always made "goal lists". I had different goals that I wanted to accomplish in my life, and I wrote them out in a list on paper. One of those was to do a different kind of interview show.

After all my years in radio, I had always wanted to do an interview-type TV show. I enjoyed talking to artists and entertainers, but I wanted to do it in a different way. I didn't want to sit in front of a fireplace, or with a couch and desk. That had been done, and I wanted to try something different.

So I came up with the idea of shooting the show in a diner. We never said what town or state the diner was in, but we assumed it was in a small town somewhere, and we'd act like the local cable TV company had sent over a little crew at lunchtime. The local sheriff would happen to play the guitar, and he'd stop by each day, and he'd be there when a star dropped in to get something to eat.

I think one of the most important pieces of the puzzle that fell into place was when we got Jimmy Capps. Jimmy is a country music legend. We knew we couldn't afford an entire band - and even if we could, that would have destroyed the idea that this was just a little diner where the stars came to relax.

It had to be scary for Jimmy to know that we shot every show "live to tape". Knowing that we are not going to stop and do a retake, even if he really messes up, is a lot of pressure to put on someone and when you also add in the fact that he is the one and only band member, that even multiples the pressure! But Jimmy is the kind of person who could handle the stress. Jimmy can play like he's an entire band. The artists don't need anything but his one guitar. He is so well-known and loved by all the country artists, and they trust him enough to sing their songs with only his guitar for their music. I don't know if we'd still be on the air if we hadn't have hired Jimmy.

Jimmy's wife Michele is someone who we get a lot of comments on. She sings harmony on most of the shows, and of course she's always there to support Jimmy. People think she is one of the cast, but I didn't want to add a sixth person to the show. She has as much visibility as any of the cast, but she's not an official cast member. But Michele adds so much to each show, when she sings with the artists. I know the Diner has also been a blessing to her. She has thanked me numerous times for allowing her to sing with her heroes.

Jimmy Capps' autobiography, "The Man in Back", came out a year before this book. Jimmy's was such a great one that it finally pushed me into doing mine. He is a man of very few words, so I am honored that he chose to write a few for my book.

"I had played on the Grand Ole Opry for more than fifty years, and I had played on hundreds of hit songs, but most people didn't know my name until I became The Sheriff on Larry's Country Diner!

Larry didn't know if the show would last more than one season, but after we had taped a half-dozen shows, I started to think, 'This show is really good. I think it might catch on.'

And it did.

Now, after more than eleven years, all of the cast is still there. Renae, Nadine, Larry, Keith and I have all managed to hang in there. Larry has gone through so many health troubles, but he is tough as a nickel steak. He's had to have some occasional guest hosts, and while they are always very good, if one of the cast members is gone, the show is just not complete. It would not be the same with any of us missing. It would be like when Don Knotts left "The Andy Griffith Show". Mayberry was never the same without Barney. Even though they continued making great shows, it never had the same feel.

I love the feeling I get when I'm doing the Diner and Country's Family Reunion. On both shows, I get to work with people I dearly love. On the CFR, for more than twenty years, I've been able to sit there and listen to those country music legends tells all of their stories.

Larry was totally responsible for the Family Reunion shows, but he always stayed behind the scenes. He paid to produce the show for more than two decades, and the viewers didn't even know he was involved in it. Of course, he enjoyed acting on TV and in the movies, so I'm sure he would have enjoyed hosting the Reunions, but he was willing to give that job to Bill Anderson. He knew what a great host Bill would be, so Larry stayed behind the camera. Larry didn't have to be the star. There are not many people who would do that.

Everybody in the Diner cast truly loves each other. They showed that love last year when I had an emergency gallbladder surgery. We were in Branson, Missouri for a week of live shows, but I got very sick after the first two shows, and was taken to the hospital, where I spent the next ten days. Instead of enjoying their free time having fun in Branson, the cast of the Diner spent the week with me. They were at the hospital round the clock. When they had to go do their show each evening, Moe Bandy and his wife came and stayed with me and Michele until all the cast got back. It really touched me that everyone was there for me.

But I was touched even more when Larry got ready to leave Branson. He gave me an envelope that contained a check for my full pay. Even though I could only do two shows, he paid me for the entire week.

I wrote my autobiography last year. I was so surprised and totally humbled at the positive response to my book. Larry probably should have written his life story before I wrote mine, but I'm sure his will be worth the wait. I can never thank him enough for letting me be a part of the Family Reunions and Diner, and now a part of his book."

– Jimmy Capps

Renae Johnson had been running my business office for a number of years. She joined my company when we started producing Country's Family Reunion. When we were planning the Diner, I asked her to be our waitress on the show. She had never been a waitress and her only TV experience had come when she was a contestant on "The Price is Right"! So of course, I thought she would be perfect! She played the role so well, people thought she was a real waitress! She really became "Renae the waitress" to the public. But she had been an important part of my group for many years. Everyone just loves Renae.

Renae's husband Phil is a multi-talented man. He has worked as our official photographer since the Diner began. He took all of the Diner photos that you see in this book. Phil has also written some very big Gospel hits, and he is a great singer. I gave him the chance to share his singing talent with our fans when I invited him to appear on the Wednesday Night Prayer Meeting Reunion. He did a wonderful job, and was one of the highlights of the entire series.

Here are a few thoughts from Renae. Hopefully she will say good things about me!

"I met Larry in church. He was one of our Sunday School teachers! My husband Phil knew him from their work in the Christian music field. I was a flight attendant with America West Airlines, but I wanted to stop flying, and was looking for something else to do.

In 1998, Larry had just completed the first Country's Family Reunion, and he was looking for a secretary. He was using temps at the time. I met with him and told him all my 'qualifications' to be a secretary. I said, 'Larry, I can serve coffee and I can answer the phone.'

He said, 'You're hired!'

Eleven years after I joined the company, Larry announced that he was going to start a weekly TV show called 'Larry's Country Diner'. As he planned the show, he told me, 'Since you are so good serving coffee, you can be our waitress in the Diner.'

The first indication that people were watching came when my husband and I were driving to Arizona. We stopped at a Dairy Queen in Arkansas, and the guy in the drive-up window recognized me as he handed us our ice cream! Phil teased me about being a 'big star' all the way to Arizona.

I wrote my book, called 'Diary of the TV Waitress', to answer questions that people always asked about the show. Those questions included things like 'Do you serve real food?' (Yes we do) and 'Is Nadine a man or woman?' (We always got that! Yes, she is a woman!)

But the number one question has always been, 'Is it a real Diner?' Of course, it is not. It was just a set on a television soundstage. But I think the main reason that people thought it was real is because I acted like a real waitress throughout the show. That was Larry's idea. When we started, he instructed me, 'Just act like there is no TV camera there. If you need to walk in front of the camera, or even the artist as they sing, go ahead and serve your food.' That also got me a few complaints from people who said, 'That white-haired lady keeps walking in front of everyone!'

I answered the phone at the office one day, and the woman on the other line said, 'I'm never watching that show again! That woman is not a waitress! I have been a waitress for years and she does not serve the food correctly.' I laughed and said, 'Well, I am Renae, and I will admit that I am not a real waitress. I'm just acting on the show.'

One of my most important jobs on the show is to remind Larry to read The Promise, as we start each show. He would often forget, and if I forgot to remind him, the viewers would just bombard our phones with calls, asking why we didn't do it. The viewers get to know us, and they really feel like we are part of their family. I think that's because we always try to keep in mind that the audience is the most important part of the show. Without them, there is no reason for us to be doing it.

I worked for Larry more than 21 years, and he always allowed me to be honest with him. If I thought he was wrong, or had screwed up on something, he always let me tell him my true opinion. I never had to hold back my thoughts, like a lot of employees do.

I would have been very content to just serve coffee and answer the phone, but Larry always pushed me to be more and do more. He was always encouraging me to step out of my comfort zone. I would never have written the books I did without his support. He always wants people to use their creative talents.

When I think of Larry, I think of his heart. In 2008, a couple weeks after my son Justin was killed in a car accident, I was in my office. And from his office, Larry could hear me crying. He came in and prayed, 'Lord Jesus, just help Renae. Ease her pain…' That meant everything to me. His first response was to pray for me. Most bosses would not do that, and that's what I appreciated about him over the years. I watched him do the same thing for many other people who were struggling, and he would just start praying for them, whether they knew it or not."

I love Larry Black."

— Renae Johnson/Renae the Waitress

Without a doubt, the most popular character on Larry's Country Diner is Nadine. As I planned the show, I wanted to have a "church lady" drop by each week. She would be the town gossip. Mona Brown went to church with us, and she did this character called Nadine. I asked her to be the church lady, and to come up with a different sign for the church each week. I wanted to close out her segment with her saying, "I've got to go change the church sign."

I knew Nadine was going to be a star when we filmed our thirteenth episode. Larry Gatlin was the guest star. He hadn't met Nadine's character yet, and when she walked in, she loudly stated: "Well, Larry Gatlin! I haven't seen you since we were separated at birth."

Gatlin was speechless, and I knew if she could make Larry Gatlin speechless, Nadine must be something very, very special!

I knew Nadine/Mona Brown wouldn't be speechless when I asked her to say a few words in my book.

"I met Larry in church. His family and my family attended the same church, and we all got to know each other very well. I had come up with a funny character that I performed at the church parties and events. I called her 'Nadine the Church Lady'.

Larry was an Elder in our church, and my husband Dave was also on the church board with him. We got to know him quite well over the years, and I really respected his willingness to speak out about important issues our church was dealing with. I also admired how open he was, when it came to praying for others, and for himself and his family. He never made any decisions without first praying and listening to see where God wanted him to go.

One day, Larry called me and told me about his idea for a TV show, and he asked me to do my Nadine character for a five minute segment on the show. None of us had any idea how long the show would last. If I had known I would have to come up with 11 years' worth of funny material, I would have probably said 'No!'

While I play the Church Lady character, I am truly thankful that Larry has allowed God to be a part of our show. I have had so many people tell me how much it means to them, that we are all willing to share our faith and talk about God on the Diner. There are not many TV shows that do that these days.

I also want to say that, while Larry gets most of the attention and press, I know that his wife is truly the backbone of his life and career. She is a very sharp person. Luann is so kind and loving, and she is devoted to Larry and their children and grandchildren. I respect her in many ways.

Larry is a very giving person. He has done so much for so many people. I thank Larry for putting his confidence in me. He had total faith in me, even though he knew I was not a professional comedian and I had no television experience!

I know all of the other cast members will say the same thing, but this is the truth…I totally feel that every member of that cast is my family. It's not just the cast members, but also the spouses of each one of us. Larry and Luann, Renae and Phil, Keith and Emy Joe, Jimmy and Michele, and of course me and Homer, we all truly love each other."

– Mona Brown/Nadine

One of Nadine's most popular episodes came when Linda Davis was our guest. Linda had the award-winning mega hit with Reba McEntire called "Does He Love You", an almost operatic duet between two women who are fighting over the same man. On the Diner, and in the spur of the moment, Linda asked Nadine to sing Reba's part of the song, and the result was one of the funniest moments in the history of the Diner.

For some reason, a lot of people think Nadine is a man! I guess it's because she has strong features and big hands. But she is indeed a woman! In real life, she is very attractive, and is just a sweet lady. Well, she's not always sweet. Nadine once told me, "You are the only man I know who could walk through a pile of manure and come out smellin' like a rose."

I also wanted to have an announcer for the show. Keith Bilbrey was one of WSM radio's most popular DJs. He also announced on the Opry, and did a lot of TV things for The Nashville Network back when it was still on. But WSM fired Keith just before we started taping the Diner. And since I knew that same feeling of losing a job, I thought I should give him a call. I'll let Keith tell you the rest of his story.

"I'd just been let go from the Opry after 35 years. I didn't know what I was going to do. I didn't know where my career was going, or even if I had a career anymore. I had been in broadcasting since I was 16 years old. It was all I ever wanted to do, and when I found myself out of work, I really wasn't qualified to do anything else. I guess I could have gotten a job as a greeter at a store. I like meeting people.

It was at that very low point in my life that Larry Black called me, and I remember the call like it was yesterday. Larry explained, 'I'm thinking about doing a show and I'd like you to be a part of it. But I can't pay you very much.' I laughed, 'Larry, you are talkin' to an unemployed man.'

Larry told the cast that we would not use any script or teleprompter. That can be a challenge, but it allows us to be ourselves, as we just ad-lib everything. But I usually write a general outline of what I want to say. I try to find out what I can about each artist, and I always write out a 'menu special' that features food related to the artists or their songs.

Larry's wife Luann came up with the line that I close the show with. That's a line that I hear a couple times a day when I'm out in public. People will yell, 'The cameras are always rollin' and we don't care!' It always makes my day, and I know they are watching.

I am truly surprised that the show has lasted as long as it has. We thought the Diner might be on for a year. We just try to have the most fun we can possibly have on each show, and I think if we are having fun, the viewers at home will have fun watching us. They can also see that the cast really is a family. Not only do I enjoy working with all these people, but I know they all love me, and I love them. We truly care about each other.

People really got emotionally invested in the show. The viewers care about us. When we have a death in our family, or if Larry is in bad health, the viewers really care. They know we are real people, and they pray for us. How many other shows have viewers who are praying for their cast members?

When I started on the Diner, I was an out-of-work radio announcer. Now, I'm busier than I've ever been. In addition to the diner, I am on the Mike Huckabee Show on TBN, and also on The Music City Roots Show. I owe all of that to Larry's Country Diner, and to Larry Black."

– Keith Bilbrey

So that was my concept for the show. Now all we had to do was get it on the air! The Country's Family Reunion was already on RFD TV, so we committed to buying another time slot for Larry's Country Diner.

I probably need to explain what I mean, when I say "buy a time slot". RFD TV works a little different than most other networks. People have no idea that we had to pay RFD to be on. RFD never paid us. We had to pay for the production of the show, plus we had to pay RFD to air the show. We lost $600,000 each year for the first two years of the Diner.

In an effort to save money, we taped four shows in one day. We filmed the first thirteen shows in a one-week period. But it still cost us $150,000 a day to tape the Diner. We lost so much money... but we were becoming stars!

We had no sponsors for the first few seasons of the show, and every time we aired a new Diner show, we were losing money. But I had faith in the show, and it was so fun to do! I was having such a ball that I announced we would keep doing it until it stopped being fun, or until all my money ran out - whichever came first!

Luckily for us, and also for the fans of the Diner, we were able to find some sponsors. We wouldn't be on the air today without Randy Little and PFI/Boot Daddy, Gus Arrendale and Springer Mountain Farms, and Ann Tarter and her Tarter gate and farm equipment company. They have all helped us pay for the production of the show. LCD has never made a profit, but our sponsors helped us pay some of our bills.

Randy Little and the guys at PFI/Boot Daddy in Springfield, Missouri are much more than just people who advertise on our show. They are true friends. We have spent much more time together off the air than on the set. Randy and I have laughed, cried, lived and almost died together. I'll get to the almost dying part later.

Randy had enjoyed great success with PFI for more than 30 years, before he began sponsoring our show. The official name of their company was "PFI Western Wear". But for some reason, I could never remember or say their three little initials of "PFI". Since I always had a brain-lock with PFI, I just called them Boot Daddy, and I said it so much that they had to spend more than

$15 000 to change the outside sign on their store to "PFI, home of Boot Daddy"!

For years, Jean Shepard kept telling me she knew someone who would sponsor our show. I didn't pay much attention to it - but one year, Gus Arrendale went on one of our cruises, and he just fell in love with us. Of course we had already fallen in love with him...everybody does!

Gus' smile lights up any room he is in, and he has such an amazing personality. His around-the-clock hard work, promotion, and his one-of-a-kind persona have helped him turn his Springer Mountain Farms into a billion-dollar company. The Diner has helped Gus sell a lot of chicken, but it has also helped make him a star.

Of course, Gus is known as the chicken man, and Ann Tarter of Tarter USA is so sweet. Like I did with Randy Little's PFI, I also had major trouble trying to remember the name of Ann's company and website. My brain-freezes on the air actually once caused Ann to have to pay to get her entire website changed! She used the web domain of Tarter Farm and Ranch Equipment... but I told the viewers to go to Tarter-Gate-Dot-Com. Ann quickly changed their domain to that, and by the time they got it done, I started directing people to Tarter-USA-Dot-Com, so they had to quickly get that website! To be honest, when we started the show, the Internet was fairly new, and I knew absolutely nothing about it. I had no idea what a domain name was, and how important it was that you sent people to the exact name!

Of the three main sponsors, Ann might be the smartest person in the room. She knows computers. In her college days, she could hack anyone's computer. She has taken the lead in her company, and she is such a wonderful person. The sponsors all like what the show does for them. It creates an image for them.

A part of the show that has been there from the start is The Promise. My family used to read a promise each morning before breakfast. We learned scripture verses that way. I can't think of any other TV shows that read a Bible scripture before they start, but the viewers at home identify with it. People say to me, "Thank you for your expression of faith on the show, and thank you for not hiding from that."

I say, "I can't hide from it. It is who we are."

Even off camera, before we start taping the shows each day, we say a prayer over the cast, crew and audience. We pray that we will touch the viewers and bless the people who watch our show.

Those prayers must have worked, because our little show began to catch on. And before we knew it, 1.5 million people were watching us each month! RFD TV has an older audience. They are moms and dads and grandmas and grandpas. They love country music. They love our country. They love God. They are exactly who we are!

For the first thirteen episodes, I featured all of my grandkids. I had three sons and ten grandkids. And for each show, we made a Western-style "wanted poster", that had a large photo of one of my grandkids on it. The poster called them a "Cereal Killer", meaning they ate cereal! It was a funny way of showing a photo of my grandkids on TV, and my sons were the fathers of the cereal killers. It was a running gag for our first shows.

We never used a script of any kind for the Diner. Everything has always been ad-libbed, all of Keith's tosses to the breaks and anything that I say. Nadine writes her jokes ahead of time, but she ad-libs them all during the show. In our first years of the Diner, we used to air segments of old Opry shows and early Country's Family Reunion shows. They were legacy pieces, which paid tribute to stars who had passed away.

Our premiere episode of Season 3 of the Diner featured a duo that not many people had heard of. I didn't know them. As a matter of fact, I kept getting their names mixed up throughout the entire show. Their names were Joey and Rory. It was love at first sight for everyone in the Diner, and for all of our viewers. We could tell there was something very, very special about this couple from the first moment we met them.

I'll get back to talking about the Diner, but first I want to say a few things about Joey and Rory.

A short time after their successful appearance on our show, Rory came to me with a request: he wanted me to help them get their own television show. He said, "I'd like to partner with you."

"No," I answered, and then I explained: "Rory, you don't need me. I can't bring anything to your show that you can't do on your own. It would be foolish for you to take me on as a partner. I would just take away from any money you will make."

But I did offer him all the advice I could. I also introduced him to the folks at RFD TV, and I promised Rory that if they ended up doing a show, I would do everything I could to get it exposed, I would even air it in one of our timeslots.

Rory purchased video cameras and hired a couple young men to help him shoot a Joey and Rory Christmas show. I was at their home when they shot some of it, and when he showed me the finished video, I thought it was one of the most special Christmas programs I had ever seen.

I kept my word to Rory, and we aired the special two times in our Country's Family Reunion spot. We also aired it twice during LCD's airtime. The owner of RFD TV, Patrick Gottsch, liked what he saw, and said he'd love to have the Joey and Rory Show on RFD. Of course, like our shows, he wanted Joey and Rory to pay for it. They did, and once they hit the air, they were able to get a sponsor to help them finance it.

Joey and Rory loved to visit our home in Red Lodge, Montana. They took their entire crew and did a lot of filming there. They even made use of a drone, and it filmed them as they rode horses and shot guns.

Rory has always given me credit for helping them. Their first appearances on The Diner and Family Reunion shows put them in front of a big TV audience. Rory says my telling him "no" was the best thing that could have happened to them. They knew they would have to do everything on their own, and it opened up Rory's mind to produce, shoot, write and direct. And his talent continued to grow, as he branched out into making movies and writing best-selling books.

When Joey got sick and was dying from cancer, I didn't understand why. She was such a wonderful person. I prayed a very sincere prayer to God as I offered, "Why not take me instead of Joey? I'm old. Take me. I don't understand why you heal me and not her. I appreciate it that you saved me, but I think you might have made the wrong choice."

When we lose someone like Joey, I think those of us that God has allowed to stay here on Earth, we probably have a deeper obligation to do what we do as best as we can. We need to be the best person we can be.

After Joey died, Rory took a bunch of people who were close to Joey up to our Montana home for three days. It was a place where they could be together, as they got away from everything for a little while. We have stayed close to Rory since then.

For the first year after Joey died, Rory would not sing or perform. He didn't want to go onstage without Joey. But we invited him to just come on and sit with us during one of our Family Reunion tapings. That eased him back into everything a little bit. Then he came on and sang, and when he felt the reaction from the audience, just total love, he finally began performing again. I'm so happy we played a small role in getting him back to where he needs to be.

The name of the book you're reading right now is based on the motto of Larry's Country Diner, "Where the cameras are always rolling... and we don't care!" My wife Luann is the one who came up with that motto. We were driving to our first taping, and Luann said, "You need something special to end the show with, something everyone will remember. You don't want to just say, 'We'll see you next week.'"

The saying comes from the fact that, once we start taping the show, we go straight through. If there are any mess-ups, we leave them in. We don't stop. We do that for a couple reasons. The first is that it saves us money! In order for us to film four shows in one day, we have to go straight through. We don't have time to do a second take. The other reason we do it that way is because it gives the show a sense of live, spontaneity that is hard to find on TV today. And the stars just love it.

It was on our very first show that we put that "the tape never stops rolling and there are no re-takes" rule to the test. Bill Anderson was the guest star on our premiere episode, and the first song ever sang on the Diner was Bill's classic, "Po' Folks". But just as Jimmy Capps started the play the song, he dropped his guitar pick on the floor. It took him about fifteen seconds to pick it up, but we just kept rolling!

But things got really interesting when Bill sang his second song. It was the big hit he'd written for George Straight called "Give It Away". He was well into the song, when Bill laughed and said, "I started this song too fast. I can't sing that fast."

Again, we kept rolling, and a minute later, Bill completely forgot the words… words to the major hit that he had written! As he continued to search his mind for the words, he looked at the Sheriff and said, "We should have rehearsed this!"

While Bill Anderson was our first-ever Diner guest, later in that show, I walked out to a table where I interviewed the legendary cartoonist Guy Gilchrist. Guy had drawn the classic "Nancy and Sluggo" comic strip. But while we taped the premiere episode, Guy created wonderful drawings of the Diner cast.

If you watch that first episode, or any episode from the first season (and you can see every one of them at www.countryroadtv.com), you will see that we had less than ten people sitting in the Diner! And our entire "crowd" was made up of our staff and family members! Our show wasn't on the air yet, and no one knew anything about it, so it was tough finding a live audience.

For our second episode, we made the unique choice of comedian James Gregory as our guest. He didn't sing, but he told the most hilarious jokes and stories throughout the entire hour.

We kept the cameras rollin', through many other instances where most other shows would have yelled, "Cut!" During the first couple seasons, Keith Bilbrey had a tough time remembering the name of the show! He called it "Larry's Classic Diner", and "The Country Café", and we just left it in.

During a show with T. Graham Brown, Renae dropped a bunch of silverware on the floor. T. Graham asked me, "Where did you get that waitress?"

On another show, Renae dropped a glass and it shattered… right in the middle of Gene Watson singing! Gene knew we weren't stopping, so he just smiled and kept right on. He didn't miss a word.

In Season 9, when Exile was performing, I accidentally (I think) hit Renae's arm, just as she walked by carrying two big plates of food. As she tried to catch them, Keith hit her arm again, on purpose. She dropped all the food. As she picked some up, she threw it at Keith. Then she and I "exchanged" pieces of pie… all over our shirts. It turned into a food fight, and it ended with food all over the floor. The Exile guys just stood there and watched, thinking, "there is no way they are going to air all of this"… but we did!

On one show, Nadine forgot her own name. On another, a very honest Jean Sheppard told me that my shirt was ugly. There was never a dull moment! The viewers tuned in because they had no idea what was coming next… none of us did!

When Vince Gill and Paul Franklin came on, Vince made a sarcastic and very funny comment toward me, and I said, "I don't have to put up with this." I grabbed my towel and walked off the set, out the door.

It was funny, but as soon as I got outside I thought, "Now what am I going to do?"

But Keith picked up and went on with the show. I went around the back and came through the kitchen door, and I started bringing food to everyone's table. Vince started laughing as he was singing. It was fun.

One of Bobby Bare's big hits is called "The Winner" - and that song is so long and has so many verses, I don't know how he can remember it all. But when he did it on the show, he only did about half of it.

When he got done, I said, "You didn't do the whole song."

"You want me to do it all?" he asked.

I said, "Yes I do!"

So he went right back into it, and included all of the verses.

When Mickey Gilley was on the Diner, he forgot the words to his all-time biggest hit, "Don't the Girls All Get Prettier at Closing Time". I'm sure he had sung that song thousands of times, but live on the Diner, he totally blanked out. He couldn't remember the second verse. Jimmy Capps was playing guitar, and he could sense that Mickey wanted to stop, but Jimmy just kept on playin'. Mickey finally stood there and said, "I have no idea where I'm at."

He kept apologizing, but I told him things like that are what made the Diner different and fun. But I could tell the mess-up was no laughing matter to him. As we went to the break, he continued trying to remember the second verse, and when we went back on the air, Mickey sang the song again, this time with the second verse! He really wanted to redeem himself. But we kept it all in the show, with no editing. It aired with the mess-up, and with Mickey's redemption.

I love to see the stars' reactions as we tape the show. They are used to doing television that is so heavily produced and scripted, with long rehearsals, constant floor direction, camera changes and re-takes. So when they come on for the first time, and see the relaxed atmosphere that we have, that really allows them to relax, too.

The first time an artist comes on, they almost always comment at the end of the show that they can't believe the whole hour has passed and that the show is already over. The Diner is freeform TV, like it used to be back in the Golden Age of TV.

Sometimes people come on the show before they have ever seen it. But when the show airs, their sales go through the roof.

The first time Exile was on, they had no idea what it was about, and how many people watched. Nadine loves Exile. She loves to dance around them when they sing, and the group loves it. After the show aired, they called Terry Choate and said, "Man, it blew our website up! Anytime you want us, just call."

We used to have Exile on every August. During one of the shows, I was talking about our cruise, and one of the Exile boys said, "We'd like to go on your cruise."

I casually said, "We'll work that out."

About four months before the next cruise, they called and said, "When do we leave?"

"What?" I asked.

They said, "On our cruise."

I looked back at the tape, and saw that I had committed to them, so I called them back and said, "Let's go!" It cost me about $20,000 to take the group and their wives, but they were worth every penny! The group has always been ready to do the show anytime we call, because they know it will sell their product and increase their bookings.

Jim Ed Brown was on many of our CFR and Diner shows. In February of 2015, he came to watch a taping of our show with Jason Crabb. Jim Ed had been undergoing cancer treatments, and had a hat on, since he had lost a lot of his hair. Even though it was Jason's show, I asked Jim Ed to come up and sing a song. He sang "Pop A Top", with Jimmy Capps playing guitar.

It turned out to be the last time Jim Ed ever sang on television. He died a few months later. He was such a sweet man. The time we spent together on "You Can Be a Star" really drew us closer together, and we stayed close through the years, long after that show. Jim Ed was always willing to do anything for us. Anytime we needed him, he would just drop everything and come on.

I loved when people would just drop in on the Diner. That really helped the show and gave it a "live feel". I really loved those impromptu interruptions, because they always served to energize the show. The Diner gave a lot of the older stars a place to show their fans that they were still around, and still singing great - and also gave newer acts the major exposure on national TV that they were unable to get anywhere else. Many of those artists saw their popularity grow and - in some cases - totally skyrocket, after they were on the show.

The Malpass Brothers' career really took off after they appeared on the Diner. They hit a note with our audience. They are a throwback to the golden era of country music, but they are two young guys who are so sincere and so talented. The Malpass Brothers were taping our show at Ray Stevens' theater. Ray happened to be there too and he had not seen them before. After they got done, he went up to them both and said, "Man, you guys are good. You might think I say that to everyone, but I don't. You guys are really great."

This past year, at our live shows in Branson, the Malpass Boys outsold all of our big-name guests! The people at the theater called us and asked, "Who are these guys? Everyone wants a ticket to their show!"

In the last few years of her life, Jean Shepard almost never missed coming to the Diner. She enjoyed just sitting in the audience and watching the show. She didn't need to be there, and sometimes maybe she shouldn't have been, because her health was so bad at the end. But she did it for Gus, and Gus did it for her. She really meant a lot to Gus.

A man who has almost the exact opposite personality as Gus is Wilfred Brimley. Wilford is the actor known for his trademark mustache and gruff demeanor. He was a curmudgeon who almost never smiled.

Wilford came on the show with the Riders in the Sky. I was surprised when he agreed to appear, because we don't have the huge multi-million viewer ratings that attract stars like him. But he had done a project with the Riders, and they brought him. He had never seen the show, but he really started warming up to us… about 45 minutes into the show! We actually got a smile and a laugh out of him, and he liked Nadine. He liked her, even though he refused to believe that she was really a woman! A few days after the show, Wilfred told some people in Nashville, "I did this TV program and they had a transvestite on there!"

When Gene Watson appeared on the Diner, people just fell in love with him all over again. Gene has fans who follow him everywhere. We always try to get him in Branson, because we know we'll sell 200 to 300 tickets just from the people who follow him from show to show. I love Gene Watson, and I thank him for his kind words earlier in this book.

Mark Wills invited Randy Owens from Alabama to come on the Diner. I was still in my wheelchair, recuperating from my fall down the mountain, and Mark was filling in for me. Randy was a little perturbed that we didn't have someone meet him at his car to help him with his guitar and stuff, but he warmed up to us as the show went on, and we really won him over when he saw that Ann Tarter was there.

Randy said, "I have your Tarter gates all over my place!" And about ten minutes into the show, he asked, "Are we on the air?"

He couldn't believe that we were just letting the cameras roll.

I am still surprised at the reaction people have to the show, and I enjoy watching it myself! I think it's a funny show, and you never know what a guest or one of the cast members will say. It's all totally unexpected, and none of us know what is going to happen. Everybody feeds off everybody. If we were trying to write a script for it, it wouldn't work.

I think the spontaneity is what grabs people. But I have never been able to understand why legends like George Jones watched the Diner. Andy Williams also loved the show. We were all especially shocked when "The Price is Right" host Drew Carey once tweeted out: "I'm watching Larry's Country Diner and trying to figure it out!"

There Drew was, in Hollywood, watching our little show! I'm surprised at all the people who watch it every week.

We knew the show was getting popular when some of the other artists and fans at the Grand Ole Opry started calling Jimmy Capps "The Sheriff".

We thought, "Wow, this show must be getting big." Jimmy had been with the Opry for more than 50 years, and now he suddenly had a new name there!

Jimmy had a new name, and I also found myself with a new title. In December of 2012, I was surprised and honored when I was named a Tennessee Ambassador of Goodwill. They gave the title to me during one of our Diner tapings. I was touched that the award recognized my positive promotion of Nashville, the state of Tennessee, and of course, Country Music.

After we added PFI/Boot Daddy as our sponsor, we started talking about taking our show on the road. Randy Little from Boot Daddy asked us to do a live version of the Diner at the Starlite Theatre, a theater he owned in Branson, Missouri.

For the first year, we didn't bring the entire cast. We didn't bring the set; I just came and introduced different artists. That didn't fly real well with the audience. They wanted to see the show they were familiar with on TV! So the next year, we brought in our set and everyone from the show.

We tried just an occasional weekend for our first Branson shows, and we played to fairly small (sometimes very small) crowds. But when we started doing a full week of shows there, our audiences quickly grew. We were also surprised when many people purchased tickets for each night and stayed for the entire week. In recent years, all of our shows in Branson have been extremely popular.

But it is very expensive to take the show on the road. When we travel with the cast, it costs $20,000 just to get started. We pay for everyone's time and travel, hotel rooms for a week, and their talent fees. The artists all work with us, and they share in the income from ticket sales... but they don't get the perk of being on a TV show, since we don't actually tape the Branson shows for television. I love doing the show live in Branson, but it is such a long drive from Nashville. It's seven-and-a-half or eight hours, no matter which way you go.

Getting the whole cast together for a week is also not easy. Keith, Nadine and Renae have day jobs. Jimmy is so busy on the Opry, and in recording sessions, that he loses so much money when he has to leave Nashville for a week. When he's in Branson with us, he isn't on the Opry or available for recording sessions.

As the Diner grew in popularity, I was amazed that, after all my years in radio, and after all my movie roles, here I was... a TV star! Luann and I were in Montana at a Perkins Restaurant, and while we were eating, three different groups of people stopped by the table and said, "We love your show. Thank you so much."

I thought, "Wow, in Billings, Montana..."

As I was writing this book, we were also in Red Lodge, Montana. Tom Kuntz, who has a restaurant and hotel there, introduced me to a 93-year-old man who just loves LCD. He watches it on the Internet. I was honored that he was such a big fan that he wanted to meet me.

My friend Dan Miller was in a Walmart parking lot in Wyoming, and he saw an older couple trying to get a wheelchair into the back of their car. Dan went over to help them, and they immediately recognized him from being on our show. They had heard about all of my health trouble, and told him, "Dan, please let Larry know that we are praying for him."

It is truly amazing how that little TV show has helped turn complete strangers into loving and caring friends, even though we might have never met in person.

That love and devotion can boost your ego… sometimes a little too much. But the Lord always has a way of humbling me. One of those humble moments came in Branson. We were having lunch at a restaurant downtown. Renae and her husband Phil had gone with us, and Nadine and her husband and Bill Bass were there as well.

Numerous people came up to say hi, and tell us how much they enjoyed our show. My pride grew a little with each fan who stopped by. During our meal, I kept glancing over at another couple, who I thought were watching us. I figured they must be shy, and didn't want to interrupt our dinner. So as we got ready to leave, I walked over to their table, and loudly asked, "How ya'll doin'?"

They quietly answered, "Fine."

I thought I would help them out, as I proudly proclaimed, "Ya'll watch the show, don't you?"

To which, they responded with, "What show?"

I very humbly walked out of the restaurant at that point. Renae, Nadine and the rest of the gang were all in the parking lot, bent over laughing at me and "my fans"!

The Diner hits a chord with the audience. It touches them in a way that other shows don't. Rural people are our strength. They have been so loyal to our shows, and they are such a sweet group of people. Larry's Country Diner is a silly little television show that is so much fun to do. One of the reasons I keep doing it, is because it is so enjoyable. There will come a time when it's over, but as long as they can prop me up behind the counter, and I can still do reasonably well, we will continue to do it.

MONTANA

When we are not in Nashville, or on a Diner cruise or in Branson, you can probably find us in Montana. Montana is such a beautiful, peaceful place. It became our second home as we were going through a stressful time. Our sons Ian and Adam each got married within six weeks of each other. And after all the planning and excitement of those weddings, I told Luann we should go somewhere we'd never gone before. We chose to go to Montana.

Our friend Dan Miller was living in Red Lodge, Montana, so we decided to spend some time with him. We flew into Casper, Wyoming, rented a car, and then drove from Casper to Jackson Hole. Dan wanted to take us on the road that CBS newsman Charles Kuralt called "the most beautiful highway in America".

The route from Jackson Hole to Red Lodge goes through the Grand Tetons, and through Yellowstone. After that, you have to travel over a huge mountain. It was only mid-October, but as we started up the mountain, it began snowing. The higher we drove, the harder the snow fell. With each turn, however, it also got more and more beautiful. As we reached the top of the mountain, Luann sighed, "I now know the meaning of the word 'majestic'." We fell in love with that mountain.

We loved snowmobiling in Yellowstone. We once snowmobiled 105 miles in one day. We could barely open our fingers when we got in! At dinner, Luann was so tired that she couldn't even lift her fork. She was totally exhausted.

As we enjoyed ourselves in the snow, I off-handedly told Dan, "I know why you live here, Dan. This is as close to Heaven as you can get on Earth."

When we returned to Montana in February of 1998, Dan said he had a real estate friend who wanted to show us some property. It was in the middle of winter, with snow up to our waist, but there was another, much bigger problem...

"We don't have any money," I told Dan. "We have no ability to buy anything!"

But Dan insisted we go and meet his friend, "just for fun."

The real estate agent drove us up a mountain, and when we got halfway up, she said, "By the way, this is not for sale."

I thought, "Why are we wasting our time?"

The people who owned the property had bought two 20 acre parcels of land. None of us had winter clothes on, but the realtor insisted we get out to look around.

When Luann stepped out of the car, she sank down to her knees in the snow. She was not a happy camper. But when we reached the edge of the property, we saw the most gorgeous, breathtaking view we had ever seen. Luann loudly proclaimed, "Dear God, I've got to have this!"

I shook my head and laughed, "There goes our ability to negotiate to try to bring down the price!"

I told the realtor, "See if they will sell it, and what they want for it."

A few days later, she called and said, "They are willing to sell! But they insist on selling both parcels together."

I knew we didn't have enough in the bank to pay for the 40 acres. Even if I could manage to swing it, I would then need a miracle to come up with the money to actually build a house on the land!

At the time, we had just started doing Country's Family Reunion. It had been bringing in good money, but we were far from rich... very far. I told Dan Miller, "We can only afford half of what they are asking."

But Dan confidently answered: "I know a guy who can help."

His name was Palmer. I didn't know him and we'd never met. But I called and told him that Dan said I should contact him. I explained that I had enough money for half of the property, but I needed a bank loan for the rest.

He said, "I have lived in Montana all my life, and I've never lost a dime on a piece of property."

He co-signed on the loan before we ever met in person.

We closed on the property six months after we had first seen it. Now if we only had a house to live in on the property... or the money to build one!

Again, Dan introduced us to another friend, this time a woman at First Interstate Bank in Billings. Since we owned 20 acres of the property, free and clear, we were able to get a building loan, and construction of our dream home began in the spring of 1999.

One request that Luann made of the builders was that she didn't want any electrical outlets showing anywhere. She wanted them imbedded into the huge logs. But drilling through all of those was very expensive. They had done about four outlets, when I found out they were going to cost me $600 each. I told them to do the rest the usual way! Luann also wanted huge, 12-foot party style decks that went around the house. We did follow through on that request, and it was one of the best ideas she ever had. We spend as much time out on the decks as we do inside.

Our log home has five bedrooms and four baths, and sits at the foot of the Beartooth Mountains. The reason we wanted so many bed and bathrooms is because we wanted the home, not only for ourselves, but also for all of our family and friends. We have a huge table that is very special. We invite all our visitors to use a wood burning set to burn their names in the table. It is a very permanent record of all of the friends and fun that have filled our home. That table is completely full of names, many famous names, and many names of folks you've never heard of. My longtime friends Mickey and Jane McElroy, and Johnny and Frannie Jones visited our Montana home eighteen times before they finally bought their own property, not far from ours.

Since our main home is still in Nashville, when we aren't in Montana, we have someone who comes in once a week to make sure that everything is quiet. Our neighbors also keep a good eye on everything for us. But we have still had a number of scares there; not from intruders, but from wildfires.

One of those fires was caused by Willie Nelson. That might be a stretch, but we do still call it the "Willie Fire". Willie Nelson had been at the rodeo grounds near Red Lodge, and a kid who was at the concert on a motorcycle lost control, had a wreck, and his motorcycle somehow started a forest fire.

I was in Nashville when our Montana neighbor Chris Benton called. I knew something was wrong when his first question was, "Do you have a hose at your house up here?"

He said a big fire was headed toward our home.

"Forget it," I said. "A garden hose won't stop it. If God wants a burnt offering, he can have it. We'll just rebuild. Don't risk your life to save our place. But I am going to pray that the wind blows the fire the other way."

The next day, the headline in the Billings newspaper was "God Changes the Wind." The fire never made it to our home.

We've had two other fires that caused the mountain to be evacuated. Each time, I prayed, and each time, God protected our home. The most recent fire was caused by someone who dumped hot ashes and set the hill on fire almost instantly. Again, we were in Nashville, and again we received a call from a neighbor on the mountain. Wally and Diane Zook had built a gorgeous house near our home.

As the fire raged, they got their horses off the hill, and then called us. "Larry, it's coming up. It's coming right toward us, and it's gonna get your house," Wally sadly informed me.

I said, "I'm just going to pray that God changes the wind again."

The next day, they sent an aerial photo that showed how the black, burned area went up that mountain, and when it got to our house and to our neighbors, it just turned and went right in-between the two houses. It barely missed us! You can't look at that picture without saying, "God saved it. It had to be God."

We call our Montana home "Legacy". It has been a real refuge. It is a place of peace. Everyone who has visited there says they sense the peace in the home. Ironically, if you stand out on the back deck and look down toward Wyoming, there is a vast valley. Long before our time, a number of different Indian tribe chiefs came together in that valley. Now it's called The Valley of Peace. All of that area just exudes peace. I don't know how it works, but you feel totally peaceful when you're there.

THE DAY I DIED

We had been looking forward to the third week of June 2015 for quite some time. Luann and I were heading to our favorite place on Earth, our home in Red Lodge, Montana. And to make the week even more fun, we had invited our friends Randy and Johnelle Little to come along. Of course, Randy is one of the main sponsors of Larry's Country Diner.

We spent June 17th at Yellowstone Park, and that evening we decided to surprise Randy and Johnelle with a unique experience. We had dinner at a very nice restaurant, and then we took everyone to where we would stay the night… in two tents. But they were very nice tents. Each one actually had a pot belly stove and king size bed! One drawback was that neither one had indoor plumbing. Randy and I didn't care, but our wives weren't real thrilled! Johnelle and Luann were also a little concerned when the "tent manager" offered us bear spray, "Just in case bears show up in the night."

But bears would be the least of our trouble in less than 24 hours.

On the morning of June 18th, we drove over the Bear Tooth Range, to our home in Red Lodge. After getting settled in, I wanted to go for a ride on our Kawasaki Mule ATV, down to the creek. Randy and Johnelle said they would ride along. Luann said she would stay at the house. It was a wise decision on her part. It was yet another smart move, possibly one of the smartest moves she ever made.

At 12:20pm, we were driving down the mountain on a narrow dirt road. About three miles down, I saw some horseback riders on the ridge above us. As we waved at them, I recognized my friend, Brad Edwards. Brad gave horseback rides, and I wanted to introduce him to Randy.

I stopped our ATV so that I could back up and drive up to the horseback riders. The dirt road we were on had just been graded. The edge of the road was loose, and a little hard to see. When you looked over the side of the road, there was nothing. Just a straight drop off.

When I put the Mule in reverse, the back tires grabbed some loose gravel.

I tried to slam the gear shift into drive, but it was too late. The driver's side rear tire caught the edge of the cliff and started pulling us over. As we rolled backwards over the edge, Randy and I looked at each other. The last thing Randy remembered from that day was looking into my eyes, knowing we were going over that cliff.

It was a 30 foot, sheer drop off. There was little rolling or bouncing. Just a 30 foot fall, straight down... with a sudden and very hard hit at the bottom.

We knew we were going over the edge. I remember as the ATV started over, it began to slide and then flip. On the way down, I could hear my bones breaking. I knew I was in big trouble. Randy fell off at some point, on the way down the hill. Johnelle had been in the back, and she grabbed the roll bar and held on for dear life. She jumped off at some point and managed to only break a finger. She was so lucky that was her only injury.

Randy and I were not so lucky.

When the ATV settled, I was under it, lying face down. My body was all twisted, and I couldn't budge the ATV. It weighed more than 1,000 pounds, and was right on top of me. I was never in great pain. I felt pressure, but not pain.

Randy was a few feet away from me. I couldn't see him, but if I could, I would have probably gone into shock (I was headed there anyway). Randy had shattered his jaw and broken his eye socket. It really messed up his eye. He had trauma to the brain, and he was bleeding profusely from his entire head and face.

I could hear the horseback riders galloping down the ridge. They were coming through the brush. There were a number of things that happened on that mountain that day... things that were gifts from God, who was watching over us the entire time.

The first gift was the group of horseback riders. One of them had been the police chief in Billings, and another was a police officer. They were both very familiar with EMT work. They took care of me, and in no time, the EMTs from the Red Lodge fire department were there. They have an incredible fire department, with an amazing search and rescue team, and they were there within minutes.

The other gift from God was a medical helicopter that happened to be flying over at the exact moment we went over the cliff. They had been on their way to Red Lodge, and they actually saw us fall off the mountain. What are the odds of that? It had to be God's perfect timing. They landed immediately.

The EMTs saw that Randy was gushing blood. He lost so much that he had lost consciousness. He came to, just long enough to see someone coming toward him with a big pair of scissors. His neck was swollen so much that they had to cut his necklace off. After doing what they could onsite, they loaded Randy onto the helicopter and airlifted him to St. Vincent's Hospital in Billings.

But getting me off the mountain would not be as easy. I was still pinned under the ATV. It was too heavy for them to try to roll it off of me, so they brought up a "jaws of life" to cut me out. I wasn't bleeding much, at least on the outside. My left elbow had been crushed, and it was covered in blood. Other than that, there were no other visible signs of how hurt I was.

Since I was lying face down, with my face in the dirt, I couldn't see anything. I knew I was under something heavy, and that I couldn't get out. As I heard the firefighters trying to free me, I told myself it was going to be awhile. I breathed deeply, breathing in through my nose and out through my mouth. I tried to relax… and then I thought about my wife. Oh no. She is going to kill me.

Johnelle called Luann, who was at our house, a couple miles up the mountain. Johnelle didn't want her to panic, so she told her we had a flat tire. She asked her to come down to get us.

The minute Luann topped one of the hills, she saw all the emergency vehicles and knew that something bad had happened. And she knew it was us. She parked at the top of the hill and came running down, looked over… and saw me under the ATV. She had to run down the dirt road and then back up, because she couldn't go straight down the cliff that we had gone over. When she got to me, she was screaming, "Larry! Larry!"

I wanted to try to keep her calm and I answered with, "Hey babe. How ya doin?"

I tried to joke with Luann and the EMTS who were working so hard to save my life. But I had now been trapped under that heavy vehicle for more than an hour, and all of the pressure was starting to set in.

I was under the ATV for more than an hour before they finally cut me out. That's when my troubles really began. When you get compressed like I did, it's hard to know how hurt you are. I didn't know that ribs on both sides of my body were broken. When you have broken ribs on both sides, you have a flailed chest. Your body is totally open, and there is nothing to contain the organs inside. Everything is just flopping around. I had broken my back. I also had a collapsed lung. When they took the pressure of the ATV off of me, my other lung started leaking. I was in serious trauma.

They carefully lifted me onto a flat board so that they could carry me up the hill. My head was toward the lower end of the board as they took me up, and it felt like I was going to slide off as they carried me. At that point, I wouldn't have cared.

They rushed me by ambulance to the hospital emergency room in Red Lodge. But as soon as they rolled me in, they realized they couldn't handle me there. I had too much trauma to my body. They loaded me into another ambulance and headed to Billings, which was 60 miles away.

This is where I received another gift from God. A lifesaving gift. On the way to Billings, the EMTs in the ambulance lost communication with the hospital. As they tried to relay all of my vital statistics, their signals somehow got disrupted, and they couldn't get any cell service up on the mountain. While they tried to contact the hospital, the EMTs were doing everything they could to keep me alive.

To be honest, I have no memory of any of this. I'm kind of glad I don't. But my wife was there for it all. It was a day she will never forget, so I'll let Luann fill in some of details.

"When they transported Larry from Red Lodge to Billings, I actually got to the hospital before he did. There wasn't room for me in the ambulance, since they were back there trying to keep him alive. So a neighbor took me, and we beat the ambulance by five minutes. When they wheeled him in, I ran to him. When I grabbed his hand, there was no response from him.

As they rushed him by very fast, the nurses told me I needed to stay outside the ER while they worked on him. A short time later, a female priest came and asked me to sit by her, a little further from the room. I'm guessing she didn't want me to hear all of the conversation and activity that was going on as they tried to save my husband's life. A little later, she asked me to go to a room down the hall, away from everyone. I knew that had to be a bad sign. I think they wanted me secluded, when they told me Larry was dead.

A half hour later, an ER doctor came in and said, 'You have one sick guy in there. He had no pulse and no respiration when he got here. But we were able to get him back.' They explained the long recovery he would have… if he managed to get through the night.

Larry mentioned the gift from God that came when the ambulance couldn't contact the hospital. We found out about that when the receiving doctor, Dr. Hatch, explained, 'I need to tell you something. We lost communications with the ambulance. Had we known his condition, what all his injuries were and what his vital signs were, we would have told them to call it in the field. That means unplug him and forget it. He's too far gone.'

But they didn't call it. They didn't give up on him, because they never got the message. I know it was God who made sure their communication didn't work."

– Luann

They hadn't given up on me. But I was still in grave danger. They still kept my wife in a far-off room, in case they had to deliver the bad news. They knew my back was broken. As soon as they got my vitals stabilized, which took two days, they took me to the operating room. The main doctor was not confident that my body could handle the surgery, and his worst fears were realized the moment they turned me over onto my stomach. Everything went haywire, and my body just collapsed. Every vital sign went crazy. I flat lined. They had to flip me back over to get me stabilized.

None of the surgeons knew exactly what was happening. But they unplugged everything on me and started over; kind of like when you're having computer trouble, and you just unplug it and then plug it back in, hoping for the best. That's what they did with my entire body! A short time later, they crossed their fingers, said a prayer, and turned me back over. The second time, I remained stable, and they were able to complete the surgery.

For the next six days, I was in the intensive care unit. I don't remember anything from my week in ICU. They kept me out most of the time.

They had to operate on my back. They put two rods in it, along with a bunch of screws to get it back together. They did surgery on my left arm. They put it in a metal cast. With broken ribs and both lungs damaged, they put me in a plaster cast that looked like a Stormtrooper's chest plate from "Star Wars".

Within 24 hours of my accident, Luann's sister Carol and her husband Bill were at our side. They dropped everything and flew to Montana. Our three sons tag teamed each other during the 33 days I was in the hospital. They sat with Luann in the waiting room, and with me in ICU. They were so supportive and helpful during the most challenging time of our life. If you've never been in a situation like this, you have no idea how comforting it can be to have family with you. I will never forget their willingness to put their lives on hold so that they could help be our support.

As I look back, it's interesting how God works things out. Luann and Carol were close growing up, but when Luann went off to college, she met and married a DJ (me) who kept her moving all over the country. When Carol and Bill got married, they settled in New Jersey where Bill had a job working for a firm that dealt with Wall Street. Our boys would spend a couple weeks in the summer with them. Then Bill went into banking and began his moving around. The sisters always wanted to live close to each other and when Bill retired from the banking, they moved to Nashville. We were blessed they were here when I had my accident. Carol and Bill are still an incredible support system, for both Luann and I, especially these past few years, as life has dealt me an interesting hand. We are also grateful that Luann's other two sisters also live fairly close. Lisa Johnson and Cristi Bullard still live in Memphis, only three hours away.

A week after my accident, after they had taken the tube out of my throat and I could finally talk, Luann asked me if I remembered anything about the previous days.

I told her, "I remember dying. I absolutely remember that. There was nothing traumatic about it. I just thought, 'Okay, I'm dead. No problem. It's Okay.' Then I thought, 'Boy, they are gonna miss me.'"

I smiled to myself and said, "Even when you're dead, you still have your huge ego." That all was as clear as I am sitting here writing about it today.

Randy Little was hospitalized for three days. They wanted him to stay longer, and he should not have left as soon as he did, but he wanted to get home to Springfield, and to his own doctors.

But I was in for a much longer stay. 33 days. It might have been the longest month of my life... but a few surprise visitors helped pass the time. I looked up one day and Larry Gatlin was standing over me. The Gatlins had been playing someplace nearby. Larry came to see me one day, and Rudy and Steve also stopped in later. My great friend Dan Miller was there a couple times.

Brad Edwards, the horseback rider who had been on the ridge when we fell over the cliff, came to see me. He and his wife also brought details of one more gift that God had given me that day on the mountain.

Brad told me, "I couldn't figure out why that 1,000 pound ATV didn't totally crush you to death. We could see it was right on top of you. So I went back to the cliff to see where you had been laying. And there was a little trench, just a little place that was hollowed out a little, and that's where you landed. Since you were a few inches down into that trench, the ATV was not totally on you with all of its weight."

I had landed in the only place that could have saved me. I was protected by that little trench. I can picture my guardian angel watching me fall over that mountain, and the angel just taking his finger and making that little groove for me to land in. The Lord has ways of protecting you in the midst of trauma. It was a miracle I landed in that spot.

When the surgeries were over, they finally put me on another floor, to start my very slow recuperation process. At first, I couldn't move on my own at all. But eventually I was able to sit up in bed. My next goal was to stand up. That took a few weeks. I spent most of my time in a wheelchair.

When news of my accident started getting out, the cards and letters started pouring in. Our viewers sent them by the thousands, and they sent up even more prayers. It made me feel so much better, knowing there were people around the country who were praying for me. I was amazed at the great outpouring of love from everyone.

By the way, we kept all of the cards and letters. They were so sweet. One of my Montana doctors had watched Larry's Country Diner. She was a fan. But most of the others went on the Internet and Googled it, so they could see who they were dealing with!

I slowly started rehabbing. I had physical therapy every day, and I also underwent mental rehab. That started easy enough, as we played games like chess and checkers. They didn't tell me at the time, but cognitively I wasn't doing real well. They performed cognitive tests, to see if my brain had been hurt.

They would show me a stick drawing and ask me to draw it. And I would think, "I can draw that simple, little house"… but I couldn't do it.

It was just a little square and triangle. But I couldn't draw it. My brain wouldn't let me. But things slowly came back to me. It was a major accomplishment when I could draw a 4-sided box.

One night, part of my therapy included going out to a nearby restaurant. A nurse went with us to Red Lobster. I was still in a wheelchair, but I ordered our food, and then I was supposed to figure out what the tip should be. But they didn't tell the waiter what was going on, and when he gave me the bill, it showed what a 10 or 20% tip would be. I got a perfect score for my "mental calculation", and then I showed my nurse what the waiter had done.

After our "night on the town", they took me back to the hospital, and Luann stayed at a little motel within walking distance. I didn't want her to stay with me at the hospital all night, every night. She needed some rest, probably more than I did.

Our Red Lobster dinner was also a test for Luann. Before they let us go home, she had to prove to them that she could care for me on her own, with no nurses around to help get me in and out of my wheelchair.

We went through practice exercises in a little apartment they had built on the fourth floor of the rehab unit. I named it "The Fantasy Suite". We had been alone in the room for less than 30 minutes, when I had to go to the bathroom. I could hang onto a railing to go by myself, but when I came back, Luann had to set me back down into my wheelchair. But she forgot to lock the chair, and as soon as I began to sit down, that wheelchair went out from under me! I fell down on the floor like a bag of rocks. Of course, she couldn't stop me from falling. She tried to catch me, but she was no match for my big body. She went running for the nurses.

The people at St Vincent's Hospital were all so great. When I got to feeling a little better, I always tried to make my doctors and nurses laugh. I wish I had stayed in contact with some of my nurses, but some of the HIPAA laws make it hard to do that. They were all very sweet and comforting. I really wanted to bring a couple of them to Nashville, to show them what I did. I talked about them on the show, but I was never able to get them there in person.

Once I was well enough to travel, we needed to figure out a way to get me home to Nashville. Because of the damage to my lungs, my doctors didn't want me to fly. They said I would have to wait another two weeks before I could fly. Our other options were renting a sprinter van, or a tour bus like our Country friends use. But no matter how plush a vehicle was, I dreaded a cross-country drive.

When Gus Arrendale from Springer Mountain Farms heard about our challenge, he immediately called. He said, "Larry, you know that my mother loves the Diner. She just called me and said, 'Gus, get him home.' You know I've got to listen to my mom, so what can I do?"

I then listened in amazement, as Gus told me he was going to pay for a medical jet to fly to Billings to get us and bring us back to Nashville. Gus said that he would pay for the entire cost.

We told the head of the rehab unit what our friend Gus was doing, but he smiled and said, "Yeah, I'll believe it when I see it."

But on the day of our flight, the doctor came in and said, "In all my years here, people have always said, 'My friend has a plane and will take me home', and it never happens. This is the first time a friend has kept their word on something so expensive."

As we left the hospital, some of the rehab nurses had tears in their eyes. They had become part of our family. An ambulance took me to the little airport in Billings. Since I was still laid flat on a gurney, there wasn't a lot of room in the plane. We had two pilots, two medical people, Luann, and me, lying flat on my back.

2 hours and 45 minutes later, we were home. As they wheeled me into our home on July 23rd, I said, "God is good. So is Gus."

I was in my bed at home for several weeks while I was trying to get better. My legs had not been broken or seriously injured in the accident, but all of the trauma to the rest of my body had affected my legs. I had to learn how to walk again. Through everything, my wife was the consummate caregiver. She was fearless and untiring. She got up at 2:00 in the morning to help me go to the bathroom. It's not easy on the caregiver to be on edge and ready to go around the clock, but she did it.

Luann always said, "Montana is so beautiful. God must live there." After my fall off the mountain, she said, "I am so glad that God was home that day."

As I look back at everything, I know that God was in control during every minute. Today, I like to say, "God is still on the throne." God is still in control. He is still on the throne. We all are destined to die. My time was not on that hill in Montana. But my day will come. It will be no great loss, because I am ready to go when the Lord calls me home.

CRUISING THROUGH LIFE

I have had some crazy ideas over the years. But one of the craziest turned out to be one of the greatest successes of our company. I knew that Larry's Country Diner and Country's Family Reunion were both very popular. Then I started thinking, "I wonder if some of the people who watch our shows would like to go on a cruise with us?" I thought that maybe a nice vacation, and the chance to meet all of our cast and some of the country music legends in person, might appeal to a few folks.

From the outside, hosting a cruise might look like fun and games, but behind the scenes, there is so much work and so much financial pressure. If you ever want to put on your own cruise, here's a little bit of what you can expect...

Getting into the cruise business was very frightening. Just the financial risk alone can scare you to death. The first time we did it, I knew we were committing our company to a risk of 1.5 million dollars!

As I considered doing a cruise, I ran into a program director I had worked with previously in Hartford, Connecticut. He had left his job, and had started putting together cruise packages for radio stations. He told me that in order to secure the ship, you needed a line of credit for 1.2 million dollars. Then I talked to another person, who told us how we could reserve 500 rooms, and we would then have a period of time before we had to pay for them. During that time, we needed to have as many advance down payments as we possibly could.

Two ladies in Fort Lauderdale had a company that worked with cruises. They helped us wade through everything for our first one, and it went very well. But after a couple of years, we realized we were leaving money on the table. If you book ten rooms, they'll give you a free room. We didn't know that when we first started, and we had booked 500 rooms. No one offered to tell us that we could probably get 50 of those rooms for free. Somebody made a lot of money on those rooms, but it wasn't us. Yes, it was an expensive lesson we learned.

My son Jared got heavily involved with our cruises a few years ago. We found that we could do everything ourselves, in-house. Jared went on a couple management cruises, where he learned things that helped us even more. He also goes on the ship we're going to use, and he sits in every theater seat to make sure that it has a good view. We don't want to sell a seat that we wouldn't want to sit in. If we need to cut back on the number of fans, we'll do that, rather than sell a bad seat. We limit the number people who can go on each cruise, based on the size of the ship's theater. If it holds 1,200 people, we'll book 600 rooms.

Choosing the right country music artists for each cruise is one of the most important aspects of each trip. We usually take nine artists. The most popular artists are those who have a certain temperament. They like to mingle with the fans and have fun with everyone. We don't want to book stars who hide in their room and don't want to meet the fans.

But our fans also don't smother the artists. They know the artists are on vacation too, so they give them enough space. I want the artists and the fans to have a good time. Unlike other cruises, we try not to overwork the artists. We only ask that they do two shows; one with Bill Anderson for CFR, and one with all the artists together. And, of course, we also have our Diner show.

Rhonda Vincent has been one of our most popular cruise guests. When she first started joining us, it seemed like Rhonda never slept the entire time she was on the cruise! She did our big shows on the ship stage, but then on her own time, she would start playing her mandolin anywhere she could on the ship. She would play in a little lounge, or outside on a deck. She would just sit down somewhere and start playing and singing, and then in no time, she'd be surrounded by astounded fans. The fans never knew where Rhonda would pop up, but they always knew that it would be a fun time! She continued that tradition every time she went on one of our cruises, and her impromptu jam sessions got so popular, she had to move them to larger locations on the ship.

All of the artists have a great time on each cruise. Johnny Lee always has fun... sometimes too much! On one cruise, we were playing a game with the audience, and Johnny started telling one of his more "colorful" stories. I cut him off and playfully yelled, "Johnny, go to your room!" Johnny got a big laugh when he answered with, "It's been a long time since I've been sent to my room!"

We pay all the expenses for the artists and our band. In addition to the cruise, we also have to pay for their flight, to get to where the ship is. It does add up. We also pay for the wives of the artists and band. Plus, I want all the spouses to know we were glad they were there, so I give them each $200 to spend on the trip. The wives all tell me, "My husband will be available, no matter what the dates are for next year's cruise!"

The cruises have worked very well for us. We just kept adding rooms each year.

We haven't had any major problems, and we are very pleased with the way they have gone. Getting paid to have a great time and take a nice vacation is one of the best ideas I have ever had.

MY THREE SONS

One thing we all have in common is our love of family, so let me tell you a little about mine.

Luann and I were married in 1965. Our first son, Ian, was born in September of 1970. Adam, our second son, came along in February 1974, and we were blessed with our third, Jared, in March of 1976.

Ian Devin Black came into the world laughing, and he has been laughing ever since.

For our first Christmas together, I gave Luann a little Pekingese dog named Kona Sha. Ian loved that little dog so much, and he was always laughing at funny things Kona did. They were together around the clock. Kona had a very flat nose, and we liked to toss a balloon in the air and watch her try to catch it. As Ian watched the balloon bounce off Kona's flat nose, he would giggle like crazy.

As he began to grow, we enrolled Ian in "Perkins Fit by Five", a swim club that taught kids to swim, walk a balance beam and climb a rope ladder. We thought it was a good program, and that he would have fun. But little did we know that God was at work, even then, in Ian's life.

When Ian was in the second grade, we noticed that he wrote his 'S's and B's backwards. He was tested and diagnosed as a classic dyslexic. After reading up on it, we found that many of those who have dyslexia are highly intelligent, with gifts and strengths in other areas, like creativity and imagination.

As I mentioned, God was at work when we put Ian in the "Fit by Five" program. While there, he learned to control his eye and hand movements. That teaching not only helped him deal with dyslexia, but was also important years later, as he pursued his career.

Ian had severe asthma when he was young. He had a lot of allergies. He was allergic to horse, dog and cat hair. Ian was once on an overnight trip with his youth group, when I got a call from them. They said he was wheezing, and that we should come get him. I drove my little MG BGT hatchback to pick him up. As we drove home, down a two lane road, we passed a little diner. It had a sign that read "Malts and Milkshakes". We had already driven past when I asked Ian if he would like to get a malt. Of course, he yelled, "Sure!"

I pulled over to the side of the road to turn around and go back to the diner. It was dark, and the rural road didn't have any lights. It also didn't have any shoulder, and we couldn't see that there was a steep drop off, right at the edge of the road. When I put it in gear to go forward, the car started to slide sideways, and I could feel it getting ready to fall down the embankment, into a very deep ravine just off the road.

I yelled, "Hold on Ian, we're going to roll over!"

The car lifted up and starting rolling. I put my arm up to the roof of the hatchback, in an attempt to keep the top of the car from crushing us as it rolled over. As we tumbled over, the car rolled onto Ian's door, then kind of flipped so that it crushed the top of the car and broke the window out - but it didn't totally pancake it down on top of us.

Our car rolled three times. My glasses were knocked off, and landed in the floorboard. Once the car stopped, we came to rest at the bottom of the hill.

Ian cried, "Dad, are you okay?"

I felt around my body, and finally said, "I think I'm okay. But we have to figure out a way to get out of this smashed up car."

I'm sure my guardian angel broke a wing that night, but we were not injured.

I managed to get my door open, stood up outside, and then reached in to pull Ian out. He looked at the car and asked, "What do we do now, Dad?"

"See that steep hill we rolled down?" I asked. "Now we've got to climb to the top of it."

Once we crested the top, we walked to the diner. I called Brother Billy Roy Moore, the Pastor of the Lord's Chapel, and asked him to come get us. He arrived a couple hours later, as Ian and I were just finishing our malts.

I have no doubt that God put his hands around my son and I as our car tumbled down that hill. It is quite ironic that, way back then, a diner was involved with an incident of me falling over a cliff. Of course, a couple decades later, a similar incident would happen... but when the owner of Larry's Country Diner fell off a Montana mountain, the outcome was much more devastating.

I once gave Ian a very unique gift. It looked very expensive, but it really wasn't. I always loved MG sport cars, and I bought one from Mike Blanton, who helped promote and manage Amy Grant's early career. As a thank-you gift, Amy had given Mike her own MGB GT but he parked it under a maple tree, and the sap from the tree fell on the top of the car, destroying the paint. So he sold the car to me for $3,500.

I drove the car for the next couple of years. When Ian was at Brentwood Academy, all of the rich kids had brand new cars their parents had given them. I couldn't afford that, but I gave Ian my MG. The rich kids had no idea what kind of car it was, but they knew it had to be expensive! Some thought it was a Jag XKE. Ian soon found out that he was driving a very cool, elite car. He drove it during his senior year, and then during his freshman year at Auburn.

But one day, someone ran into him, and just nailed the side of his car. I had the car brought back to town and had it completely rebuilt. It received a new interior and paint job. Ultimately, I sold it to Jimmy Velvet, who put it in his Cars of the Stars Museum. He billed it as Amy Grant's car! I guess she was a lot more famous than Larry Black, even though I drove it much more than she did. Jimmy displayed it with one of Amy's gowns. The best part about the deal was that he paid me $3,500... the exact amount I had paid for the car, many years earlier!

Ian always wanted to be a graphic design artist. When I saw his first artwork, I wasn't confident that it was going to work, but I didn't discourage him. When he went to Auburn, he majored in Art. In his second year, one of his teachers told him he needed to do something else. But during one of his college breaks, he came back to Nashville and did an internship at Sony Music. The art director at Sony liked Ian, and had him work on several projects. He designed album covers for some big names.

At that time, Sony was shifting from guys drawing with pencil and pen to computer-generated art. They put in computers, and had everybody go through a six-week course. Ian got the benefit of that, and when he went back to college, they were just beginning to do the same thing; but now, he was way ahead of the professor! He was able to answer all the questions his teachers and other students had.

One year, Ian went down to Biloxi, where my brother's son was doing air brush work. Ian learned how to use the air brush as well, and he made t-shirts and license plates. The next summer, he told us he wanted to try doing his own air brush business in Orange Beach. We bought him an air compressor, and he headed off. He had been dating a girl named Holly. Her mom and dad owned a condo right on the beach, and they let him stay there for free.

Ian worked eight hours a day at a souvenir shop, creating t-shirts and license plates. In just three months, he made $19,000! He did that a couple times, and by his senior year in college, he was trying to decide what he should do after school. The starting salary for a professional graphic design artist was $17,000 to $19,000 a year. I told him that he should go back to the beach, and he could make more there in just a few months than he could in an entire year in Nashville.

He and Holly had decided to get married. George King, who owned a Christian Music record company in Nashville, offered him a job as art director for the company. George later told me that Ian's resume wasn't that extensive, but the reason he hired him was he knew that anyone who could stand there for eight hours a day and have customers looking over their shoulder, saying what they were wanting, would be someone who was a great worker.

Ian learned how to operate with printers, and he learned about color and typeset. In addition to graduating from Auburn with a degree in Graphics Design, Ian's time with George King's company was like an additional year of college. Ian designed ads for major magazines and created CD covers. Then he started doing freelance work.

We were filming Country's Family Reunion, and Ian began doing all of our graphic design work for that. He came to work for me full time ten years ago. Every time you watch one of our video projects, you see lots of Ian's work. His quiet demeanor and easygoing way works well with artists, sponsors, and the rest of the staff.

While Ian was born in Ithaca, New York, Adam was born in Rochester. From day one, Adam was a bundle of energy! When he was still in diapers, we were trying to move him from his crib to a bunk bed with Ian. But he kept getting out of bed and running down the hall to our room.

I walked him back to bed three times, and each time, I got more and more stern as I commanded, "Stay in bed!"

I probably shouldn't say this, but I did it, so I might as well fess up. The fourth time I had to take him back to bed, when I shut his door, I stopped in the dark hallway and waited. I heard his feet hit the floor once again, and as he started opening the door, I slammed the door in his face. It scared him so bad that he ran back to bed. Probably not perfect parenting, but he did stay in bed.

Adam was a bit of a daredevil, who seemed to have no fear. He would wonder away from the house, still in his diapers. We had an above-ground pool in our backyard. Adam was still just crawling when he headed to the water. In an instant, I saw him slide over the edge of the pool and sink to the bottom. A friend, who was closer than I was, jumped in and pulled Adam up out of the water.

A couple years later, Adam gave me another scare… we were getting ready to leave church one Sunday morning, and I was supposed to be watching Adam. But someone stopped me to talk about something, and while I had my head turned, Adam took off. I looked around the church, and then went outside - just in time to see him heading for the street, getting ready to run out into the busy East Avenue.

I took off after him just as I saw a car coming. I grabbed Adam just as the car screeched to a stop right before it hit him. It taught me that you have to constantly be vigilant. You have to always pay attention to what your kids are doing.

Adam also taught me another lesson. He was just a little guy when we lived in Ithaca, New York. One winter day, I was inside, watching the boys playing out in our backyard. It was snowing, and Adam was trying to get up on a big bench that we had out there.

With his bulky snow suit and heavy boots, he struggled to move. I went out and lifted him up, so he could stand on the bench. As soon as I walked back in, I heard him yell to his brothers, "Hey guys! Look what I did!"

At that exact moment, God spoke to me, saying, "How often do you do that Larry? How many times has your Heavenly Father helped you do something, but then you tell everyone, 'Hey guys! Look what I did!'"

That stayed with me forever. It was a life lesson that I learned from my son.

Adam never ceased to amaze us. He was a great student, a great actor, and he excelled in the Forensics Society as part of their oratory and debate team. As a senior, Adam won the national championship. He also won a scholarship to Western Kentucky College where, as a senior, he also became a national champion, this time at the college level.

Adam went on to teach speech and drama at Brentwood Academy for eight years. But he was looking for something new to do, and he left his teaching job. In the CFR chapter of this book, I detailed how a conversation Adam had while he was borrowing a bed led to the success of our Country's Family Reunion shows. Adam started working full time with our Gabriel Communications company. One of his first duties was to be in charge of all of our country music infomercials that started ten years after the first CFR had aired.

Adam has the ability to write commercials, edit content and direct productions. Today, Adam is President of our company. He does a great job, as he keeps everyone focused on our goals and tasks. He and his wife, Jenny, have been married 25 years.

Our third son, Jared, was also born in Rochester. While our son Ian came into the world giggling, Jared came in rockin'... at least at bedtime. He completely wrecked his crib! He would stand in the crib, start rocking it, and banging it against the wall. He put a huge hole in our plaster wall. He rocked all night long, every night, until he had totally destroyed the crib.

After seeing what he did to his crib, it shouldn't come as any surprise that today Jared is a "muscle man". He has always been into physical fitness, since he was thirteen years old. He started out as a pudgy little boy, like me - but when he became a teenager, he asked for a weight set. My friend Dan Miller agreed to work with him. He put him on a weightlifting schedule, and his body began to drastically change. He is quite a hunk today.

The winters are long in New York. We had a big, old house that was hard to heat. A pot belly stove was the only heat we had for our kitchen, but when it was fired up, it would heat up the entire house. Sometimes, even if it was below zero outside, that old stove could make it so hot inside that we'd have to open the kitchen door to cool everything down.

And Jared always wanted to touch that kitchen stove. We were constantly shouting, "No!", as we swatted his fingers away. But one day, he ran up to the very hot stove and put both hands on it.

He screamed and screamed. His hands were covered in blisters, but he learned to never touch that stove again.

While we are teenagers, or in our twenties, we often take the simple things in life for granted. I think that sometimes our children help us get back to seeing and appreciating those things. One night, we were driving outside of Nashville, and Jared looked up at the stars and was just in awe. He was so amazed at the night sky. I thought, "We should all be in awe of that sight." A few minutes later, Jared had the same sense of awe… when we stopped at a gas station candy machine. He couldn't believe it had Fig Newtons! It really didn't take much to entertain Jared!

Jared was a very serious boy. Luann always said that he seemed to be trying to figure out if he wanted to be with this family! In his early teens, however, he finally discovered his "silly" side, as he helped Adam with a little video show that they produced in our garage.

Jared advanced out of the garage when he landed a commercial for Opryland. He got to go on all the rides, and they filmed him, and then paid him! He made more money in two days of fun at Opryland than his brothers did mowing grass all summer!

Jared wanted to be a physical therapist. He went to the University of Evansville for two years, and finished his schooling at the University of Massage Therapy in Salt Lake City, Utah. That's where he met Stephanie, the girl who would become his wife. Before he left Utah, Jared remembered a time during a youth retreat where he was told that God had a plan for his life. Now he felt that the Lord was calling him into a different profession. He and Stephanie moved to Nashville, and he enrolled at Trevecca Nazarene University.

After earning his Master's Degree in Arts, Religion and Biblical Studies of Theology, Jared took a job as a youth pastor at New Hope Community Church. He became associate pastor at a church near Leiper's Fork, Tennessee, but they had financial problems; he told them they had too many people on the payroll, and that one of the people they should cut was him! Jared has always excelled at breaking the most complex thing down to its simplest form... even if it meant he would be out of a job!

When we decided to move our Country's Family Reunion fulfillment center out of Salt Lake City, we leased a building near where Jared lived in Petersburg. After several years in various ministries, Jared joined his brothers in our business. We made him the head of fulfillment, and then all of my sons were working for the company.

Our boys have grown into fine young men, and they have all chosen wives well. They have given us ten grandchildren. Our three sons are truly the best thing we have ever done!

When I was a kid, I had no idea what I wanted to be when I grew up. In high school, I thought I might go on to be a cartoonist. I liked to draw, and I liked to be funny, so I thought "cartoonist" would be a good career choice. Of course I loved being in plays and loved entertaining a crowd, but I didn't know if a fat kid like me could make it into the movies. But as I watched my father's career, I also considered being a missionary or preacher. Today, I think it's interesting that my three boys have ended up pursuing the same dreams that I had when I was a little boy. Ian is an artist, Adam is an actor, and Jared is a preacher. I've had three sons that I could encourage in whatever they were doing.

Early in this book, I wrote about the night my mother, my brother and I spent at Union Station in Nashville. Almost 70 years later, I found myself in the very same spot. My sons had asked me to meet them at Union Station so that we could talk about "something important."

That "something important" was the future of our company.

I asked them, "If I die tomorrow, who takes over the company?"

Ian said, "Adam does."

I was surprised, since Ian was the oldest. But they all agreed that Adam had the gift to take over everything. The joy of our three sons is that they are all gifted in different areas. They work well, because there is no competition between them. My sons all have different talents. Jared is the most spiritual. Ian is the most outgoing, and he can work a room. Adam has the most business sense. He can think through things.

My boys grew familiar with seeing their dad banged-up, or being taken to the hospital. When they were teens, we flew to Park City, Utah to visit Dan Miller. The boys were skiing together, and Dan and I were off on our own, when I fell so hard that I thought I had broken my shoulder.

Our boys were at the top of the hill when they saw a bunch of medics helping someone at the bottom of the mountain. They looked at each other and said, "That must be dad." Of course it was. After being treated at the medical clinic, I was relieved to be told that my shoulder wasn't broken, but the doctor warned me to be extra careful for the next couple of weeks. On the way out the door, I slipped on the ice and fell right on that shoulder!

I suffered another vacation accident in 1986. We took our kids and Luann's sister Carol, her husband Bill, and their kids, to a water park in New Jersey. The Big Kahuna Water Slide was beckoning, so the kids took off. Then Bill and I decided it would be fun to go down the 50-foot, straight drop slide. Bill went first, and I jumped on the slide right behind him. I outweighed Bill by 100 pounds, and I caught up to him in just a second. As Bill hit the water, I instantly hit Bill... with my face. Blood was everywhere. It covered the water, and covered my face and body. We spent the rest of the day in a hospital emergency room, while they treated my broken nose.

Being as accident-prone as I have always been, you can probably see what's coming with this one... in late 2003, I thought I needed a motorcycle. Luann happened to be out of town, settling her mother's estate in Memphis, when I bought a brand new motorcycle. It was beautiful. I hadn't had it six months when I wrecked on the way to Jared's house. I was knocked out for about 20 minutes, when an old farmer came by to help wake me up.

Even though I was always working two or three jobs at a time, those jobs also had lots of downtime, and that allowed me to spend a lot of time with my kids. When we moved to Nashville, I recorded the Larry Black Show in our garage, so I was home a lot. Even when I had an office downtown on Music Row, I wasn't there that much. But Luann did most of the raising of our family on her own. Once we had all three of our boys, she decided to not work outside the home. We felt that her most important work was being there for our kids.

When our boys were little, we never went on a real vacation, because we couldn't afford it. We did get to go to Disney World in Florida, thanks to my parents. By then, my dad had become a counselor. He realized that, after all his years of preaching, he would have no retirement money, so he went back to college and got his Master's Degree in Counseling. He somehow qualified for free tickets to Disney, so he let us use them. My parents lived about 40 minutes from Orlando, and we always stayed with them for free, so the trip cost us almost nothing.

Then we started taking the boys to Pigeon Forge, Tennessee each Memorial Day Weekend. It was a close, fairly inexpensive getaway. And those trips were the beginning of something my wife called HISH.

Luann came up with the idea for HISH, which stands for "Hooray It's Summer Holiday". Each summer, she always wanted to try and do something special for the boys and, eventually, our grandchildren. Luann always liked putting on big productions, making big meals or hosting huge cookouts.

We continued our tradition of trips to Pigeon Forge with our kids and our grandkids. We rented a tour bus and took them all to Pigeon Forge. That's when the fun really began! We rented a hotel room, and the boys rode go karts, we swam, and did all the water slides. Our HISH events seemed to grow each year. One summer, we brought in the biggest inflatable water slides available, and set them up in our yard. The water slides were huge. We also had little pools for the smaller kids who couldn't do the big slides, and we ended the day with a picnic.

Adam was a huge Miami Dolphins fan. He loved Dan Marino, and Luann had found out that the closest Miami would be playing to Nashville was in Indianapolis. So we rented a tour bus, and our entire family went to Indy to watch the Dolphins play the Colts. That was Adam's gold medal memory. He still has the game ticket.

Jared has three girls and two boys, Adam has a son and a daughter, and Ian has three sons. When the grandkids were little, Luann would do "Cousin Buddies" and "Big Boy Sleepover" events. We were always having sleepovers for our grandchildren. Sometimes we'd have one just for our granddaughters. They were called "Girly Girls" nights, and Luann would take them to get their hair and nails done, and then they'd spend the night.

Some of our most special times as a family have come at our home in Montana. We go skiing and sledding in the winter, and during the other seasons, we sightsee, or just enjoy the beautiful mountains. Those are special memories with our family.

The first Christmas we had the house there was 1999. We rang in the year 2000 on that mountain. If you remember, 2000 was also Y2K, and people thought all the computers and banks were going to crash and go haywire when we turned over from the year 1999 to 2000. So I had taken a few thousand dollars in cash with me, just to make sure we had money to get back to Nashville with.

That year, Luann came up with the idea of our family burying a time capsule.

We only had two grandsons at that point, but Luann had everyone write letters to themselves, and to each other. She even wrote letters to her grandchildren who had yet to be born. We put all the letters inside a Ziploc bag, then I put the large bag into another container, and buried them under a tree in our yard.

Ten years later, we got everyone together again and we dug up those letters. But for some reason, Ian's wife, Holly, didn't want to see what she had written a decade earlier. She and Ian had a big argument about it, and she told him she was flying back to Nashville and would not take part in the opening of the time capsule. But she ended up staying. When she read the letter she had written a decade earlier to her first son Nathan, she started crying. Nathan was just a tiny baby when Holly had written this letter, and now he was standing next to her. She was just sobbing.

She cried, "This is the best thing that ever happened to me."

It was such a precious and moving experience for the entire family. We had videoed it when we buried the letters, and we had a camera going when we dug them up and read them. I think it ought to be a Ziploc commercial! Those bags preserved the history of our family. Everything was just pristine. The next Christmas, I took all the letters and made a leather satchel for them to be kept in, and I gave each family member their letters and their own satchel.

Luann has always had great ideas to do stuff like that. She even made our Christmas cards into a fun event for the entire family. Each year, we got everyone together for a major photo shoot for our Christmas card. Luann would come up with a new idea or theme, and all the outfits and costumes we would wear. These were very elaborate.

Dean Dixon took most of those photos. He's done album covers for so many artists. Scott Moore, who designed the set for our TV show, even built huge sets for our photo shoots at Dean's studio in Germantown. The kids just loved it. They loved dressing up. People who were on our Christmas card list also loved it. They told us that they always waited for our card to arrive. They never knew what we were going to do for our next photo shoot.

Once the last grandbaby was born, we decided that we would cut back on the big, elaborate cards... but we still do some huge photo sessions with our family. Fortunately, all of our family lives close by, and we've been able to round them all up for our photo shoots. They are photos that our whole family will cherish as the years go by.

WITH A LITTLE HELP FROM MY FRIENDS

"I feel like I've known Larry Black my entire life. But I think we first met when he interviewed me on his morning show on WSM radio. We got to know each other a little bit, and then I started filling in for him when he needed a day off! I was comfortable doing radio since I had started out as a disc jockey when I was a teenager in Georgia. At the time, Larry's acting career was going pretty good, and he needed to be away quite often. So I would get up before the sun came up, and take Larry's place on WSM.

Many years later, Larry called and asked me to meet him for lunch at the Amerigo Italian Restaurant in Nashville. As we ate, he explained how he wanted to do a 'Country Music version of the Bill Gaither Gospel Homecoming shows'. Larry had gone to Bill and asked him to partner with him. Bill said he was too busy, but he gave Larry his blessing to do the similar show.

Larry asked me to be the host of the show, and I jumped at the chance. Of course, I had much more of a background in country music than Larry did. But I admired the fact that he was willing to put in all the work, as well as all of the money, but he let me get the spotlight as the host.

Country's Family Reunion has been a blessing to my career, and to the careers of so many other artists. In 1997, I still had my best songwriting years ahead of me, but as far as my recording career, my records weren't getting played on the radio anymore. But the Family Reunion kept my face out in front of the public, and it helped boost our concert attendance.

I also had the honor of being the guest on the very first Larry's Country Diner episode. I was Larry's guinea pig! The Diner is as close as you can get to a live TV show these days. People ask me what Larry is really like, and I say, 'with Larry, what you see is what you get. He is the same person off the air as he is on TV.' I've gotten to know Larry's entire family. His wife, Luann, is just wonderful, and all of his sons are great.

When he had his accident in Montana, I was heartbroken and so worried about him. During his long recovery, they asked me to fill in for him on one of the Diner shows. I tried to do my best, but there is only one Larry!

Before they start filming every Diner and Family Reunion, Larry gathers the artists and crew, and in front of the audience, he says a very public prayer. He asks for the Lord's blessing on the production, everyone involved in it, and on the viewers who will be watching it.

Larry is a very kind and generous person. When we tape the Reunion, as soon as we're done, Larry gives us an envelope, with our check inside. That is quite rare. Usually the artists hear, 'The check is in the mail,' but Larry pays everyone on the spot.

He is generous in other ways, too. I've visited Larry's home in Montana a half-dozen times. It is such a great place to go clear your mind and get away from everything. He was so generous to let his friends and many of the artists use his home. It was amazing that he opened it up and let us spend time there.

I respect Larry Black, and I just have so much love for him."

– Bill Anderson

Bill Anderson is an incredible friend. People might be surprised to find out that there are just a few country music artists who I am very close friends with. I have a lot of acquaintances. Some are closer than others, but as far as intimate friends, I don't think I have very many. Gene Watson is a friend. Gene is very loyal, and I try to return that loyalty to him. I also consider T. Graham Brown, Ray Stevens and Ronny Robbins to be close friends. There are a few others who I'm sure will be mad that I didn't name them here… but if they are real friends, they will understand!

But here's the real tragedy: I don't spend very much time with any of them. I don't go to their concerts, I don't get on their bus and travel with them for a weekend, we don't visit each other's homes. I'm only with them when we are taping our shows. I hate that. But all of us are always so busy, we don't seem to make the time to get together.

The one exception to that rule is a group of pals I see every Saturday morning. A couple years ago, Buddy Kalb invited me to have breakfast with them. They had been getting together for many years already, and the small group of 8-10 people originally included Norro Wilson, Chet Atkins and George Lindsey. Now our group includes Ralph Emery, Don Cusic, Jim Stephanie, Ronny Robbins, George Gruhn, Blake Chancey,

Bergen White, Ray Stevens, and a few others; some in the music industry, and some who are not.

We meet at a local restaurant every Saturday morning at 8:00, push two tables together, have breakfast, and tell stories and jokes for a couple hours. Ray Stevens never misses. He finishes his show at his theater after midnight on Friday, and he's meeting us for breakfast bright and early the next morning.

I have a peculiar way of identifying friends. Jesus only had twelve guys. Just three of those twelve were his intimate friends. The others were followers, his disciples. (They only had Instagram! Ha!) In the Bible, there's a Proverb that says you can't have too many true friends. You can't maintain a close friendship with a lot of different people. You can have three or four, but you run out of time to spend with many more than that.

When I was playing racquet ball, I had racquetball friends. They are still good acquaintances, but I haven't seen any of them since I had back surgery and stopped playing. You're friends when you are playing, but when you stop, your closeness also ends.

The great radio DJ Charlie Monk is a real friend. We go all the way back to when I was eighteen and working at a radio station across town from him. We were both in Mobile, Alabama. I didn't know him then, but we both worked the Junior Miss America Pageant. When I moved to Nashville, he called me. He was already here. I would help Charlie in any way, and I know that he would help me.

Dan Miller, Bob and Laura Whyley, Bruce and Jill Coble, Mark and Linda Turner, Stan and Cathy Negvesky, Lee

Groitzsch, Tom Piggott, and Scott and Nedra Ross are close friends. Richard and Dorathy Pippin have been such wonderful friends. They always take care of our car in Montana. They are huge country fans, and they have also helped some of the artists who've visited our home there. Mickey and Jane McElroy are true friends. They bought a place near us in Montana. When I had my accident there, Mickey and Jan flew up so they could help us as I recuperated. Those are real friends. And, of course, I consider our Diner family as some of my true friends.

A REAL DINER

One of the most interesting things about the Larry's Country Diner TV show is the fact that many, many people thought we were in a real Diner. From the very beginning of the show, many viewers thought we were in a regular restaurant. And to this day, ten years later, some people still think that!

As the show got more popular, people started coming to Nashville to see the "real" Diner. But the Diner didn't exist! We had always filmed the show on a set we had built on a TV soundstage at a complex called North Star Studios, where the RFD TV Network was also based. But many people just refused to believe that there wasn't a real Diner they could walk into.

We'd sometimes have people driving around our offices after they'd found our business address. They'd slowly drive by, and finally park and come knock on the door. We knew what they were going to ask… "Where is the Diner?"

I was always in my office, and Renae was usually there too, so they were just thrilled to meet us. But they were always shocked when we told them it was just a TV show.

With each visitor who dropped in (and there were MANY), we began to think that maybe we should build a real Diner. It was just a thought, for a year or so. Then I started asking advice from some of my friends who had owned restaurants. They all gave me the exact same advice. I so wish I had listened to them!

Everybody I talked to, including Bill Anderson, who had an experience with the chain of Po' Folk restaurants, tried to talk me out of it! Bill said, "Larry, don't ever do a real diner."

Ray Davis, who owns the Texas Rangers, told me, "If you ever want to buy a restaurant, please call me, and I'll spend all day and all night, until you get over that idea!"

Trying to build the real Diner might have been the biggest mistake of my life. It cost me so much money, and it put so much stress on me. That stress was nowhere to be seen when we officially broke ground on the project on September 17, 2015. Bill Anderson, Jeannie Seely, Ronnie McDowell, T. Graham Brown, Exile, and all of the show's cast joined us for the groundbreaking celebration. Local political leaders, and even the heads of Nashville's Convention and Visitor's Corporation, gave speeches about how the real Diner was going to help bring the tourists to the entire Nashville area.

We had found the perfect property, located just across the road from our offices. It was three acres, just off of I-40 in Bellevue, Tennessee - and just outside of Nashville. It was a great location for tourists coming off the interstate. As we celebrated our groundbreaking, we were already planning for our grand opening in the spring of 2016.

Spring did come. But the Diner did not.

On paper, at least initially, it looked like a no-brainer that it would be a huge success. We had a popular, weekly television show that would be an hour-long commercial for our restaurant. We knew that thousands of viewers would come to visit. You know that saying, "If you build it... they will come."

But we couldn't build it. We tried. But we ran out of money!

In our original agreement, I was supposed to pay one million dollars for the three acres. That was just for the land, and not the diner building. At the time, our DVD sales were going great. We had money pouring in. But almost at the exact moment that I signed that million dollar contract... our DVD sales started plummeting.

To make a very long story short... everything that could go wrong, did go wrong. As soon as we had broken ground, we found out that the ground we were on was actually a lake. We had to bring in thousands of tons of rock to fill it all in. That cost us hundreds of thousands of dollars, almost before we had even started.

The total cost was supposed to be 1.5 million dollars, but it then blew up to 3.2 million - and that was just to open it! We still had to pay all the expenses of employees and running the place! We should have built a simple square or rectangle restaurant, but our little Diner quickly turned into a 6,700 square foot facility, which would seat 135 people. We also wanted to produce the TV show from there, and we knew we needed very high ceilings. So we built a huge, multi-faceted roof.

We just did it all wrong with the real Diner. I did everything I could to raise money, but after three and a half years, I finally gave up. I had to sell the property, and the real Diner never got built.

In the last couple of years, we made a different deal with RFD, which eased our money worries a bit. We also started taping the show at the Ray Stevens CabaRay Showroom that Ray had just built near Bellevue. With that change, we could start selling tickets to our Diner tapings. We had never charged people to come and watch the show being taped; we just let them in for free. Because of that, for ten years, we had an ever-growing, waiting list of fans who all wanted to come and sit in the Diner.

After our first tapings at Ray's place, we were able to pay all of our production bills, and even made a little profit. That was the first time we'd ever made money in the history of producing the show!

So the show went on, but I had to give up on my dream of a real Diner. If I hadn't, we could have lost the entire company. But I really wasn't all that sad that there would not be a Diner. I was actually relieved, just to have it all go away. I knew that I had more important things to worry about… mainly trying to stay alive, as my health started to nosedive.

"AND WE DON'T CARE!" – Says Father Time

I have a plaque in my office that features a version of a quote by Hunter S. Thompson. It reads, "Life is not a journey to the grave with the intention of arriving safely in a pretty and well preserved body, but rather to skid in broadside, thoroughly used up, totally worn out and proclaiming 'What a Ride!'"

I look at that quote on my wall every day.

When I had my accident in Montana, my sons all stepped right into the roles they had planned on when we'd talked about what would happen if I would die. It turned out to be a great blessing, because it gave them the chance to do the job before I actually died! If I had been healthy, I never would have let them take over.

But I wasn't healthy, and little did I know that my health was going to get even worse. I went from having a broken body, with lots of broken bones, to having a very sick body. The last four years have been something else. To be very honest, it hasn't been easy, and I do get discouraged at times.

Just a few months before my fall down the mountain, I had total knee replacement surgery. I was still rehabbing that, when I had the accident in Montana. Over the past decade, I had undergone two back surgeries, and also a heart surgery. I bounced back from all of those in no time. Nothing had ever slowed me down.

But this time would be different.

While I was still recovering from all my Montana injuries, I had two major gallbladder attacks. I was back in the hospital in January of 2016 to get my gallbladder taken out. One year later, I developed a urinary tract infection, caused by E. coli. The doctor put me on an antibiotic, and left me on it for two years. That move almost killed me.

In 2018, my health began to really go south. I had begun writing this book, and I honestly did not know if I was going to get it finished before I died.

We had just come back from our Diner cruise, and I was totally exhausted. I knew I was sick, but the doctors were at a complete loss as to what was wrong. They knew I was dying, but they could not come up with what was killing me.

I was also told that I had anemia. They didn't know the cause, but thought I was losing blood. As we headed back home from the hospital, I prayed, and during that prayer I heard God say, "Touch the hem of his garment. Just reach out to Jesus and he will heal you and make you whole." I clung to that message. "Touch the hem of his garment".

They ran every test known to man. They all came back negative. But everyone knew my blood was not right. I was also having shortness of breath. They sent me to a cardiologist, and were going to do a heart cath. I was so anemic, they thought I was having heart trouble again. I was on the gurney, preparing for the procedure, when the doctor said he couldn't do it. My blood count was too low, and it was too dangerous to proceed.

The cardiologist announced, "I think you have a blood marrow problem," and contacted another colleague who was in the hospital. They then changed the plan from having a heart cath to doing a bone marrow biopsy. One doctor suspected I had leukemia, but once tests ruled that out, they were still at a loss as to why my bone marrow was not producing red blood cells.

I was sent to a hematologist, and when he had finally made a diagnosis, it was not a good one. He said I was in the beginning stages of MDS. As soon as we got home, Luann got out one of her medical books and looked up Myelodysplastic Syndrome, and she began to cry. It said that I would die within eighteen months to five years.

When I returned to the doctor, I told him, "I just want to feel better."

Coldly, the doctor stated, "This is the best you are ever going to feel. But you have had a good life, haven't you?" I couldn't believe my ears.

I began losing weight at a rapid pace. I had no strength at all, and could hardly walk. I started needing blood transfusions, at first one every three weeks, then that increased to once every two weeks. I knew that my end was near when I had to have three transfusions in one day.

We were reaching the bottom. It was the end of the line. We sat down with the boys, and they decided we would shut down the show. I was catatonic, sitting in my chair all day, slowly deteriorating. I knew I couldn't do it anymore.

We called all the cast members together, and I told them, "That's it, we're done."

But I just couldn't admit that it was really over, so I added: "But if we decide to do more..." Everyone laughed. All of the cast members said, "It has been a fun run." When we started the show, none of us thought it would last as long as it had. Everyone was accepting of the show coming to a close. They all understood.

We did take a couple months off, and we aired a few more reruns. But I just couldn't say goodbye to the show. They sometimes had to bring me in on a wheelchair and prop me up behind the counter, but I managed to get through the shows.

After more hospital visits and tests, I was told I was having bone marrow failure.

Bone marrow failure is when the bone marrow fails to produce red blood cells. The doctor kept saying, "We'll do another biopsy in three months."

And when that came back negative, he said we'd do another one in three more months. But I was running out of months. No one had a clue of what was causing it.

One day, the doctor advised me to go off all the supplements and medicine that I could possibly give up. He also asked, "Have you ever been exposed to any toxins?"

It was at that moment that my wife began to save my life. Remember earlier in this book, when I wrote that Luann's dream was to work in the medical or science field? While she dropped out of college to marry the man she loved, she never gave up her love for medicine. She always said that she wanted to be a diagnostician. She wanted to be able to look at someone's symptoms, and then come up with the answer as to why they were sick.

She did exactly that, as her husband prepared to die.

When Luann went to pick up more of the medication I had been prescribed, she started reading each label very closely. One of the bottles was a low dose antibiotic Bactrim prescription that I had been taking since June of 2016. After a quick scan of the dosage instructions, she threw them in the garbage.

But then something inside her said, very loudly, "Take it out of the trash and read every word."

It had been a long, rough day, and Luann was worn out. But she read every word of the ingredient and instruction paper. And there it was…

"Rare and serious side effects; bone marrow failure."

I heard her scream with joy across the house. "Larry! I have found it! I know why you are having bone marrow failure!"

I had been taking that drug for two years, and the entire time, it was slowly killing me. Once I stopped using the drug, my blood count started coming back, until it was almost perfect. Not one doctor, with all of their state-of-the-art (and very expensive) tests, had been able to come up with what was wrong with me. But my wife, who didn't finish college, was able to figure it out. She knew my life depended on it. I have no doubt that Luann saved my life. Without her, I would not be here today. I also think that it was God himself who whispered to her to get those drug instructions out of the trash. It had to be.

For the next few months, my health started coming back. I also noticed that my mental state and brain function were getting sharper. But I was still facing serious health issues.

About the time I finally felt that I was going to live, I got to a point where I couldn't walk. I had done so much damage to my back over the years, and now I was paying the price. All those motorcycle and car wrecks and that one big parachute jump that went wrong had caught up with me. I was in so much pain when I tried to walk that I finally started using a wheelchair.

But my doctors assured us that they could rebuild me. I underwent extensive surgery on July 30th, 2019. They took out a lot of the old metal that had been holding my back together, and replaced it with titanium. Hopefully, that surgery will give me much more mobility, and I can get back to walking like a normal 75-year-old man.

In 2017, while I concentrated on trying to stay alive, my three sons stepped into full time administrative roles with the company. They have guided us into new directions I would have never taken us to. They have gotten us into the digital age. Luann and I are very proud of our sons, and of our grandchildren. They are, without a doubt, our greatest accomplishment.

I'm also proud and very thankful that my kids have all come to a relationship with God. They did that on their own. I might be the greatest Christian in the world (I'm not), but that will not get my kids to Heaven. I like to say that God has no grandchildren. He only has sons and daughters. He doesn't have grandkids. That means that your kids will not go to Heaven just because you are going. They will have to come to the Lord themselves.

I give my wife most of the credit for how great our children and grandchildren have turned out. As I write this, I remember the best decision I ever made (other than deciding to follow the Lord). 54 years ago, I made the decision to marry Luann. Has it been easy? I'm sure not for her! She was willing to move twelve times in the first thirteen years we were married... just to follow her husband and his dream of making it in radio. Back then, "follow me" meant much more than just making a keystroke on a website.

There were many times in our marriage when Luann had to remember those vows she had said - "in sickness and in health", and "for richer or for poorer". As she was saying those words, if she could have seen into her future, she probably would have thought, "What am I getting myself into?!"

But through it all, we are still here... and I love her all the more for it.

This past winter, we headed back to our home in Montana. When the snow starts falling up on the mountain, there is no more beautiful sight. But it doesn't take long before that snow starts to really pile up. We had dinner downtown, and then started driving up the mountain. Halfway up, the snow was blowing so hard that it was caused a whiteout.

Luann was very scared. She asked, "Can you see the road? Because I can't see anything!"

I assured her, "Yeah, we're fine."

I couldn't see a thing… but I didn't want her to know that.

The windshield wipers were all iced up, and barely moving. We managed to get to the 3 ½-mile dirt road that leads to up our house, crossed a little creek… and then we saw lights coming down the mountain. The road is so narrow that you don't want to meet anyone coming the other way, especially when neither driver can see anything! So I pulled over and waited. When the truck reached us, we saw that it was Tom and Liza Kuntz. They live right across from us on the mountain.

Tom pulled up to my door and said, "Larry, just follow my tracks. I'm going downtown to get the plow for my truck, but just follow my tracks."

We did as he instructed, and it was a true blessing from the Lord. There are no markings on the road to show you where the edge is, so we stayed in his tracks, and followed them all the way.

He told us the next day, "Man, I'm glad we came down when we did. By the time we got back with the plow, we couldn't see any tracks."

I thanked the Lord for his perfect timing. I often think about the instructions Tom gave me, as we headed up that snowy, ice covered mountain. I think the words he said that day were really the words that the Lord has told me throughout my entire life...

"Follow my tracks. Just follow my tracks and you'll be okay."

I know if I continue to do that, that I can get through anything.

Larry

THANK YOUS

Thank you to all the behind the scene workers who have helped make Larry's Country Diner and Country's Family Reunion a success over the years.

Jamie Amos

Patrick Kennedy

Terry Choate

Nick Palladino

Scott Moore

Elaine Hensley

James Reed

Libby Joiner Mitchell

Jan Reams

Judy Lawrence

Catherine Malkiewicz

Larry Bearden

Stephenie Dodson

Martha Armstrong

Cherokee Hart

Shipley Landiss

Lynn Edwards

Dan O'Connell

Russ Sturgeon

Steve Anderson

Eden Ramage

David Wright

Ingrid Grasman Reed

Donna Dillard

Pam Carter

Don Carr

Brandon Tait

Jeff Wills

Jack Lawrence

Bryan Blumer

Curt Casassa

Jay Rockholt

Matt McElroy

Russell Mehringer

JT Dekker

Austin Blackwell

Tom Gregory

Mark Carver

Tim Roberts

Mike Hughes

DINER GUESTS

My sincere thanks to all of these wonderful artists who have appeared on Larry's Country Diner.

45 RPM

Aaron Tippin

Ashley Campbell

Asleep at the Wheel

B.J. Thomas

Baillie and the Boys

Barbara Fairchild

Bill and McKenna Medley

Bill Anderson

Billy Dean with Hannah

Billy Grammar

Billy Yates

Bobby Bare

Bobby Osborne

Bradley Walker

Buck Trent

Buddy Green

Buddy Jewell

Carl Jackson

Carolyn Martin

Charlie Daniels

Charlie McCoy

Chris Golden

Collin Raye

Con Hunley

Craig Campbell

Crystal Gayle

Dailey and Vincent

Dallas Frazier

Dallas Wayne

Dan Miller

Darin and Brooke Aldridge

Darrell McCall

Daryle Singletary with Mike Johnson

David Ball

David Frizzell

Dean Miller

Deana Carter

Deborah Allen

Dickey Lee

Doyle Dykes

Doyle Lawson and Quicksilver

Ed Bruce

Eddy Raven

Exile

Freddy Weller

Gary Chapman

Gary Morris

Gene Watson

George Hamilton IV

Georgette Jones

Gordon Mote

Guy Penrod

Helen Cornelius

Holly Pitney

Hot Club of Cowtown

James Gregory

Jamie O'Neal

Jan Howard

Janie Fricke

Janie Price

Jason Crabb

Jean Shepard

Jeannie Seely

Jeff and Sheri Easter

Jeff Taylor

Jenee Fleenor

Diner Guests

Jett Williams

Jim Ed Brown

Jim Glaser

Jim Lauderdale

Jimmy C. Newman

Jimmy Capps

Jimmy Fortune

Joe Stampley

Joey and Rory

John Anderson

John Berry

John Conlee

Johnny Counterfit

Johnny Lee

Johnny Rodriquez

Justin Trevino

LaDonna Gatlin with Phil Johnson

Lari White

Larry Cordle

Larry Gatlin and the Gatlin Brothers

Larry Mahan with Hoot Hester

Leona Williams

Linda Davis and Lang Scott

Lorrie Morgan

Lulu Roman

Mac Wiseman

Mandy Barnett

Margo Smith

Mark Chestnutt

Mark Lowry

Mark Wills

Martin Family Circus

Marty Raybon

Michael Peterson

Michele Capps

Mickey Gilley with Paul Harris

Mike Flint

Mike Snider

Mo Pitney

Moe Bandy

Mountain Faith

Neal McCoy

Orthophonic Joy

Quebe Sisters

Paul Overstreet

Ralph Emery

Randy Owen

Ray Pillow

Ray Stevens

Rebecca Lynn Howard

Red Steagall

Restless Heart

Rhonda Vincent and the Rage

Ricky Skaggs

Riders in the Sky

Robin Young

Rodeo and Juliet

Ronnie McDowell

Ronnie Reno

Ronny Robbins

Roy Clark

Russ Varnell

Shane Owens

Shawn Camp and Lauren Mascitti

Shelly West

Shenandoah

Sierra Hull

Sonny Curtis

Southern Raised

Steve Hall and Shotgun Red

Suzy Bogguss

Sweethearts of the Rodeo

Sylvia

T Graham Brown

T.G. Sheppard

Teea Goans

The Bellamy Brothers

The Church Sisters

The Cleverlys

The Dillards

The Glory Bugles and Coldwater Jane

The Grascals

The Isaacs

The Malpass Brothers

The Martins

The Oak Ridge Boys

The Roys

The Steel Drivers

The Texas Tenors

The Time Jumpers

The Whites

Tim Menzies

Tony Jackson

Tracy Lawrence

Vince Gill with Paul Franklin

Wade Hayes

Wilford Brimley

Williams and Ree

Wilson Fairchild

COUNTRY FAMILY REUNION SERIES

Country's Family Reunion	1997
Country's Family Reunion 2	1998
Christmas	1998
Gospel	1999
Reunion Celebration	1999
Grassroots to Bluegrass	1999
At the Opry	1999
At the Ryman	1999
Generations	2001
Nashville	2008
2010	2010
Bill Anderson's 50th Celebration	2010
Grand Ole Time	2010
Songwriters	2010
Gettin' Together	2011
Old Time Gospel	2011
Salute to the Kornfield	2011
Second Generations	2011
Kinfolk	2012
Salute to the Opry	2012
God Bless America Again	2013
Simply Bluegrass	2013

Home for Christmas	2014
Honky Tonk	2014
Tribute to Ray Price	2014
Sweethearts	2014
Tribute to Merle Haggard	2016
Wednesday Night Prayer Meeting	2017
Kickin' Back	2017
Another Wednesday Night Prayer Meeting	2018
Country's Unbroken Circle	2018
Gospel Classic	Compilation
Lookin' Back	Compilation
Lookin' Back Again	Compilation
Precious Memories	Compilation